9041

The Art and Practice of Diplomacy:

A Selected and Annotated Guide

by
Robert B. Harmon

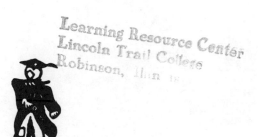

The Scarecrow Press, Inc.
Metuchen, N.J.   1971

To
John Ray, Pat, Patti Jan and Michael

> A democracy moves forward
> only so fast as the strength of the
> body politic will permit; the muscles
> and heart and digestive tract of the
> mass regulate the speed, either
> ahead or in reverse...
>
> J. Reuben Clark, Jr. 1871-1961
> Former Under Secretary of State,
> 1928-1929; and United States
> Ambassador to Mexico, 1930-1933.

Preface

I have compiled this volume for the student who would like to know a little more about contemporary diplomacy as an important factor in international affairs. More than is usually the case, I suppose, its audience is anyone who finds it useful, such as teachers, college students, students majoring in international relations, or perhaps the interested non-student. It is designed to guide both specialists and laymen through the labyrinths which comprise current diplomatic practice.

The goals of this work, I hope, reflect the needs of its audience. More than providing simply an annotated bibliography, I have attempted to supply the user with helpful background information which will make the works cited more useful. I have also included a chapter of illustrations and documents which will also make the subject matter of diplomacy more meaningful when placed in proper perspective. Along with its advantages the discerning student will notice that this work has a number of shortcomings. I have not included many works on the diplomatic relations among various nations or the memoirs of leading diplomatists. These will be added in future editions.

My debts to others in compiling this work are many; however, I am particularly grateful to my wife, who typed the final manuscript, and to my children who tolerated my effort to complete the job. Whatever defects and shortcomings this work may have are the sole responsibility of the author.

RBH

Acknowledgments

I wish to thank the following publisher for permission to quote from copyright works. Also I am appreciative to the following governments and governmental agencies for their valuable assistance.

Portions of Chapter VII are reproduced from Conduct of American Diplomacy, 3rd Ed. , by E. Plischke, by permission of Van Nostrand Reinhold Company, a division of Litton Educational Publishing, Inc. , Litton Industries, Princeton, N. J. , 1967, and from International Relations: Basic Documents, 2nd Ed. , by E. Plischke, by permission of Van Nostrand Reinhold Company, a division of Litton Educational Publishing, Inc. , Litton Industries, Princeton, N. J. , 1962.

A number of documents reproduced in Chapter VII were obtained from the U. S. Department of State and the British, Canadian and French Consulates in San Francisco.

Contents

ix

Introduction

Within the international realm the contacts that governments have with each other and the manner in which this intercourse is carried on are generally subsumed under the name of diplomacy. As a technique of state action, diplomacy is essentially a process whereby communications from one government go directly into the decision-making apparatus of another. Considered in this manner diplomacy is in the final analysis the one direct technique of state action in that it exerts its diplomatic power upon the crucial personnel of the other government or governments. In this sense, diplomacy can be considered the central technique of foreign policy.

Diplomacy has many procedures. They range from highly formal devices such as notes, aides-mémoires, and communiqués at one extreme to more informal and almost casual conversation at the other. At bottom, diplomacy is a method of negotiating between sovereignties, and although the elaborate ritual and protocol that surround the practice may sometimes seem pretentious and time-consuming, they have their roots in the very nature of the task. By diplomatic means a state transmits its position on an issue to another state and receives that state's response. Whatever changes may take place in the respective positions are registered diplomatically, and the eventual elaboration of whatever relationship develops also lies in the hands of the diplomats.

There are a number of distinct functions that can be detected in diplomacy. Which one or ones the diplomat may be called upon to perform depends, naturally, on the nature of the policy his government is following.

First of all diplomacy is largely a technique of coercion. Withdrawal of diplomatic relations is, in effect, a coercive element. Coercion may also be applied in negotiation by an ultimatum, by the establishment of a rigid time-limit for the conclusion of an agreement, or by the registration of a formal or informal protest or complaint.

xi

Secondly, diplomacy can also be considered as a technique of persuasion. The advancement of arguments on the one hand and the proffer of a quid pro quo on the other, both persuasive devices, are within the exclusive province of diplomatic technique. It is true, of course, that the actual line between coercion and persuasion is often fuzzy at best and that the two approaches frequently coalesce into one another. Yet there is a real and distinguishable difference both in motivation and atmosphere, and most diplomatic initiatives are cast at least initially in a persuasive form.

In a third way diplomacy is uniquely a procedure of adjustment. That is, it is designed to further the task of enabling two nations to modify their respective positions on an issue in order to reach an amiable relationship. Finally, diplomacy is a technique for reaching agreement. Formal written agreements are as binding an international commitment as world politics offers, and these can be brought into existence only by diplomatic means. It must be emphasized, however, that agreement may involve either coercion, persuasion, or adjustment and that no agreement is possible unless both sides wish one. On the other hand, even a strong interest in formalizing an accommodation would be pointless were there not instruments and procedures for reaching one.

Diplomacy, therefore, is an exciting and very important area of activity in the contemporary world. A glance at one's daily newspaper will provide ample proof of this conclusion. Increased understanding of this complex process by citizens and students will enhance the role of any government in world affairs. 1

I

The Nature and Objects of Diplomacy

Within the international arena the foreign policy objectives of nation states are pursued in a variety of ways. The determination of what method a state will employ depends in large measure upon its internal and external strength, an estimate of the forces arrayed against it, the importance of the policy objective, and an estimate of the consequences of a certain policy in terms of its long range, intermediate, or short range results. Diplomatic methods include such things as negotiation, persuasion, propaganda, mediation and conciliation, economic pressure, invocation of international judicial procedures, collective action through international security agencies, threat or demonstration of force, forceful measures short of war, full-blown war, or self-imposed isolation just to mention a few. Simply stated then-- diplomacy is a method or means by which a nation state conducts recurrent international transactions and adjusts to changing world conditions. [2]

The various ways in which the term "diplomacy" has been employed in the study of international relations has produced some confusion. A distinguished scholar has noted a number of common usages applied to this term: foreign policy, international negotiation, administrative machinery or processes to facilitate negotiation, a functional branch of foreign service, and the personal qualities which contribute to persuasive negotiation. [3] Diplomacy in actuality should be distinguished from foreign policy or international law since it is confined simply to the art or practice of conducting negotiations internationally and the administrative management of such negotiations. When we speak of negotiation here we are referring not only to the final formulation of the terms of an agreement but also to defining areas of agreement by continuous reporting of the position of the state to which a diplomat is accredited, and effective representation of that position. Negotiation also refers to building relationships of mutual confidence and understanding which will inspire agreement.

13

In some cases it is useful to think of diplomacy, when
applied to conflicting national interests, as a type of negotiation to which war stands as the extreme alternative. When
skillfully used, diplomacy, assessed in terms of a nation's
various strengths and weaknesses, can be employed to avoid
the unpleasantness of war. Still, one ought not to exclude the
possibility that diplomacy can be used not to avoid but de-
liberately to provoke a war. There are other instances where
diplomatic negotiations are conducted between nations on matters which present little or no conflict of national interests
but which may to mutual advantage be better organized or
regulated. These areas include the regulation of international
trade, transport and the like as well as the provision of
economic, military or technical assistance, the arrangement
of defense alliances or the development of international administrative organizations. [4]

In modern international intercourse, diplomacy is
distinctively an instrument of the government of nation states
and has a number of important implications. First, the
negotiators represent not themselves but their respective
governments. They do not make policy but attempt to
implement it. Second, the manner in which diplomacy is
conducted by a particular government may reflect to some
extent the peculiarities of that state's political and economic
system. Third, the extent of reliance upon diplomacy tends
to be in inverse ratio to the growth of effective international
constitutional or institutional apparatus.

Below are cited a number of materials which wholly
or in part demonstrate the nature and objects of diplomacy.

1.   Audisio, G. Idea storica erazionale della diplomazia
         ecclesiastica. Roma, 1864. 320p.

      A study of the church's role in the conduct of diplo-
      matic relations.

2.   Barraza, Rafael. Vademècum diplomático. Managua,
         Editorial Rodriguez, 1943. 80, 2p.

      A brief look at the broad sweep of diplomacy.

3.   Beladiez, Emilio. Diplomacia y diplomáticos. Madrid,
         Imprenta Maestic, 1960. 177p.

A general treatise on the function of consular
officials and ambassadors in diplomacy.

4.   Bernard, Montague. Four lectures on subjects con-
      nected with diplomacy. London, Macmillan, 1868.
      205p.

      Contents - Lecture I. The Congress of Westphalia;
      Lecture II, Systems of policy; Lecture III, Diplomacy,
      past and present; Lecture IV, The obligation of
      treaties.

5.   Bonneval, Henry. Études diplomatiques. Paris, Firmin
      Didot frères, 1857. 350p.

      Primarily a history of French foreign relations with
      some relation to general diplomatic practice.

6.   Bourgeois, Leon Victor Auguste. La diplomatic du
      droit ... Paris, Delagrave, 1909. 47p. (Conciliation
      international. Bulletin, 1900. no. 8)

      A short essay on the problems of diplomacy and
      international law.

7.   Braun, Werner. Démarche, ultimatum, sommation: eine
      diplomatischvölkerrechtliche studie. Berlin, G.
      Stilke, 1930. 84p.

      Discusses the diplomatic process and attempts to
      analyze briefly a number of problem areas.

8.   Cagiati, Andrea. La diplomazia dalle origini al xvii
      secdo. Siena, Cantagalli, 1946. 179p. (Bibliografia:
      p. 169-177)

      An overview of diplomacy in the 17th century.

9.   Callieres, François de. On the manner of negotiating
      with princes: On the uses of diplomacy, the choice
      of ministers and envoys, and the personal qualities
      necessary for success in missions abroad. Trans-
      lated from the French by A. F. Whyte. Paris,
      M. Brunet, 1716. Notre Dame, Ind. , University of
      Notre Dame Press, 1963. 145p.

      Considered a classic in the field. In modern trans-
      lation this early work delineates the early diplomatic

practices of continental Europe.

10.   Carnegie Institute in Diplomacy, University College,
         Dar es Salaam, 1965. Report and general in-
         formation. Compiled by David Kimble. Dar es
         Salaam, University College, Institute of Public
         Administration, 1965?   42 leaves.
         (Bibliography: p. 28-29)

         A brief outline of the study of international re-
         lations with some detail given to the subject of
         diplomacy.

11.   Chambrun, Charles, ed.   L'esprit de la diplomatie.
         Paris, Correa, 1944.   458p.

         An examination of diplomatic practice with em-
         phasis upon the French experience.

12.   Chazelle, Jacques.   La diplomatie.   Paris, Presse
         universitaires de France, 1962.   126p.   (Que
         sais-je? no.   129; Includes bibliography)

         A brief study of the role of diplomacy in inter-
         national relations.

13.   Corbett, Percy Ellwood.   Law in diplomacy.
         Princeton, N. J., Princeton University Press,
         1959.   290p.

         A study, by an experienced scholar in international
         law, of the question: "What role does legal reason-
         ing and legal rules play in the diplomacy of na-
         tions?" The work is based largely on British,
         American and Soviet experience and practice.

14.   Czartoryski, Adam Jerzy.   Essai sur la diplomatie.
         Paris, Amyot, 1864.   332p.

         A very light and general examination of European
         diplomacy during the 19th century.

15.   "Diplomacy in transition," Journal of International
         Affairs, XVII, no. 1 (1963), pp. 1-69.

         Excellent articles covering the changing nature of
         modern diplomacy.

16. Dirksen, Hervert von. Diplomatie, Wesen, Rolle
     und Wandlung. Nürnberg, A. Abraham, 1950.
     24p. (Nurnberger rechtsund sozialwissenschaft-
     liche Vertrage und Schriften, Nr. 3)

     A brief overview of diplomacy and its problems.

17. Economie. La diplomatie. Lausanne, Comptoir
     suisse, 1954.

     A general analysis of the nature and objects of
     diplomacy.

18. Fabius, Dammes Paulus Dirk. Democratie en
     diplomatie. 's-Gravenhage, M. Nijhoff, 1920.
     61p.

     A very brief discussion of the foundations of dip-
     lomacy.

19. Florio, Franco. Nozioni di diplomazia e diritto
     diplomatico. Milano, Giuffre, 1962. 294p.
     (Bibliography: p. 277-278)

     Analyses the various aspects of diplomacy and in-
     cludes a discussion of diplomatic and consular
     practice.

20. Forgac, Albert A. Essai sur la diplomatie nouvelle.
     New ed. Paris, A. Pedone, 1950. 38p. (Bib-
     liography: p. 35-38)

     A small pamphlet concerning the democratization
     of diplomacy.

21. Fraga Iribarne, Manuel. Guerra y diplomacia en
     el sistema actual de las relaciones internacionales.
     Madrid, Ediciones Europa, 1960. 356p. (Bib-
     liographical footnotes)

     An interesting essay on war in international re-
     lations and its relationship to diplomatic practice.

22. Garden, Guillaume. Traité complet de diplomatie,
     ou Théorie géneral des relations extérieures des
     puissances de l'Europe. Paris, Treuttel et Wurtz,
     1833. 3v.

Perhaps the most complete of the early works on
European diplomatic history and practice.

23.   Genet, Raoul. Traité de diplomatie et de droit dip-
       lomatique. Paris, A. Pedone, 1931-32.   3v.

This work is one of the most extensive treatises
on diplomatic procedure. V. 1, deals with diplomatic agents, V. 2, with diplomatic action, and
V. 3, with the organization and functioning of international conferences.

24.   Gentet, Ferdinand. Droit diplomatique et procédure
       internationale. Genève, Imprimerie Maurice
       Reymond, 1900.   64p.   (Includes bibliographies)

A short overview of the role of diplomacy within
the international arena.

25.   Gerbore, Pietro. Formen und Stile der Diplomatie.
       Reinbek bei Hamburg, Rowohlt, 1964.   299p.
       (Bibliography: p. 287-291)

A documented work of general scope on the nature
of diplomatic style in international politics.

26.   Hayward, Charles William. What is diplomacy.
       London, G. Richards, 1916.   256p.

A series of case studies in European diplomacy
and diplomatic practice.

27.   Heatley, David Playfair. Diplomacy and the study
       of international relations. Oxford, The Clarendon
       Press, 1919.   292p.

A valuable source book. Its tone is scholarly and
gives evidence of much painstaking care in its
preparation.

28.   Hill, David Jayne. The contemporary development
       of diplomacy. A paper ... St. Louis: 1904. 18p.

A speech on the art and practice of diplomacy.

29.   International Seminar for Diplomats, Klessheim,
       1959? Diplomatie unserer zeit. La diplomatie

contemporaine. Contemporary diplomacy.   Edited
by Karl Braunias and Gerald Stourch.   Graz,
Styria, 1959.   330p.

Lectures, in English, French and German, on
diplomacy and the diplomatic profession.

30.   Johnson, Edgar Augustus Jerome, ed. The dimen-
       sions of diplomacy, by McGeorge Bundy and others.
       Baltimore, Johns Hopkins Press, 1964.   135p.

       A series of scholarly lectures dedicated to the
       theme of diplomatic practice and, above all, ex-
       cellence.

31.   Kertesz, Stephen Denis, ed. Diplomacy in a changing
       world.   Edited with M.A. Fitzsimons.   Notre
       Dame, Ind. , University of Notre Dame Press,
       1959.   407p.

       A symposium of essays on "the problems and re-
       sources of diplomacy in a world characterized by
       radical departure from the past. " The topics
       covered range from general issues of diplomacy
       and diplomatic practice to the diplomacy of various
       nations, large and small.

32.   Krauske, Otto. Die entwickelung der ständigen dip-
       lomatie vom fünfzehnten jahrhundert bis zu den
       beschlassen von 1815 und 1818.   Leipzig, Duncker
       & Humbool, 1885.   245p.   (Bibliographical foot-
       notes)

       An overview of world diplomacy within the scope
       of international law and relations.

33.   Krekeler, Heinz L. Die Diplomatie.   München, Wien,
       Olzog, 1965.   254p.   (Geschichte und Staat, v.
       110/111; Bibliography: p. 247-250)

       A series of essays on diplomacy in general and
       diplomatic practice in particular.

34.   Krishna Murty, G.V.G. Dynamics of diplomacy.
       Delhi, National, 1968.   343p.   (Select bibliog-
       raphy: p. 333-335)

A basic discussion of modern diplomatic methods
as seen from the Indian experience.

35.   Krizman, Bogdan. Sto je diplomacija. Zagreb,
       Stamparija "Vjesnik" NFH, 1952.   127p.

       A short work on the art and practice of diplomacy.

36.   Lippmann, Walter. The stakes of diplomacy. New
       York, Holt, 1915.   235p.

       Entertaining but rather too cynical criticism of the
       political features of modern diplomacy. Now some-
       what out of date.

37.   Mably, Gabriel Bonnot de.   Diplomatische varhand-
       lungen. Edited by Albert Ritter.   Berlin, W.
       Borntrager, 1918.   278p.

       An essay on different aspects of diplomatic practice.

38.   Manning, Charles Anthony Woodward.   The nature of
       international society. New York, Wiley, 1962.
       220p.

       In what he calls an essay in meta-diplomatics for
       beginners, the author grapples, in an original and
       sprightly fashion, with a number of troublesome
       and ambiguous concepts on international relations
       and diplomacy.

39.   Moshamm, Franz Xavier von.   Europäisches gesand-
       schaftsrecht. Landshut, F. S. Hagen, 1805.
       467p.

       A general treatise on diplomacy and ambassadors.

40.   Nicolson, Sir Harold George.   Diplomacy.   3d ed.
       New York, Oxford University Press, 1963.   268p.
       (Home University library of modern knowledge,
       192p; Bibliography: p. 263)

       The history, elementary rules and practice of dip-
       lomacy lucidly set forth for the layman.   The
       author, a trained diplomat himself, devotes par-
       ticular attention to recent changes in the methods
       of diplomacy.

41.   Numelin, Ragnar Julius.   The beginnings of diplo-
        macy; a sociological study of intertribal and
        international relations.   London, Oxford University
        Press, 1950.   372p.   (Bibliography: p. 316-365)

        A sociological study of intertribal and interna-
        tional relations by a Finnish diplomat.

42.   _____.   Les origines de la diplomatie; traduit du
        suédois par Jean Louis Perret.   Paris, Flam-
        merion, 1945.   269p.

        An excellent discussion of the primitive roots of
        the art and practice of diplomacy by a noted
        scholar and former diplomat.

43.   Oliver, Robert Tarbell.   Culture and communication;
        the problem of penetrating national and cultural
        boundaries.   Springfield, Ill., Thomas, 1962.
        165p.   (American lecture series, publications
        no. 506; Includes bibliography)

        A discussion of the problems surrounding inter-
        national communications and the diplomatic inter-
        course of nations.

44.   Panikkar, Kavalam Medhava.   The principles and
        practice of diplomacy.   Bombay, Asia Pub. House,
        1956.   99p.

        A basic study of diplomatic practice.

45.   Pecquet, Antoine.   Le l'arte de négocier avec
        succès pour l'avantage de son souverain.   New
        ed.   Francfort & Leipzig, Aux dépens de la
        compagnie, 1764.   160p.

        This work covers the difficulties involved with
        diplomatic negotiations between sovereigns.

46.   _____.   Discours sur l'art de négocier.   Paris,
        Chez Nyon Fils, 1737.   168p.

        A brief but provocative study on the role of
        diplomacy in negotiations between nations.

47.   Peralta Peralta, Jamie. La institucion diplomática.
        Santiago, Editorial Juridica de Chile, 1951.
        pp. 438-546. (Bibliography: p. 543-546)

        A reprint of an article on the art and practice of
        diplomatic affairs.

48.   Pipkin, Charles Wooten. The diplomacy of peace
        and international cooperation. New York, League
        of Nations Association, 1930. 24p.

        A short overview of diplomacy in action to settle
        international disputes.

49.   Pokstefl, Josef. Co je diplomacie. Vyd. 1. Phaha,
        Svoboda, 1966. 132p. (Abeceda mezinarodnich
        vztahu, sv. 29)

        Although somewhat brief, this is a fairly stable
        and general discussion of diplomacy and its prob-
        lems.

50.   Pradhan, Bishwa. Foreign policy and diplomacy.
        Delhi? 1964. 96p. (Bibliography: p. 95-96)

        An essay on the development of foreign policy and
        diplomatic practice.

51.   Pritiwitz und Gaffron, Friedrich Wilhelm von.
        Aussenpolitik und Diplomatie; eine Skizze. Mun-
        chen, Isar Verlag, 1951. 26p. (Politische Bild-
        ung; schriftenreihe der Hochschule fur Politische
        Wissenschaften Munchen, Heft, 20)

        A summary of diplomatic practice in the formu-
        lation of foreign policy.

52.   Quaroni, Pietro. Aspetti della diplomazia contem-
        poranea. Oriete e occident. Conferenze.
        Venezia, C. Ferrari, 1956. 60p.

        A brief excursion into the difficulties of diplo-
        matic negotiations.

53.   Redlich, Marcellus Donald Alexander von. Interna-
        tional law as a substitute for diplomacy. 2d ed.
        Chicago, Independent Publishing Co., 208p.

(Bibliography: p. 205-208)

A capable survey of the history of international relations and the practice of diplomacy, as a background for the thesis that the abolition of war is dependent on the further development of international law.

54.   Regala, Roberto. Diplomacy in a changing world. Manila, 1961. 11, 1p.

The text of a speech briefly enumerating the problems involved in modern diplomatic practice.

55.   Rennell, James Rennell Rodd. Diplomacy. London, Benn, 1929. 79, 1p. (Bibliography: p. 80)

A brief treatment of the complexities of diplomatic relations.

56.   Roetter, Charles. The diplomatic art, an informal history of world diplomacy. Philadelphia, Macrae Smith, 1963. 248p.

A brief but well written general account of diplomatic history emphasizing the nature of the subject.

57.   Santa Pinter, José Julio. Humanismo y política exterior. Buenos Aires, 1959. 61p. (Ediciones Humanismo, 7; Bibliography: p. 55-61)

A general treatment on international relations with special emphasis accorded to diplomacy and diplomatic and consular service.

58.   _____ . Teoría práctica de la diplomacia. Buenos Aires, R. Depalma, 1958. 353p. (Includes bibliography)

This work covers the theory and practice of diplomacy and has good bibliographic coverage.

59.   Szilassy, Gyula. Traité pratique de diplomatie moderne. Paris, Payot, 1928. 256p.

The author, a former Austro-Hungarian diplomat,

supplies an admirable guide to the practice of diplomacy, and in this field the book is almost unique.

60.   Tarle, Evgenii Viktorovich. La tattica della diplo-
         mazia borghese. Milano, Edizioni sociali, 1952.
         126p.

         Includes information on the role of diplomacy in
         international politics.

61.   Ugarteche, Pedro. Educación diplomática antigua y
         moderna. Buenos Aires, Emece, 1964.   119p.
         (Seleccion Emece de obras contemporaneas)

         A brief essay on the general practice of diplomacy.

62.   Vidal y Saura, Gines.   Tratado de derecho diplomá-
         tico, contribución al estudio sobre los principios
         y usos de la diplomaccia moderne.   Madrid, Ed-
         itorial Rees, 1925.   576p.

         A very general work on all aspects of the diplo-
         matic arts.

63.   Wakelin, John.   The roots of diplomacy; how to
         study inter-state relations.   London, Hutchinson
         Educational, 1965.   186p.   (Bibliographical foot-
         notes)

         A basic treatise on the study and teaching of inter-
         national relations with emphasis upon diplomacy.

64.   Webster, Sir Charles Kingsley.   The art and practice
         of diplomacy. New York, Barnes & Noble, 1962.
         245p.

         A selection of lectures and articles by a leading
         British diplomatic historian who died in 1961.

65.   Wellesley, Sir Victor.   Diplomacy in fetters.   New
         York, Hutchinson, 1944.   224p.   (Bibliographical
         footnotes)

         A former diplomat discusses the forces which he
         believes hamper British diplomatic officials in
         their task of forwarding the Commonwealth's long-
         term interests.   Among these are lacks of coor-

dination between political and economic policies
and the failure of the government to give a firm
lead to public opinion on foreign affairs.

66.   Wesendonk, Otto Gunther von. Diplomatie. Eine
       einführung in ihr wesen und ihre methoden. Rad-
       olfezell am Bodensee, Heim-Verlag Adolf Dress-
       ler, 1933.   101p.

       A general treatise on the role of diplomacy in
       international affairs.

67.   Winter, Hellmuth.   Système de la diplomatie; rédigé
       préalablement en ébauche pour servir de base et de
       guide aux cours de diplomate théorique et pratique.
       Berlin, Chez Logier, 1830.   69p.

       A brief essay on diplomatic practice within inter-
       national law and relations.

68.   Zechlin, Walter.   Diplomatie und diplomaten.   Stutt-
       gart, Deutsche verlags-anstalt, 1935.   230p.

       A competent outline history of modern diplomatic
       institutions and procedures.

69.   _____ .   Die Welt der Diplomatie.   2. Aufl.   Frank-
       furt am Main, Athenaum-Verlag, 1960.   288p.

       A basic work covering the total spectrum of dip-
       lomacy, diplomats and diplomatic practice.   An
       extension of the above work.

Diplomats

        During the past century the functions of diplomats
have been steadily modified.   They were once the personal
representatives of monarchs, but obviously cannot have such
a personalized role in the present scheme of things when
they so often represent mass democracies and large bureau-
cratic structures.   Improvements in communication have
deprived diplomatic negotiators of their former freedom to
work out their own compromises.   Foreign offices insist
on controlling the finest details of a continuing negotiation.
Transportation has been improved to such a level of speed
and reliability as to permit much diplomatic intercourse to

go on in an atmosphere of multilateral conference rather
than the intimate head-to-head sessions of an earlier era.

The diplomat residing abroad has innumerable special
functions.   First in the list of tasks is that of representation.
He symbolizes his own country in all its dealings with his
host.   Second, the diplomat is charged to a major--although
declining--extent with negotiation of all manner of questions.
Third, the diplomat is par excellence a medium of communication between his own government and that of his host.
Finally, and of major importance only in recent times, diplomats have developed a real public relations mission in
explaining and interpreting their own culture to the citizens
of the state to which they are accredited. [5]

The following section includes mostly the memoirs
or reminiscences of those who have had extensive diplomatic experience.   Their lives are an important source
for understanding the complexities of the diplomatic process.

70.   Abetz, Otto Friedrich.   Histoire d'une politique
          franco-allemande, 1930-1950; mémoires d'un am-
          basadeur.   Paris, Stock, 1953.   356p.

          A diplomatic perspective on Franco-German foreign
          relations particularly during the German occupation
          of France from 1940-1945.

71.   Acheson, Dean Gooderham.   The pattern of respon-
          sibility; edited by McGeorge Bundy from the record
          of Secretary of State Dean Acheson.   Boston,
          Houghton Mifflin, 1952.   309p.

          A well rounded account of the record of Mr.
          Acheson in his role as Secretary of State.

72.   Akzin, Benjamin.   Propaganda by diplomats.   Wash-
          ington, Digest Press, American University Grad-
          uate School, 1936.   22p.

          An examination of the diplomats' efforts to influ-
          ence public opinion and the techniques he uses.

73.   D'Auvergne, Edmund Basil Francis.   Envoys extra-
          ordinary; the romantic careers of some remarkable
          British representatives abroad.   London, Harrap,

1937.   317p.

Relates the role of a number of British diplomats
in European politics. Attempts to portray the
romantic aspects of diplomatic life.

74.   Beaulac, Willard Leon.   Career ambassador.   New
York, Macmillan, 1951.   262p.

Informative and instructive memoirs of an American diplomat most of whose career has been
spent in Latin America and Spain.

75.   Bemis, Samuel Flagg, ed.   The American Secretaries of State and their diplomacy.   New York,
Cooper Square Publishers, 1963   (Vol. 1-17
so far issued)

An important set of volumes detailing and documenting the foreign policy of the Secretaries of
State.

76.   Bowers, Claude Gernade.   Chile through embassy
windows, 1939-1953.   New York, Simon and
Schuster, 1958.   375p.

Mr. Bowers served as American Ambassador to
Chile for 14 years from 1939-1952.   This informal
narrative, based on personal correspondence, on
his extensive diary and his own recollections, provides a useful source for the recent history of
Chile, its society and manners, and on its relations with the United States.

77.   Bowles, Chester.   Ambassador's report.   New York,
Harper, 1954.   415p.

Mr. Bowles, who was American Ambassador to
India for 18 months from 1951-1953, reports cap-
ably and with imagination on his mission.   In
general the work deals less with issues of diplomacy than with the more fundamental problems of
the 20th century.

78.   Boyce, Richard Fyfe.   The diplomat's wife.   New
York, Harper, 1956.   230p.

A book of helpful advice for wives of American
Foreign Service Officers.

79.   Briggs, Ellis Ormsbee.   Farewell to Foggy Botton;
       the recollections of a career diplomat.   New York,
       McKay, 1964.   306p.

       A former diplomat states his views and criticism
       of the United States Foreign Service.

80.   Byrnes, James Francis.   Speaking frankly.   New
       York, Harper, 1947.   324p.

       An account of the author's activities as Secretary
       of State in the early part of the Truman Adminis-
       tration.   An important source of information for
       the period covered.

81.   Cambon, Jules Martin.   The diplomatist.   London,
       P. Allan, 1931.   151p.

       A basic discussion of the career diplomat and the
       problems of diplomatic negotiations.   Covers his-
       torically up to the League of Nations.

82.   Cambon, Paul.   Correspondence, 1870-1924 ... avec
       un commentaire et des notes.   Paris, B. Grasset,
       1940-   3v.

       The correspondence of a noted French diplomat
       and statesman with emphasis upon European poli-
       tics from 1871-1924.

83.   Campbell, Sir Gerald.   Of true experience.   London,
       New York, Hutchinson, 1948?   183p.

       Memoirs of a diplomatic and consular career,
       which included extended experience in the United
       States since 1920.

84.   Cardozo, Michael H.   Diplomats in international
       cooperation: stepchildren of the Foreign Service.
       Ithaca, N.Y., Cornell University Press, 1962.
       142p.

       An interesting study of the uncertain status of a
       new breed of United States diplomat--those assigned

to international organizations such as O. E. E. C.,
NATO and European Communities.

85.   Clemens, Severus.   Der beruf des diplomaten; bet-
      rachtungen über die diplomatische berufsmentalität.
      Berlin, Deutsche verlagsgesellschaft für politik
      und geschichte m. b. h., 1926.   107p.

      A pioneer essay on the psychology of the diplomat
      by a former member of the German diplomatic
      service.

86.   Cleugh, Eric Arthur.   Without let or hindrance;
      reminiscences of a British Foreign Service Officer.
      London, Cassell, 1960.   223p.

      A serious reflection on the British Foreign Ser-
      vice.

87.   Cobban, Alfred.   Ambassadors and secret agents;
      the diplomacy of the First Earl of Malmesbury
      at the Hague.   London, Cape, 1954.   255p.
      (Bibliography: p. 219-224)

      The account of the Ambassadorial function in the
      external politics of the Netherlands, 1714-1798.

88.   Craig, Gordon Alexander, ed.   The diplomats: 1919-
      1939.   Edited with Felix Gilbert.   Princeton,
      N. J., Princeton University Press, 1953.   700p.
      (Bibliographical footnotes)

      Seventeen authors collaborated in this diplomatic
      history of the inter-war years.   Based for the
      most part on the careers of individual diplomats
      and officials in the foreign offices, the biographical
      approach is of particular value in showing the
      vicissitudes of the old art of diplomacy under the
      political and social changes of our present era.

89.   Cresson, William Penn.   Diplomatic portraits;
      Europe and the Monroe doctrine ... Boston,
      Houghton, Mifflin, 1923.   270p.   (Bibliography:
      p. xvii-xviii)

      A look at European diplomats and their view of
      the Monroe doctrine.

90.   Daniels, Josephus. Shirt-sleeve diplomat. Chapel
        Hill, N. C., University of North Carolina Press,
        1947.   547p.

        The memoirs of the former Ambassador to Mexico.

91.   Davies, Joseph Edward. Mission to Moscow. New
        York, Simon & Schuster, 1941.   683p.

        Mr. Davies became U.S. Ambassador to Russia
        late in 1936 and served in Moscow during a fate-
        ful period in Soviet history.   He took his job
        seriously and traveled about the country exten-
        sively and talked with all conditions of men from
        Stalin down to the Mushik.   He shows himself in
        these memoirs to have been a cannier judge of
        men and events than many a professional diplomat.

92.   Dennett, Raymond, ed. Negotiating with the Russians.
        Edited with Joseph E. Johnson.   Boston, World
        Peace Foundation, 1951.   310p.

        A highly instructive symposium of the experience
        of ten Americans who have had the responsibility
        of negotiating with the Russians on a variety of
        issues over the last decade.

93.   Dodd, William Edward. Ambassador Dodd's diary,
        1933-1938.   Edited by William E. Dodd, Jr. and
        Martha Dodd.   New York, Harcourt, Brace, 1941.
        464p.

        As a professional historian, Mr. Dodd was well
        equipped to place the Nazi movement in its proper
        perspective and to understand its implications
        ahead of some of his more superficial contempor-
        aries.   He went to Germany in the summer of
        1933 already disliking the Nazi regime.   This diary
        reveals that in his reports home he portrayed
        the true character of the Nazi Government and the
        men who ran it.

94.   Dunham, Donald Carl. Envoy unextraordinary. New
        York, John Day, 1944.   166p.

        Reminiscences of a young American who spent 8
        years serving as a vice-consul in Berlin, Hong

Kong, Athens and Aden.

95.   Einstein, Lewis. A diplomat looks back. Edited by
        Lawrence E. Gelfand, with a foreword by George
        F. Kennan. New Haven, Yale University Press,
        1968.   269p.   (A bibliography of Lewis Einstein's
        published writings: p. 251-256)

        The evocative and perceptive memoirs of a dis-
        tinguished American diplomat, spanning half a
        century.

96.   Freidin, Seymour. The experts. With George
        Bailey. New York, Macmillan, 1968.   398p.

        A study of the influence of journalism on Amer-
        ican foreign policy. They analyze reports made
        by members of the diplomatic service, by news-
        paper reporters and by television commentators,
        and seek to show that this reportage is based on
        misinformation and vanity.

97.   Gibson, Hugh. A diplomatic diary. London & New
        York, Hodder and Stoughton, 1917.   296p.

        The diary of the first secretary to the American
        legation in Brussels.

98.   Glasgow, George. Continental statesmen. London,
        G. Bles, 1930.   238p.

        Interesting character sketches and appreciations
        by an English liberal.

99.   Graebner, Norman A., ed. An uncertain tradition;
        American Secretaries of State in the twentieth
        century. New York, McGraw-Hill, 1961.   341p.
        (Includes bibliography)

        A symposium of essays on 14 American Secretaries
        of State of the twentieth century--from John Hay
        to John Foster Dulles.

100.   Grew, Joseph Clark. Turbulent era; a diplomatic
        record of forty years, 1904-1945. Edited by
        Walter Johnson, assisted by Nancy H. Hooker,
        Boston, Houghton Mifflin, 1952.   2v.   (1560p.)

This record is based largely on Mr. Grew's
diary and letters.   Valuable as a historical source,
the sections of interest revolve around the events
leading up to Pearl Harbor.

101.   Griscom, Lloyd Carpenter.   Diplomatically speaking.
        Boston, Little, Brown, 1940.   476p.

        The entertaining and often enlightening memoirs
        of an American who enjoyed quite a career as a
        diplomat in various ports of the world before and
        during World War I.

102.   Hardinge, Charles Hardinge.   Old diplomacy: the
        reminiscences of Lord Hardinge of Penshurst.
        London, J. Murray, 1947.   288p.

        An informative record of 45 years in the British
        diplomatic service, ending in 1922.   During this
        time the author held several high posts.

103.   Hassell, Ulrich von.   Im wandel der aussenpolitik,
        von der französischen revolution bis zum welt-
        krieg.   3 aufl.   München, F. Bruckmann, 1940.
        244p.

        A former Ambassador of Germany at Rome dis-
        cusses a number of European diplomats.

104.   Hatch, Alden.   Ambassador Extraordinary Clare
        Boothe Luce.   New York, Holt, 1956.   254p.

        An interesting biography of Mrs. Luce who served
        her country in a distinguished manner.

105.   Hayes, Carlton Joseph Huntley.   Wartime mission in
        Spain, 1942-1945.   New York, Macmillan, 1945.
        313p.

        Mr. Hayes served as American Ambassador in
        Madrid from 1942 to 1943.   His primary assign-
        ment was to keep Franco from making any more
        trouble for the United States than could be helped.

106.   Hayter, Sir William.   The Kremlin and the Embassy.
        New York, Macmillan, 1967.   160p.

A description of the author's diplomatic experience
while serving as the British Ambassador.

107.   Heinrichs, Waldo H. American ambassador; Joseph
        C. Grew and the development of the U. S. diplo-
        matic tradition. Boston, Little, Brown, 1966.
        460p.   (Bibliography: p. 441-446)

        This book is an intriguing case study of the limi-
        tations of diplomacy when overpowering national
        ambitions and emotions complicate the issues.

108.   Holman, Ada Augusta (Kidgell). Memoirs of a
        premier's wife. Sydney, Angus and Robertson,
        1948.   198p.

        An interesting look at Australian diplomacy by
        the wife of one of its premiers.

109.   Hugessen, Sir Hughe Montgomery Knatchbull. Dip-
        lomat in peace in war ... London, J. Murray,
        1949.   270p.

        The correspondence and reminiscences of a British
        career diplomat in the 20th century.

110.   Hull, Cordell. The memoirs of Cordell Hull. Pre-
        pared with the assistance of Andrew Berding.
        New York, Macmillan, 1948. 2v. (1804p.)

        Mr. Hull retraces his career, with emphasis on
        his nearly 12 years as Secretary of State. He
        reveals a man deeply attached to certain principles
        and on the whole sure that his policies were the
        best ones for putting those principles into effect.

111.   Huntington-Wilson, Francis Mairs. Memoirs of an
        ex-diplomat. Boston, B. Humphries, 1945. 373p.

        Reminiscences of a former U. S. diplomat and
        under-Secretary of State who traveled extensively
        in Europe and South America and lived for nine
        years in Japan where he was second secretary in
        the legation at Tokyo.

112.   Huyn, Hans. Tragedy of errors: the chronicle of a
        European. Tr. by Nora Wydenbruck. London,

Hutchinson, 1939.   256p.

An Austrian diplomat analyses critically the rise
of National Socialism in Europe.

113.   Kelly, Sir David Voctor.   The ruling few, or the
human background to diplomacy.   London, Hollis
& Carter, 1952.   449p.

Intelligent reflections on an extended diplomatic
career by the former British Ambassador to the
Soviet Union.   As the title indicates, it is the
author's belief that the function of the diplomat is
to size up and maintain communication with the
few who rule a country, regardless of its form of
government.

114.   Kennan, George Frost.   Memoirs, 1925-1950.   Boston,
Little, Brown, 1967.   583p.

The interesting recollections of our former Ambassador to the Soviet Union.

115.   Lane, Arthur Bliss.   I saw Poland betrayed: an
American ambassador reports to the American
people.   Indianapolis, Bobbs-Merrill, 1948.
344p.

Mr. Lane was American ambassador in Poland
from July 1945 to early in 1947.   He went to
Warsaw disliking the communists, and the longer
he stayed the more he disliked them.   This is
an angry book, well-informed though not attempting to cover all of the facets of the post war
situation in Poland.

116.   Lombard, Mrs. Helen Cassin (Carusi).   Washington
waltz; diplomatic people and policies.   New York,
Knopf, 1941.   271p.

Breezy, irreverent gossip about the great and near
great in the diplomatic world.

117.   Miller, Hope Ridings.   Embassy Row; the life &
times of diplomatic Washington.   New York, Holt,
Rinehart and Winston, 1969.   286p.

A light-hearted expose of the diplomatic life in
our nation's Capitol.

118.   Mott, Thomas Bentley. Twenty years as military
        attache. New York, London, Oxford University
        Press, 1937.   342p.

        Most of Colonel Mott's career was devoted to
        smoothing the path of political and military mis-
        sions in various parts of the world.   He served
        on Mr. Root's staff during the latter's visit to
        Russia in 1917 and on General Pershing's staff
        during the war.   He thus has many interesting
        things to say about important persons and events.

119.   Phillips, William. Ventures in diplomacy.   Boston,
        Beacon Press, 1953.   477p.

        Memoirs of a distinguished professional diplomat
        whose career extends back to 1903.   In the Second
        World War, Mr. Phillips was President Roosevelt's
        representative in India, then political adviser to
        SHAEF, and in 1940 a member of the Anglo-Amer-
        ican Commission to Palestine.

120.   Reinsch, Paul Samuel. An American diplomat in
        China.   Garden City, N.Y., Doubleday, Page,
        1922.   396p.

        A useful narrative by the American minister to
        China from 1913 to 1919.

121.   Richardson, Norval. My diplomatic education.   New
        York, Dodd, Mead, 1923.   337p.

        The writer of these memoirs has seen 14 years in
        the diplomatic service.   A worthwhile narrative of
        diplomatic life, of foreign lands and customs.

122.   Russell, William Richard. Berlin embassy.   New
        York, Dutton, 1941.   307p.

        Interesting sidelights on how the average German
        reacted to the war, by a young American who
        served for a time as clerk in the U.S. consulate
        in Berlin.

123.   Schwerdtfeger, Rudolf. Die völkerrechtliche son-
       derstellung der diplomatischen agenten. Berlin,
       Frendsdorf, 1914.   84p.   (Bibliography: p. 5-7)

       A short and oversimplified essay on the functions
       of diplomats in the international sphere.

124.   Seabury, Paul.   The Wilhelmstrasse: a study of Ger-
       man diplomats under the Nazi regime.   Berkeley,
       University of California Press, 1954.   217p.
       (Includes bibliographies)

       This able study of the position of German diplomats
       and the Foreign Office under the Nazis explores
       both the anomalous position of the civil service in
       a totalitarian regime and the broader aspects of
       the function of the bureaucrat and technician in the
       modern state.

125.   Spaulding, Ernest Wilder.   Ambassadors ordinary
       and extraordinary.   Washington, Public Affairs
       Press, 1961.   302p.

       An informal sketch of a number of the ambassadors
       and ministers who have represented the United
       States abroad in the course of its history.

126.   Stuart, John Leighton.   Fifty years in China: the
       memoirs of John Leighton Stuart, missionary and
       ambassador.   New York, Random House, 1954.
       346p.

       For many years a missionary and educator, Dr.
       Stuart was appointed U. S. Ambassador to China
       in 1946, a post he held until December 1952.
       Written calmly and without rancor, it is none the
       less quite critical of several aspects of U. S.
       policy, especially the publication of the White
       Paper on China in 1949.

127.   Thornton, Percy Melville.   Foreign secretaries of
       the XIX century to 1834.   2d ed. London, W. H.
       Allen & Co., 1881-83.   3v.

       One of the most detailed biographical works on
       British statesmen of the 19th century.

128. Wilson, Hugh Robert. Diplomacy as a career.
      Cambridge, Mass., The Riverside Press, 1941.
      52p.

      A brief view of the career possibilities of the
      foreign service.

129. _____. The education of a diplomat. New York,
      Longmans, Green, 1938-41. 2v.

      The author reminisces on his career in the Amer-
      ican diplomatic service in many parts of the
      world during thirty years. Mr. Wilson makes
      no revelations, but does provide a few interesting
      insights on the countries in which he served.

130. Zacharias, Ellis Mark. Secret mission: the story of
      an intelligence officer. New York, Pitman's sons,
      1946.   433p.

      Memoires and behind-the-scenes recollections of
      an American naval officer for many years con-
      cerned with Far Eastern intelligence. Contains
      a number of revelations on Japanese diplomacy
      before and during the war.

Diplomatic Etiquette and Protocol

     Etiquette and protocol are interesting facets of dip-
lomatic practice. The function of etiquette is to provide
an amiable means by which certain diplomatic activities
may be carried out. The role of protocol involves the
order by which these activities can proceed. Every individual is affected by etiquette and protocol to some degree.
For example, when a person eats at a restaurant he expects
to be waited on in his turn. If someone else arrives later
and gets served before him, he justly feels slighted and, in
all probability, protests in some manner. The same is true
when one stands in line to buy a ticket to a football game.
He would undoubtedly object to another person's crowding in
ahead of him. He is sensitive about his own place in line.
He wants the other fellow to abide by the rules.

     Thus it is we find that in the course of time most
human relationships have come to be governed by a series
of accepted practices. When these practices are ignored,

trouble is usually encountered and is accompanied by confusion and even conflict. The same holds true in the intercourse of nations: the dangers are more extensive where
established procedure is violated. Slights take on an ex-
ceedingly grave character. Any failure to conform to the
customary courtesies may result in an international incident.
Upon occasion, such incidents have brought nations to the
brink of war.

For the most part, protocol is rooted in the sound
knowledge of human relationships. It is both practical and
purposeful in that it reflects the observance of mutual respect and consideration among nations. It allows international affairs to be conducted in an atmosphere of courtesy
and friendliness. It is the mode of behavior most favorable
to the achievment of understanding and cooperation.

Protocol has been described simply as the body of
acceptable practice which has developed between the nations
of the world in their continual contacts with each other.
It is the recognized system of international courtesy. In
the final analysis it plays an important role in carrying out
a successful foreign policy. [6]

131.   Buchanan, Wiley T.   Red carpet at the White House;
       four years as Chief of Protocol in the Eisenhower
       administration.   With Arthur Gordon.   New York,
       Dutton, 1964.   256p.

       The author, Chief of Protocol during Eisenhower's
       second term as president, discusses his diplomatic
       responsibilities in connection with the state visits
       of foreign dignities and rulers.

132.   Moreno Salcedo, Luis.   A guide to protocol.   Rev.
       ed. Manila, Distributed by University Book Supply,
       1959.   280p.   (Bibliography: p. 269-271)

       A general handbook on diplomatic etiquette and
       outline of Philippine diplomatic practice.

133.   Radlovic, I. Monte.   Etiquette & protocol; a hand-
       book of conduct in American and international
       circles.   New York, Harcourt, Brace, 1957.
       240p.

A general treatise on the formal etiquette used
in diplomatic gatherings.

134.   Serres, Jean Charles.   Manuel pratique de protocole.
Vitry-le-Francois, Marne, Editions de l'Arquebuse,
1960.   475p.

A handbook for French diplomatic officials outlin-
ing procedures and practices in formal meetings
etc.

II

Historical Evolution of Diplomacy

Modern diplomatic practice contains many elements
inherited from Greek and Roman tradition. Although they
made no permanent diplomatic missions, they did send
emissaries upon an ad hoc basis to transact particular
business. The ancients accepted the rule of safe conduct
and protection for diplomats, at least within the recieving
state, probably conceiving it in terms of religious sanction.
The Romans made no major contribution to diplomatic practice; however, they did carry on foreign relations with other
nations with certain ceremonial activities.

The origins of diplomatic archives may be attributed
to the Romans. These later became the core of the foreign
office structure. It was their practice to issue state letters
of recommendation, passports, safe conduct, etc. to those
authorized to travel upon imperial roads. In 13th century
England essential documents relating to foreign relations
were dispersed in a number of depositories. From the
keeping of documents came the establishment of an official
service to handle them in Britain. This service became
the forerunner of the foreign service. At times these
keepers of records were sent on diplomatic missions. Permanent foreign missions were the initiative of the Italian
city states in the 15th century. This created a need for
more diplomats. Francis I of France (1515-1547) was
probably the first ruler to organize systematically a diplomatic corps. Although present notions of recruitment and
training of career diplomats originated only in the nineteenth
century, the whole period of post-Renaissance history wit-
nessed a steady growth of career diplomacy as a profession
attracting men of ability and position.

The conduct of diplomacy among the Italian states
of the Renaissance produced an unfortunate tradition of
duplicity, cunning, and unscrupulous maneuvering for advantage which continues to be associated with diplomatic

activities in the modern world. While such tactics are
appalling, modern international politics suggests that there
is still need, not for deception and bad faith, but certainly
for cool appraisal and unsentimental marshalling of force.

The character of modern career diplomacy owes more
to French than to the Italian example. Whereas the Italian
practice of diplomacy reflected an unstable political system
dominated by autocrats or oligarchs, French diplomatic
practice on the other hand since the period of Richelieu
has reflected the increasing sense of constitutional restraints
within the state and orderly standards in external relations.

From the French experience came the practice of
public and secret diplomatic maneuvering and the maintenance
of permanent embassies and numerous missions. Their
diplomatic agents were classified and the career diplomat
was a man of high quality both in rearing and education.
This led to a strengthening of ties among diplomats whose
togetherness has withstood the test of time.

Of works in this area, the following are illustrative:

135.   Acheson, Dean Gooderham.   Power and diplomacy.
        Cambridge, Harvard University Press, 1958.
        137p.

        These four lectures on the position and responsi-
        bilities of the U.S. develop certain familiar themes
        each critical of Republican policies.

136.   Alberi, Eugenio, ed.   Relazioni degli ambasciatori
        veneti al Senato; raccolte, annotate.   Firenze,
        Societa editirice florentina, 1839-63.   15v.

        An extensive account of Venetian foreign affairs
        with primary diplomatic documents on European
        history.

137.   Albrecht-Carrie, Rene.   A diplomatic history of
        Europe since the Congress of Vienna.   New York,
        Harper, 1958.   736p.

        A scholarly and thoughtful general diplomatic his-
        tory from the Vienna settlement to the Hungarian
        and Middle Eastern crises of 1956.

138.   Alting von Geusau, Frans Alphons Maria.   European
       organizations and foreign relations of states; a
       comparative analysis of decision-making.   Leyden,
       A. W. Sythoff, 1962.   290p.   (Studies on politics,
       no. 10; Bibliography: p. 266-278)

       A discussion of the change in the foreign policy-
       making process resulting from the creation of
       multilateral organizations among European states.

139.   Archives diplomatiques pour l'histoire du temps et
       des états.   Stuttgart et Tubingue, J. G. Cotta,
       1821-26.   6v.   (Vols. 1-2 German and French
       on opposite pages)

       Contains a vast number of diplomatic documents
       on European politics from the Congress of Vienna
       in 1815 to the revolutionary period culminating
       in 1848.

140.   Asmundo, Michele.   La diplomazia europea.   2d ed.
       Catania, Tip. di. G.   Pastore, 1905.   278p.

       An overview of European politics and diplomacy.
       Not very detailed or analytic.

141.   Audisio, Guglielmo.   Idée historique et rationnelle
       de la diplomatie ecclésiastique.   Louvain, C.
       Peeters, 1865.   520p.

       A concentrated treatise on Catholic diplomacy in
       international affairs.   Treats the power of the
       Papacy in temporal affairs.

142.   Barthelemy, Joseph.   Démocratie et politique étrang-
       ère; cours professé à l'Ecole des hautes-études
       sociales en 1915-1916.   Paris, F. Alcan, 1915.
       531p.

       A history of European diplomacy with special em-
       phasis upon the First World War and the problems
       of foreign relations for democratic nations.

143.   Beard, Charles Austin.   Cross currents in Europe
       today.   Boston, Marshall Jones, 1922.   278p.
       (Bibliography: p. 176-278)

An excellent view of European diplomatic history
for the period covered.

144.   Benedetti, Vincent.   Studies in diplomacy; from the
        French of Count Benedetti.   New York, Macmillan,
        1896.   323p.

        A brief history of European diplomacy covering
        the Franco-Prussian War and the Triple Alliance.

145.   Blaga, Corneliu S.   L'évolution de la diplomatie;
        idéologie moeurs et technique.   Paris, A. Pédone,
        1938   v. 1   (Bibliography: v. 1, p.   481-483)

        An extensive treatise on the evolution of European
        diplomacy.

146.   Broglie, Albert i. e.   Jacques Victor Albert.   His-
        toire et diplomatie.   Paris, Calmann Levy,
        1889.   460p.

        A short and cursory attempt to cover the broad
        expanse of world diplomatic history.

147.   Brooks, Philip Coolidge.   Diplomacy and the border
        lands; the Adams-Onis treaty of 1819.   Berkeley,
        Calif., University of California Press, 1939.
        262p.   (University of California publications in
        history, v. 24; References: p. 220-231)

        A wide ranging book covering the Washington
        treaty of 1819 and the historical background of
        Spanish-American diplomatic relations.

148.   Brunner, Sebastian.   Der humor in der diplomatie
        und regierungs-kunde des 18.   jahrhunderts ...
        Wien, W. Braumuller, 1872.   2v. in 1.

        A somewhat flamboyant attempt to disclose the
        ins and outs of the German court in the European
        diplomatic tradition.

149.   Buchanan, Meriel.   Diplomacy and foreign courts.
        New York, J. S. Sears, 1928?   13-288p.

        A historical study of court life in Russia and other
        European countries and the diplomatic maneuverings

of courtiers.

150.   Bullard, Arthur. The diplomacy of the great war.
        New York, Macmillan, 1916. 344p. (Biblio-
        graphy: p. 325-333)

        A decidedly useful work. The author has kept a
        fairly judicial attitude, not expecting to find super-
        human virtue or vice on either side.

151.   Child, Richard Washburn. A diplomat looks at
        Europe. New York, Duffield, 1925. 301p.

        A diplomatic perspective of European politics prior
        to World War I and after.

152.   Craig, Gordon Alexander. War, politics and diplo-
        macy; selected essays. New York, Praeger,
        1966. 297p. (Bibliographical footnotes)

        An analysis of the problems of war and its rela-
        tionship with diplomacy. Has good documentation
        and provides some new insights into some histor-
        ical events.

153.   Cuttino, George Peddy. English diplomatic adminis-
        tration, 1259-1339. London, Oxford University
        Press, 1940. 195p. (Bibliography: p. 171-
        178)

        A good historical account of British diplomatic
        relations for the period covered.

154.   Debidour, Antonin. Histoire diplomatique de l'Europe
        depuis l'ouverture du Congrès de Vienne jusqu'à
        la fermeture du Congrès de Berlin (1814-1878) ...
        Paris, F. Alcan, 1891. 2v.

        A detailed and documented diplomatic history of
        Europe from 1789-1900.

155.   Demiashkevich, Michael John. Shackled diplomacy;
        the permanent factors of foreign policies of nations.
        New York, Barnes & Noble, 1934. 244p.

        A study of the permanent factors in diplomacy, in
        which the author comes to the not very astonishing

conclusion that ideas of revenge, of "national
mission" and of vital interests are the motive
forces now dominant.

156.   Escott, Thomas Hay Sweet.   The story of British
diplomacy; its makers and movements.   London,
T. R. Unwin, 1908.   419p.

There are no new facts and no original reflections
in this loose and verbose sketch of English diplomatic history.

157.   Essen, Leon van der.   La diplomatie; ses origines
et son organisation jusqu'a la fin de l'ancien
régime.   Bruxelles, Editions P. D. L., 1953.
205p.

A short history of diplomacy.   Greatly over simplified but useful as an overview.

158.   Eytan, Walter.   The first ten years; a diplomatic
history of Israel.   New York, Simon and Schuster,
1958.   239p.

A somewhat official survey of Israel's diplomatic
history.

159.   Fifield, Russell Hunt.   The diplomacy of Southeast
Asia: 1945-1958.   New York, Harper, 1958.
584p.   (Bibliography: p. 520-566)

A wide-ranging study of the diplomatic problems
and crises connected with the emergence of independence movements in the Philippines, Indonesia,
Burma, Indochina and Malaya.

160.   Furnia, Arthur Homer.   The diplomacy of appease-
ment: Anglo-French relations and the prelude to
World War II, 1931-1938.   Washington, D. C.,
University Press, 1960.   454p.

A detailed look at the diplomatic interlude leading
up to World War II.

161.   Ganshoff, Francois Louis.   Le Moyen Age ... Paris,
Hachette, 1953.   331p.   (Histoire des relations
internationale, t. 1; Includes bibliographies)

A general history of international relations with a
focus upon the diplomacy of the middle ages.

162.   Glasgow, George.   From Dawes to Locarno; being
       a critical record of an important achievement in
       European diplomacy, 1924-1925.   New York,
       Harper, 1926.   185p.

       The Labour view of the Locarno settlement, con-
       taining the more important documents on the neg-
       otiations.

163.   Gooch, George Peabody.   Before the war; studies in
       diplomacy.   New York, Russell & Russell, 1967.
       2 v.   (Bibliographical footnotes)

       In this masterly work a leading British historian
       reviews the policies of the Great Powers.   Its
       only weakness is that it is largely confined to
       official material, neglecting movements of opinion
       and economic forces.

164.   _____.   Recent revelations of European diplomacy.
       New York, Russell & Russell, 1967.   475p.

       A detailed history of European diplomacy.

165.   _____.   Studies in diplomacy and statecraft.   New
       York, Longmans, Green, 1942.   373p.

       Ten essays by a noted British diplomatic historian
       of which five concern the background of the First
       World War and one deals with "British Foreign
       Policy, 1919-1939. "

166.   Graham, Robert A.   Vatican diplomacy; a study of
       church and state on the international plane.
       Princeton, N. J., Princeton University Press,
       1959.   442p.   (Bibliography: p. 397-419)

       This authoritative study describes the functions,
       development and operation of papal diplomacy in the
       relations between the Holy See and secular states.

167.   Hill, David Jayne.   Course in European diplomacy.   Wash-
       ington, D. C. The Columbian University, 1899. 153p.

An outline history of European diplomacy used
for a course on the subject.

168. _____. A history of diplomacy in the international
development of Europe. New York, Longmans,
Green, 1905-14. 3v. (Contains bibliographies)

An exhaustive study of the history of diplomacy.
It is carefully written and profusely documented.

169. Hurewitz, Jacob Coleman, ed. Diplomacy in the
Near and Middle East; a documentary record.
Princeton, N. J., Van Nostrand, 1956. 2v.
(Includes bibliographical references)

A most useful compilation of documents relating
to European diplomacy and concerning the Near
and Middle East from 1535 to the present. The
second volume is devoted to the years since the
outbreak of the First World War.

170. Jensen, De Lamar. Diplomacy and dogmatism, Ber-
nardino de Mendoza and the French Catholic
League. Cambridge, Harvard University Press,
1964. 322p. (Bibliography: p. 241-310)

This is an authoritative work on the diplomacy of
the Holy Alliance and de Mendoza.

171. Kennedy, Aubrey Leo. Old diplomacy and new, 1876-
1922, from Salisbury to Lloyd-George. London,
J. Murray, 1922. 414p. (Bibliography: p. 397-
399)

An exposition of English diplomacy for a period
of forty-six years. The author deplores the
deceit and trickery of the old diplomacy but
challenges the expediency of the new with the
entire absence of secrecy.

172. Kertesz, Stephen Denis. The quest for peace through
diplomacy. Englewood Cliffs, N. J., Prentice-
Hall, 1967. 182p. (Bibliographical footnotes)

An authoritatively written discussion of modern
diplomatic history. Material is well organized; however, no new ideas or novel interpretations are offered.

173.   Langer, William Leonard.   The diplomacy of im-
       perialism, 1890-1902 ... 2d ed. with supple-
       mentary bibliographies.   New York, Knopf, 1951.
       797p.

       Emphasizes the uses of imperialism to further diplo-
       matic objectives of world politics in the 19th century.

174.   Lefebvre, Armand Edouard.   Histoire des cabinets
       de l'Europe pendant le consulat et l'empire, 1800-
       1815. 2d ed.   Paris, Amyot, 1866-69.   5v.

       An exhaustive diplomatic history of Europe from
       1789-1815 and the Congress of Vienna.   Also deals
       specifically with french diplomatic relations during
       this period.

175.   Lodge, Sir Richard.   Studies in eighteenth century
       diplomacy, 1740-1748.   London, J. Murray, 1930.
       421p.

       An outline history of European politics and diplomacy.

176.   Mackay, B. Laurence.   Die moderne diplomatie, ihre
       entwicklungs-geschichte und ihre reformmöglich-
       keiten.   Frankfurt am Main, Rütten & Loening,
       1915.   175p.

       A short history of modern diplomacy.

177.   Mattingly, Garrett.   Renaissance diplomacy.   Boston,
       Houghton Mifflin, 1955.   323p.

       A scholarly and original book.   Its theme is the
       evolution of the function of the diplomat.

178.   Maulde La Claviere, Marie Alphonse René de.   La
       diplomatie au temps de Machiavel.   Paris, E.
       Leroux, 1892-93.   3v.

       An excellent and extensive treatment of diplomatic
       history during the renaissance.   Well documented
       and written.

179.   Mayer, Arno J.   Political origins of the new diplo-
       macy, 1917-1918.   New Haven, Yale University
       Press, 1959.   435p.   (Yale historical publica-
       tions, Studies, 18)

A detailed study of the emergence in both military camps of powerful new themes respecting war aims and diplomacy in the year that followed the March revolution in Russia and the entry of the United States into the conflict.

180.   Medrano Matus, Duilio.   El derecho diplomático a través de la historia.   León, Nicaragua, 1949. 50p.   (Bibliography: p. 50)

An overview of diplomatic history coupled with the historical development of diplomatic and consular practice of nations.

181.   Miruss, Alexander.   Das europäische gesandschaftrecht, nebst einem anhange von dem gesandschaftsrechte des Deutschen bundes, einer bucher kunde des gesandschaftsrechts und erlauternden beilagen. Leipzig, W. Englemann, 1847.   2v.   in 1.

A discussion of diplomatic history to the middle of the 19th century.   Also includes a good bibliography on diplomacy.

182.   Moore, John Bassett.   The history of European diplomacy from the development of the European concert prior to the peace of Westphalia to the treaty of Berlin, 1878.   New York, Columbia University, 1902.   191p.

An excellent view of European diplomatic history. Main disadvantage is its brevity and, thus, lack of depth.

183.   Morey, William Carey.   Diplomatic episodes; a review of certain historical incidents bearing upon international relations and diplomacy.   New York, Longmans, Green, 1926.   295p.   (References, p. 295)

Stimulatingly informative, this book deals with significant controversies in the field of diplomacy.

184.   Mowat, Robert Balmain.   Diplomacy and peace.   New York, R. M. McBride, 1936.   295p.

A readable but not greatly original book, being
in the main a reconsideration of the old diplomacy
and a critique of some current tendencies.

185.   . The fight for peace. Bristol, Eng.,
           Arrowsmith, 1937.   155p.

An uninspired review of international affairs during
the late 1930's.

186.   . A history of European diplomacy, 1451-
           1789. New York, Longmans, Green, 1928.   311p.

A useful but cursory survey.

187.   . A history of European diplomacy, 1815-
           1914. London, E. Arnold, 1933.   308p.

Good but oversimplified.

188.   . A history of European diplomacy, 1914-
           1925. New York, Longmans, Green, 1931.   343p.

A useful survey which suffers somewhat from its
brevity and consequent over-simplification.

189. Mowrer, Paul Scott. Our foreign affairs; a study
     in national interest and the new diplomacy. New
     York, Dutton, 1924.   348p.

An appraisal of the problems and responsibilities
involved in the position of the United States as a
world power by one of the most competent American foreign correspondents.

190. Namier, Lewis Bernstein. Diplomatic prelude, 1938-
     1939. London, Macmillan, 1948.   502p.

A classic study by one of the greatest historians
of the events immediately preceding the outbreak
of war. Somewhat outdated by subsequent documented publications.

191. Nanke, Czeslaw. Historia dyplomacji. Krakow,
     Nakl. S. Kaminskiego, 1947-   v. 1-   (Biblio-
     tecka Szkoly Nauk Polityczngen, uniwersyteta
     Jagiellonskiege, 4)

A series of volumes documenting the history of
diplomatic affairs.

192.   Neilson, Francis. How diplomats make war. New
        York, B. W. Huebsch, 1916.   382p.

        A history of European politics and diplomacy from
        the Franco-Prussian War up to the First World
        War.

193.   Petrie, Sir Charles Alexander. Diplomatic history,
        1713-1933. New York, Macmillan, 1949.   384p.
        (Bibliography: p. 371-374)

        A brief work tracing the main themes of diplo-
        matic history. The author is a leading British
        historian.

194.   . Earlier diplomatic history, 1492-1713. New
        York, Macmillan, 1949.   251p. (Bibliography:
        p. 239-241)

        A general history similar to the work cited above.

195.   Phillipson, Coleman. The international law and
        custom of ancient Greece and Rome. London,
        Macmillan, 1911.   2v.   (Bibliography: v. 1,
        p. 1-26)

        The first systematic work yet published on the
        subject. It attempts to expound and evaluate
        legal conceptions rather than to trace their origins.
        Over all it is a careful and scholarly treatise
        and it is magnificently documented.

196.   Picavet, Camille Georges. La diplomatie française
        au temps de Louis XIV (1661-1715) institutions,
        moeurs et coutumes. Paris, F. Alcan, 1930.
        330p.   (Bibliography: p. 329-334)

        A history of French foreign relations and diplomacy
        during the time of Louis XIV

197.   Potemkin, Vladimir Petrovich, ed. Histoire de la
        diplomatie. Translated from the Russian by
        Xenia Pamphilove and Michel Eristov. Paris,
        Librairie de Madicia, 1946-47.   3v.   (Bibliog-

raphy: v. 1, p. 531-558, v. 2, p. 420-443)

Originally published in Russian this excellent work
on diplomatic history is well documented and has
several excellent bibliographies.

198.   Rohden, Peter Richard.   Esplendor y ocaso de la
        diplomacia clásica; traducción directa del alemán.
        Madrid, Revista de occidente, 1942.   252p.

A general diplomatic history of Europe with
special attention given to Austrian foreign relations.

199.   Sarkissian, Arshag Ohannes, ed.   Studies in diplo-
        matic history and historiography in honor of G.
        P. Gooch.   New York, Barnes & Noble, 1962.
        393p.   (Bibliographical footnotes)

An appropriate festschrift with contributions by an
impressive assembly of diplomatic historians.   A
fair number of the articles deal with the twentieth-
century practice of diplomacy.

200.   Schreiner, George Abel.   The craft sinister; a diplo-
        matico-political history of the great war its
        causes-diplomacy and international politics and
        diplomatists as seen at close range by an Amer-
        ican newspaper man who served in Central Europe
        as war and political correspondent.   New York,
        G. H. Geyer, 1920.   422p.

An interesting point of view.

201.   Schuman, Frederick Lewis.   Night over Europe; the
        diplomacy of nemesis, 1939-1940.   New York,
        Knopf, 1941.   600p.

In the synthesis of European diplomatic history,
the author discusses Europe's descent into the
abyss from Jan. 1939 to the end of the Third
Republic in the summer of 1940.

202.   _____.   War and diplomacy in the French republic;
        an inquiry into political motivations and the con-
        trol of foreign policy.   New York, McGraw-Hill,
        1931.   452p.   (Bibliography: p. 433-438)

After investigating French action in various
crises, the author goes beyond the usual diplomatic
narrative and devotes many chapters to foreign
relations and the mechanism of French diplomacy,
as well as the role of Parliament, the press and
patriotic associations.

203.   Scott, James Brown, ed. Diplomatic correspondence
between the United States and Germany, August
1, 1914-April 6, 1917. New York, Oxford University Press, 1918. 378p.

A collection of correspondence concerning the
First World War. Extremely useful for source
material.

204.   _____. Diplomatic documents relating to the outbreak of the European war. New York, Oxford
University Press, 1916. 2v.

An extremely valuable collection of diplomatic
documents relating to the causes of the First
World War.

205.   Straelen, Henricus van. New diplomacy in the Far
East, a blue print for the training of future diplomats. London, Luzac & Co., 1944. 40p.

A short study by a former diplomat on his ex-
periences and their application for training others
for the Foreign Service.

206.   Thompson, James Westfall. Secret diplomacy; es-
pionage and cryptography, 1500-1815. With Saul
K. Padover. New York, F. Ungar Pub. Co.,
1963. 290p. (Bibliography: p. 265-282)

An outstanding treatise on the practice of secret
diplomacy and the art of cryptography as a part of
that type of diplomatic practice.

207.   Ugarteche, Pedro. Diplomacia y literatura, autores
célebres y obras famosas. Lima, 1961. 93p.

An altogether too short account of the problems of
diplomatic history.

208.   Weiske, Carl August.   Considerations historiques
        et diplomatiques sur les ambassades des Romains
        comparées aux modernes.   Zwickam, Frères
        Schumann, 1834.   117p.

        A wide ranging view of diplomacy and diplomatic
        history up to the 1830's.

III

Modern Diplomatic Methods

Diplomatic affairs in the nineteenth century have been considered the era of the old diplomacy. Twentieth century influences have tended to reshape and modify the old practice. Perhaps the greatest impact upon diplomacy has come from the revolution in communications and transportation. Up to the nineteenth century communications were so slow and uncertain that foreign officers had to rely upon diplomatic expertise in the field. The importance of the diplomat's capacities is no longer decisive with respect to decisions to be taken during the course of negotiations, although it may still be very great in the cogency and persuasiveness of presentation.

Personal Diplomacy

The increased use of modern air transport coupled with telephone communication has made the frequent personal contacts by political heads of government and conferences among foreign ministers and other governmental officials possible to a greater degree. President Franklin D. Roosevelt was particularly fond of personal diplomacy and the direct approach. This approach is not without its limitations, however, since frequent journeys from capitol to capitol by foreign ministers may arouse an infinity of distracting press, radio, and television speculation.

Popular Diplomacy

Another influence which has a large bearing on modern diplomacy has been the drift toward what has been called popular or democratic diplomacy. This type of negotiation is frequently associated with President Wilson's Fourteen Points (1918) in which he describes diplomatic relations in this manner: "Open convenants of peace, openly arrived at, after which there shall be no private international understanding of any kind, but diplomacy shall proceed

always frankly and in the public view. "[7]   Much to his dis-
appointment President Wilson found it impossible to negotiate openly at the Paris Peace Conference.   A confusion of
terms occurs when we speak of popular or democratic diplomacy, for insofar as diplomacy is concerned with negotiation, it is physically impossible to conduct it by popular
action.   What is really meant is the demand for popular
control of foreign policy, but even this has given rise to
popular suspicion of the professional diplomat and has en-
couraged political leaders to undertake negotiations formerly
assigned to diplomats and to conduct them in the full spot-
light of publicity.   What this implies is that while the public
should be concerned over its foreign policy, diplomatic
negotiations swayed by public demands can wreak havoc with
the entire diplomatic effort.

        The items cited below are representative of materials
within these areas of diplomatic action.

209.   Best, Gary Lee.   Diplomacy in the United Nations.
        An Arbor, Mich. , University Microfilms, 1960.
        263 leaves.   (Bibliography: leaves. 232-241)

        A good treatise on diplomatic practice within the
        United Nations.

210.   Black, Eugene Robert.   The diplomacy of economic
        development, and other papers.   New York,
        Atheneum, 1963.   176p.

        Discusses economic development as a diplomatic tool.

211.   Burton, John Wear.   Systems, states, diplomacy and
        rules.   London, Cambridge University Press, 1968.
        251p.   (Bibliography: p. 245-247)

        An attempt to relate systems theory to contemp-
        orary international relations.   Only partially
        successful but refreshingly free of jargon.

212.   Cottam, Richard W.   Competitive interference and
        twentieth century diplomacy.   Pittsburgh, University
        of Pittsburgh Press, 1967.   243p.   (Bibliograph-
        ical footnotes)

        An analysis of the development of American diplo-
        matic relations since 1900.

213. Council on Foreign Relations. Diplomacy and the
      communist challenge: a report on the views of
      leading citizens in twenty-five cities, edited by
      Joseph Barber. New York, 1954. 46p.

      A brief overview of U. S. diplomatic efforts to
      combat the influence of Communism in foreign
      affairs

214. Culbertson, William Smith. International economic
      policies; a survey of the economics of diplomacy.
      New York, D. Appleton, 1925. 575p.

      One of the best treatments of post-war policies by
      a former member of the U. S. Tariff Commission.

215. The Diplomatic persuaders; new role of the mass
      media in international relations. John Lee, editor.
      New York, Wiley, 1968. 205p. (Bibliography:
      p. 197-199)

      A scholarly study on public relations, public ad-
      ministration and the role of mass media in the con-
      duct of diplomacy.

216. Eller, George. Secret diplomacy. London, S. Swift,
      1912. 214p.

      A cursory history of European diplomatic methods
      since 1871.

217. Feis, Herbert. The diplomacy of the dollar; first
      era, 1919-1932. Baltimore, Johns Hopkins Press,
      1950. 81p. (Albert Shaw lectures on diplomatic
      history)

      Mr. Feis shows how the United States has used
      its economic power to foster its diplomatic en-
      deavors in the interim period between the two
      world wars.

218. Granet, Pierre. L'évolution des méthodes diplo-
      matiques. Paris, A. Rousseau, 1939. 168p.
      (Bibliography: p. 163-165)

      An overview of the modern techniques of diplomacy.

219.   Hale, Oron James. Publicity and diplomacy, with
        special reference to England and Germany, 1890-
        1914. New York, D. Appleton, 1940. 486p.
        (Virginia University. Institute for Research in the
        Social Sciences. Institute monograph, no. 27)

        A painstaking historical monograph with an excel-
        lent analysis of this diplomatic problem.

220.   Huddleston, Sisley. Popular diplomacy and law.
        Rindge, N. H. , R. R. Smith publisher, 1954.
        285p.

        A quite polemical treatment by an experienced
        journalist of the important issue of "expert diplo-
        macy versus popular diplomacy."   The author is
        wholly in favor of old methods and bewails the day
        when Wilson "joined the sorry pack of idiots" and
        came out for open diplomacy.

221.   International communication and the new diplomacy.
        Edited by Arthur S. Hoffman. Bloomington,
        Indiana University Press, 1968. 206p. (Indiana
        University international studies; Bibliographical
        references included in "Notes" p. 199-206)

222.   Jessup, Philip Caryl. Parliamentary diplomacy; an
        examination of the legal quality of the rules of
        procedure of organs of the United Nations. Leyden,
        A. W. Sijthoff, 1956. 140p. (Bibliography: p.
        137-138)

        A good discussion by a noted scholar on the role
        of the United Nations in the world diplomatic arena.

223.   Latham, Sir John Greig. Open diplomacy. Melbourne,
        Australian Institute of International Affairs, 1953.
        22p.

        A general discussion of the evolution of open diplo-
        mach particularly since the First World War.

224.   Nicolson, Harold George. The evolution of diplomatic
        method. London, Constable, 1956. 93p.

        This work traces the history of diplomatic practice
        and procedure from ancient Greece to the present

225.   Pearson, Lester B. Diplomacy in the nuclear age.
        Cambridge, Mass., Harvard University Press,
        1959.   114p.

        A discussion of the problems of the diplomat and
        diplomacy under the changed and trying circum-
        stances of our time.

226.   Plischke, Elmer. Summit diplomacy; personal diplo-
        macy of the President of the United States. College
        Park, Bureau of Governmental Research, College
        of Business and Public Administration, University
        of Maryland, 1958.   125p.   (Bibliographical
        footnotes)

        A brief exploratory study of personal presidential
        diplomacy since Washington.

227.   Ponsonby, Arthur Ponsonby. Democracy and diplo-
        macy; a plea for popular control of foreign
        policy. London, Methuen, 1915.   198p.

        A plea for the application of the democratic prin-
        cipal to foreign affairs. Argues that British con-
        sular and diplomatic service is adequate to modern
        needs.

228.   Regala, Roberto. The trends in modern diplomatic
        practice. New York, Oceana Publications, 1959.
        209p.

        A group of lectures pertaining to diplomacy in
        general and diplomatic methods.

229.   . World peace through diplomacy and law.
        Dobbs Ferry, N. Y., Oceana Publications, 1964.
        270p.   (Bibliographical footnotes)

        Ambassador Regala, a distinguished jurist and
        diplomat, shows how the rule of law can respond
        to and influence the course of international rela-
        tions. He believes that through codification and
        progressive development, international law can be
        strengthened sufficiently to respond effectively to
        the social and economic needs of the world, as
        well as eventually to supress nuclear weapons.

230.   Reinsch, Paul Samuel. Secret diplomacy, how far
        can it be eliminated? New York, Harcourt, Brace,
        1922.   231p.   (Bibliography: p. 225-226)

        An historical survey of the methods of diplomacy,
        followed by a stimulating discussion of the pos-
        sibilities of eliminating secret diplomacy and es-
        tablishing popular control.

231.   Scott, James Brown. The development of modern
        diplomacy. Washington, D. C., American Peace
        Society, 1921.   37p.

        Contains information on the principles of the bal-
        ance of power, the peace settlement of contro-
        versies between nations by means of arbitration,
        congresses, or judicial decisions.

232.   Seelos, Gebhard. Moderne Diplomatie. Bonn, At-
        henaum-Verlag, 1953.   99p.

        Along with a general discussion of the problems
        of diplomacy this work also treats the diplomatic
        and consular service of the Federal Republic of
        Germany.

Diplomacy by Conference. 8

        Another major influence which has affected diplomacy
is the increasing utilization of international conferences. The
use of the term "diplomacy by conference" in recent years
has become quite common. In the early intervening years
between the Congress of Westphalia (1641-1648) and the present day, diplomatic negotiations by conference were cumber-
some and difficult to work out. Since that time the working
out of details has become somewhat less difficult and flex-
ible. It must be noted that although the widespread use of
conferences has been accepted as a fact of international life,
they rarely succeed unless there has been careful planning
and exchange of views through regular diplomatic channels.

        Conference diplomacy is a more complex process of
negotiation than is personal or direct diplomacy, and its
procedures are generally more formal. An international
conference convenes upon invitation, which usually specifies
the time, place, and purposes of the meeting. (See Chapter

VII, p. 248.   1.   Invitation to attend International Conference).

        The structure of the conference will vary according
to the circumstances under which it is called. Smaller
gatherings are inclined to be rather informal, whereas the
important, multilateral conclave will be more formal and
complicated in structure. (See Chapter VII, p. 251. 2.
Conference Structure: San Francisco Conference, 1945).
Generally a rather definite conference pattern is emerging
comprised of plenary deliberations, committee meetings,
secretariat work, and administrative services. The latter
two of these are customarily furnished by the host state,
which therefore designates not only official representatives
and alternatives, together with policy and technical advisory
staffs, but also various secretariat and other personnel
(See Chapter VII, p. 252. 3.   Conference Delegation Structure: United States as Host State). The delegation representing the guest state is less comprehensive, although it does
include delegates and alternatives, policy and technical ad-
visers, and a unilateral secretariat to service the delegation (See Chapter VII, p. 252.   4.   Conference Delegation
Structure: United States Delegation Abroad).

        The chairman who presides over the plenary sessions
of the conference, although elected, usually is the ranking
delegate of the host state. Sometimes there are exceptions
to this (See Chapter VII, p. 253. 5.   Conference Chairman-
ship: Select Illustrations). The conference is serviced by a
secretariat, headed by a secretary general, who usually is
a national of the host state (See Chapter VII, p. 254. 6.
Conference Secretary General: Select Illustrations). A fixed
agenda limits the discussion of items. This is published in
advance, customarily at the time of invitation (See Chapter
VII, p. 255. 7.   Conference Agenda: Select Illustrations).

        Although they differ markedly in detail, the conduct
of business of international conferences tends to exhibit
a generally uniform pattern.   (See Chapter VII, p. 257.
8. Conference Procedure: Flow Chart). The larger the conference, the more complex is the institutionalization of its
business and the more complicated are its rules of procedure.
Some smaller conferences--even though they may be important, such as post war Council of Foreign Ministers'
meetings--may be conducted informally, perhaps even without the taking of votes. Conferences of a more important
nature, however, require substantial regularized procedures

(See Chapter VII, p. 258. 9. Conference Rules of Procedure: Suggested Table of Contents;) (See Chapter VII, p. 259. 10. Conference Rules of Procedure: Excerpts).

One of the most important procedural factors is the formula for voting, which in accordance with the principle of "equality," usually provides each participating state with a single vote, and under the rule of "unanimity" requires the consensus of all states in order to reach a decision. Whereas equality still generally persists in usage, unanimity is more and more supplanted by majority rule (See Chapter VII, p. 262. 11. Conference Voting Formulae: Select Illustrations).

Official records are kept of important sessions, occasionally those of important committees (See Chapter VII, p. 264. 12. Conference Committee Action: Verbatim Minutes), but particularly those of a plenary nature (See Chapter VII, p. 265. 13. Conference Plenary Action: Verbatim Minutes). The final result may be a single treaty or agreement. If, however, there are a number of agreed instruments--including treaties, executive agreements, resolutions, declarations, and the like--they may be signed separately and, in addition, a "final act" covering all of the work of the conference may be signed as the ultimate, inclusive action of the conference (See Chapter VII, p. 266. 14. Conference Final Act: Select Illustrations).

The following are representative works dealing with this method of diplomatic action:

233.   Acheson, Dean Gooderham. Meetings at the summit: a study in diplomatic method; an address ...
Durham, University of New Hampshire, 1958.
27p.   (Distinguished lecture series)

A speech exploring the problems involved in summit diplomacy.

234.   Eubank, Keith. The summit conferences, 1919-1960.
Norman, University of Oklahoma Press, 1966.
225p.   (Bibliography: p. 210-216)

The author sketches vignettes of several diplomatic summit conferences and concludes--not surprisingly --that "the formal summit conference could serve

as the occasion for the signing of a final agreement, not the negotiations which should have been
pursued by the professionals. "

235.   Garner, William R.   The Chaco dispute; a study of
        prestige diplomacy. Washington, Public Affairs
        Press, 1966.   151p.   (Includes bibliographical
        references)

        A detailed study of a specific dispute and the ne-
        gotiations which resulted in its settlement.

236.   Hamlin, Douglas L. B. , ed. Diplomacy in evolution;
        30th Couchiching Conference. Toronto, Published
        for Canadian Institute on Public Affairs by Univ-
        ersity of Toronto Press, 1961.   128p.   (Bibliog-
        raphy: p. 125-127)

        A collection of essays and discussions by various
        scholars at a conference on the changing role of
        conference diplomacy in today's world.

237.   Hankey, Maurice Pascal Alers Hankey. Diplomacy
        by conference; studies in public affairs, 1920-
        1946. New York, Putnams, 1946.   179p.

        These lectures and papers going back to 1920 deal
        less with diplomacy than with affairs, particularly
        as regards defense within the British Common-
        wealth.

238.   Kaufmann, Johan. Conference diplomacy: an intro-
        ductory analysis. Leiden, A.W. Sijthoff, New
        York, Oceana Publications, 1968.   224p.   (Bib-
        liographical references included in "Notes" p. 204-
        213)

        Mr. Kaufmann carefully analyses the effects of
        international conferences upon the diplomatic pro-
        cess. Well written with a good bibliography.

239.   Pastuhov, Vladimir D. A guide to the practice of
        international conferences. Washington, Carnegie
        Endowment for international Peace, 1945.   266p.
        (C. E. I. P. Division of International Law. Studies
        in the Administration of International Law and Or-
        ganization, no. 4; Bibliography, p. 263-266)

A one-time member of the League Secretariat
draws upon his experience and his exhaustive
research to present a systematic, documented
analysis of procedure at international conferences.

Negotiation and Treaty-Making. [9]

Among those things which diplomats do, the conclusion
of a treaty is one of the more important.   Principles governing treaty-making occasionally are contained in multilateral arrangements (See Chapter VII, p. 269.   1.   Treaty
Principles: Inter-American Convention).

The treaty-making process is comprised of a number
of distinct steps.   The first is negotiation and signature,
the procedure for which follows recognized principles of
protocol that sometimes are reduced to written regulations
(See Chapter VII, p. 271.   2.   United States Treaty Procedure).   Treaty texts usually adhere to generally accepted
format (See Chapter VII, p. 272.   3.   Treaty Form: Inter-
American Protocolary Principles; 4. Treaty Form: United
States Instructions).

The second major step involves legislative approval.
Some states prescribe approval and ratification procedure
by law (See Chapter VII, p. 275.   5.   Treaty Approval:
United States Ratification Procedure).   After certified copies
have been prepared, the procedure in the United States is
as follows: the Secretary of State submits the treaty to the
President, he in turn transmits it to the Senate with his
recommendation, and the Senate approves by "resolution"
(See Chapter VII, p. 276.   6.   Treaty Approval: Senate Resolution).   Occasionally, especially in recent times with
respect to treaties establishing international organizations,
both houses of Congress may approve the treaty by regular
congressional act (See Chapter VII, p. 276. 7.   Treaty
Approval: Congressional Act).

In case of legislative amendment to the treaty, such
modification must be re-negotiated with the other signatories.
It is more common practice, however, to approve the original text subject to specified reservations (See Chapter VII,
p. 277.   8.   Treaty Approval: Reservations--Select Illustrations).

Step three constitutes treaty ratification which is an

executive act customarily effected by a "ratification instrument" (See Chapter VII, p. 278.   9.   Treaty Ratification:
Instrument of Ratification) or, at times, by an "Instrument
of acceptance. "

Ratification must be officially communicated to other
signatory states.   For a bilateral treaty this step is com-
pleted simply by an "exchange" of ratification instruments,
while in the case of a multilateral treaty the instruments
generally are "deposited" with a specified government, which
notifies the signatories when the treaty goes into effect.   In
many cases the consummation of ratification is formalized
in a separate "protocol" (See Chapter VII, p. 279. 10.
Treaty Ratification: Protocol of Ratification).   Non-signatory
states subsequently may "adhere" or "accede" to some
treaties (See Chapter VII, p. 280.   11.   Treaty Ratification:
Accession and Adherence).   In order to become logically
binding, the treaty is proclaimed by the executive and becomes a part of the law of the land (See Chapter VII, p.
281.   12.   Presidential Treaty Proclamation).   In keeping
with President Wilson's insistence upon "open diplomacy, "
states have undertaken to register and publish their treaties
since 1920 (See Chapter VII, p. 283. 13.   Treaty Registration
and Publication: United Nations Rules; 14.   Treaty Registration and Publication: Select Illustrations).

In some exceptional instances a treaty may be tem-
porarily suspended, particularly in time of war (See Chapter
VII, p. 286.   15.   Treaty Suspension During War).   A treaty
may also be terminated by the fulfillment of its terms or
by supersession with a subsequent treaty (See Chapter VII,
p. 287.   16.   Treaty Termination: Supersession--Select Illustrations), by expiration (See Chapter VII, p. 288.   17.   Treaty
Termination: Select Expiration Clauses), or by denunciation
(See Chapter VII, p. 289.   18.   Treaty Termination: Instrument of Denunciation; 19.   Treaty Termination: Note Termin-
ating Executive Agreement).

The termination of a treaty differs markedly from
treaty violation.   The latter often is alleged, and then if the
treaty contains a denunciation clause it is likely to be denounced by the "injured" signatory.   However, if it does
not contain such a provision it may be deemed no longer
binding by the "injured" signatory (See Chapter VII, p. 291.
20.   Treaty Termination: Diplomatic Note of Termination).
The validity of unilateral termination, however, may be
rejected if it is unfavorable to the interest of the other

signatories (See Chapter VII, p. 291. 21. Treaty Termination: Denial of Validity of Unilateral Termination).

Below is cited a number of works which are related
to the treaty-making process:

240.   Allen, Florence Ellinwood. The treaty as an instru-
       ment of legislation. New York, Macmillan, 1952.
       114p.

       A well written documentation of the difficulties of
       international bodies in the conclusion and applica-
       tion of treaties.

241.   Arnold, Ralph, comp. Treaty-making procedure; a
       comparative study of the methods obtaining in
       different states. London, Oxford University Press,
       1933.   69p.

       This useful little volume summarizes both custom
       and law for forty-seven countries.

242.   Blix, Hans. Treaty-making power. New York,
       Praeger, 1960.   414p.   (Includes bibliography)

       A massive treatise devoted to two questions: the
       competence of diplomatic agents to negotiate
       treaties for their governments, and the competence
       of governments to bind the states they represent.

243.   Bot, Bernard R. Nonrecognition and treaty relations.
       Leyden, A. W. Sijthoff: Dobbs Ferry, N. Y.,
       Oceana Publications, 1968.   289p.   (Summary
       in Dutch; Bibliography: p. 263-270)

       A useful monograph with a heavy legal emphasis.

244.   Crandall, Samuel Benjamin. Treaties, their making
       and enforcement. 2d ed. Washington, D.C., J.
       Byrne, 1916.   663p.

       A synthetic look at the treaty making process.
       The work is well written and scholarly.

245.   Dumont, Jean, baron de Carlscroon. Corps universal
       diplomatique de droit des gens ... Amsterdam,

Chatelam, 1726-31.   8v.

246.   _____. Supplément. 1739.   5v.

A large and extensive collection of treaties and
other documents related to diplomacy, international law and relations.

247.   Garden, Guillaume de. Répertoire diplomatique,
annales du droit des gens et de la politique extérieure. Paris, J. Claye, 1861.   2v.

A detailed treatise on treaties and their formulation. Contains a large collection of diplomatic
source materials and documents with special emphasis on French diplomatic and consular service.

248.   Hudson, Manley Ottmer, ed. International legislation; a collection of the texts of multipartite
international instruments of general interest beginning with the Covenant of the League of Nations.
Washington, Carnegie Endowment for International
Peace, 1931-1950.   9v.

An outstanding collection of important international
documents.

249.   Jones, John Mervyn. Full powers and ratification,
a study in the development of treaty-making procedure. Cambridge, Eng., The University Press,
1949.   182p.   (Cambridge studies in international and comparative law, II; Bibliographical
footnotes)

An excellent treatise on diplomatic negotiations
in the conclusion of treaties.

250.   Treaties and alliances of the world; an international
survey covering treaties in force and communities
of states. New York, Scribner, 1968.   214p.

This collection of documents is designed to present
the state of affairs with regard to groupings of
States and their principal treaties with each in
force on April 1968.

251.   United Nations. Treaty series; treaties and interna-
       tional agreements registered or filed and recorded
       with the Secretariat of the United Nations ... v. 1,
       1946/47-

       A compilation of treaties and international agree-
       ments registered or filed and recorded with the
       secretariat at the United Nations.

252.   U. S. Treaties, etc. United States treaties and
       other international agreements. Washington, Dept.
       of State, 1953- v. 1- (Annual)

       Includes all treaties to which the United States is
       a party that have been proclaimed during the cal-
       endar year.

253.   _____ . Treaties, conventions, international acts,
       protocols, and agreements between the United
       States of America and other powers. Washington,
       Govt. Print. Off., 1910- v. 1-

       A fairly complete compendium except for postal
       conventions and Indian treaties.

254.   Young, Oran R. The politics of force; bargaining
       during international crises. Princeton, N. J.,
       Published for the Center of International Studies,
       Princeton University, by Princeton University
       Press, 1968.   438p.   (Bibliographical footnotes)

       An excellent analysis of bargaining under interna-
       tional crisis conditions, making fine use of case
       materials. Conceptually indebted to Schelling but
       also breaks new ground.

IV

Foreign Affairs Administration
Part I

The term diplomacy as is being used here also includes the day to day administration of a nation's foreign relations. Career civil servants in foreign relations are a long established tradition in most western nations. They maintain a very interesting and at times difficult relationship with the political officers of a nation state.

Diplomatic and Consular Service

Most of the works cited below deal with diplomatic and consular service in general. The specific management of these services requires a large force of career and clerical servants who perform distinct roles within the total diplomatic structure.

255.   Allué Salvador, Miguel. La condición juridica de los cónsules; ensayo históricocrítico. Zaragoza, M. Salas, impresion, 1909. 113p.

A general discussion of diplomatic and consular service with special attention given to the functions of consuls.

256.   Antokoletz, Daniel. Tratado teórico y práctico de derecho diplomático y consular, con referencias expeciales a la República Argentina y a las demas Repúblicas Americanas. Buenos Aires, Editorial Ideas, 1948. 2v.

An important study of diplomatic and consular law. Well documented.

257.   Arduino, Marcello. Consoli, consolati e diritto consolare. Milano, U. Hoepli, 1908. 277p.

Includes some information concerning the function
of consulates but concentrates on Italian practice.

258. _____. Diplomazia ed agenti diplomatici.   Milano,
     1909.   269p.

     A short treatise dealing with the general functions
     and problems of diplomatic and consular service.

159. Beauvais, Armand Paul.   Attachés militaires, atta-
     chés navals et attachés de l'air.   Paris, A.
     Pedone, 1937.   214p.   (Bibliography: p. 203-
     212)

     The institution of attache is examined in its his-
     torical, military and juridical aspects.

260. Bertoni, Karol.   Praktyka dyplomatyczna i kinsularna.
     Krakow, S. Kaminski, 1947+   v. 1+   (Biblioteka
     Szkoly Nauk Paolitycznych Uniwersytetu Jagiellon-
     skiego, 6; Includes bibliographies)

     A series of volumes dealing with diplomatic and
     consular service in general.

261. Bettanini, Antonio Maria.   Lo stile diplomatico;
     propedentica allo studio della diplomazia.   Milano,
     Societa editrice "Vita e pensiero", 1930.   258p.
     (Bibliography: p. 257-258)

     An undetailed survey of diplomatic and consular
     practice.

262. Blishchenko, Igor'Pavolvich.   Das Diplomaten-und
     Konsularrecht.   With W. N. Durdenewski.   Berlin,
     Staatsverlag der Deutschen Demokratischen Repub-
     lik, 1966.   548p.   (Added title page in Russian;
     Bibliography: p. 528-548)

     An introspective analysis of the functions of dip-
     lomatic agents.   Contains an excellent bibliography.

263. Blücher, Wipert von.   Wege und Irrwege der Diplo-
     matie.   Wiesbaden, Limes Verlag, 1953.   184p.

     A discussion of the nature of diplomacy and the
     requirements for a diplomat.

264. Borel, François. Formulaire des consulats. Saint-
Petersbourg, Imp. de. A. Pluchart, 1808. 154p.

A concentrated but brief survey of consular and
diplomatic practice.

265. _____. De l'origine et des fonctions des consuls.
Leipsic, L. Voss, 1831. 278p.

A history of the origins and development of consular functions and treaty obligations.

266. Bratt, Eyvind. Diplomater och Konsuler. Stockholm,
Kooperativa forbundets bokforlag, 1943. 64p.

Covers briefly the problems of diplomatic and
consular service.

267. Buck, Philip Wassenstein, ed. Control of foreign
relations in modern nations. New York, Norton,
1957. 856p. (Includes bibliography)

A substantial symposium of studies of both the
organization and content of foreign policy in the
world today. The treatment is by country or
region: the United States, Latin America, The
United Kingdom and the Commonwealth, Asia,
France, the Netherlands and the USSR.

268. Bursotti, Giovanni. Guide des agents consulaires.
Ouvrage spécialement consacré l'utilité des consuls
de Sa Majesté la roi du Royaume des Deux-Siciles.
Naples, Impr. de. C. Catanee, 1838. 2v.

A detailed and scholarly work on the activities and
functions of diplomatic and consular officials.

269. Cahier, Philippe. Le droit diplomatique contemporain.
2d ed. Genève, Libr. Droz, 1964. 534p.
(Publications de l'Institut Universitaire des hautes
études internationales, 40; Bibliography: p. 493-
504)

A good overall survey and account of recent developments in the field of diplomatic law, particularly
taking notice of the modification of traditional diplomatic procedures and the initial attempt made

at Vienna in 1961 to codify rules on diplomatic
relations.

270.   Contuzzi, Francesco Paolo.   Trattato teorico-pratico
di diritto consolare e diplomatico nei raffronti
coi codici (Civile, commerciale, penale e guidizi-
ario) e con le convenzioni internazionali in vigore.
Torino, Unione tipografico-editrice torinese, 1910-
11.   2v.

A comprehensive treatise on early twentieth-century
consular law and diplomatic service.

271.   Corsini, Vincenzo.   Diritto diplomatico consolare,
parte generale.   Milano, Giuffré, 1958.   191p.

A general work on consular law and the diplomatic
service.

272.   Cortina, Jose Justo Gomez de la Cortina.   Prontuario
diplomatico y consular y resumen de los derechos
y deberes de los estrangeros en los paises donde
risden.   Mexico, Impr. de J. Cumplido, 1856.
171p.   ("Notes": p. 103-171)

A discussion of diplomatic and consular practice
with emphasis on the regulations covering aliens
and consuls.

273.   Coulon, Henri.   Des agents diplomatiques, de leurs
fonctions, de leurs droits, de leurs devoirs,
d-après le dernier état de la jurisprudence et de la
doctrine.   Paris, Marchal et Billard, 1889.
162p.

An interesting study of diplomatic agents and their
multifarious functions.

274.   Cussy, Ferdinand de.   Règlements consulaires des
principaux états maritimes de l'Europe et de
l'Amérique; fonctions et attributions des consuls:
Prérogatives, immunités et caractère public des
consuls envoyés.   Leipzig, F. A. Brockhaus,
1851.   492p.

An interesting treatment of diplomatic and consular
practice along with maritime law and the functions

of diplomatic agents.

275. Delepoule, Eugene. Exposé théorique de la fiction d'exterrito-rialité par rapport aux personnes en droit international public. Paris, A. Rousseau, 1897. 154p. (Bibliographical footnotes)

276. Dietrich, Victor. De l'inviolabilité et de l'exemption de juridiction des agents diplomatiques et consulaires en pays de chrétienté. Paris, Marescq, 1896. 198p. ("Index bibliographique" p. v-1x; Bibliographical footnotes)

An interesting and provocative treatise on diplomatic privileges and immunities along with consular service in Christian countries.

277. Droin, Cesar. L'exterritorialité des agents diplomatiques. Genève, Impr. Chapalay & Mettier, 1895. 205p. (Bibliography: p. 199-202)

Originally a thesis, this work covers the role of ambassadors within the framework of diplomatic and consular service.

278. Erice y O'Shea, José Sebastián de. Derecho diplomático. Madrid, Instituto de Estudios Políticos, 1954. 2v. (Bibliography: v.2, p. 573-583)

An excellently developed treatise, well documented and precise, on diplomatic and consular practice.

279. _____. Noras de diplomacia y de derecho diplomático. Madrid, Instituto de estudios políticos, 1945. 2v. (Bibliography: v.2, p. 368-375)

A compendious guide to the history, law and practice of diplomacy, with emphasis on the Spanish experience.

280. Esperson, Pietro. Diritto diplomatico e giurisdizione internazionale marittima, col commento delle disposizioni della legge italiana del 13 maggio 1871, sulle relazioni della Santa sede colle potenze straniere ... Roma, E. Loescher, 1872-77. 2v. in 3.

A general treatise on international law and relations in the nineteenth century.   Contains a good
deal of information on maritime and consular law.

281.   Essen, Jan Louis Frederik van.   Ontwikkeling en
        codifictie van de diplomatieke voorechten ...
        Arnhem, S. Gouda Quint, 1928.   227p.   (Bibliog-
        raphy: p. 222-227)

        A general treatment on diplomatic and consular
        service along with problem of exterritoriality and
        the codification of international law.

282.   Feller, Abraham Howard, ed.   A collection of diplo-
        matic and consular laws and regulations of various
        countries.   Edited with Manley O. Hudson.   Wash-
        ington, Carnegie Endowment for International
        Peace, 1933.   2v.

        An important reference source for early consular
        law and regulations.

283.   Féraud-Giraud, Louis Joseph Delphine.   États et
        souverains; personnel diplomatique et consulaire,
        corps de troupe; navires et equipages; personnes
        civiles devant les tribunaux étrangers ...   Paris,
        A. Pedone, 1895.   2v.   (Bibliothèque inter-
        nationale et diplomatique, xxxiii-xxxiv; Bibliog-
        raphy: v. 1, p. 9-22)

        An extensive treatment on personnel practices in
        the diplomatic service of nations.

284.   Forgac, Albert T.   New diplomacy and the United
        Nations.   New York, Pageant Press, 1965.   173p.
        (Bibliography: p. 158-173)

        A rather far reaching but somewhat cursory treat-
        ment of diplomacy in general and the United Na-
        tions in particular.

285.   Frei, Paul Henri.   De la situation juridique des
        représentants des membres de la Société des
        nations et de ses agents (commentaire de l'article
        y, alinea 4 du Paule de la Société des nations).
        Paris, Recueil Sirey, 1929.   118p.   (Bibliog-
        raphy: p. 3-5)

Deals mainly with the League of Nations and its
role in world diplomacy. Contains an excellent
general discussion on diplomatic and consular
service.

286. Garden, Guillaume de. Code diplomatique de l'Europe,
      ou Principes et maximes du droit des gens mod-
      ernes. Paris, Amyot, 1853. 251p.

      Primarily an excellent discussion of international
      law as it affects diplomatic and consular service.

287. Gerbore, Pietro. Il vero diplomatico. Milano,
      Longanesi, 1956. 424p. (La Vostra via, v. 23)

      A detailed and well-documented treatise on diplo-
      matic and consular service in various nations.

288. Gerster, Jürg. Der militarattaché; seine völker-und
      landesrechliche stellung mit besonderer berucksich-
      tigung der schweizer verhaltnisse ... Zurich,
      Juris-verlag, 1959. 105p. (Bibliography: p.
      xiii-xv)

      Deals with the role of military attaches in diplo-
      matic and consular practice with emphasis upon
      the Swiss experience.

289. Guesalaga, Alejandro. Derecho diplomático y consular,
      con los ultimos casos de controversias entre los
      estados. Buenos Aires, Imp. de J. Penser, 1900.
      393p. (Bibliography: p. 391-393)

      A wide ranging discussion on diplomatic and con-
      sular service within the scope of international law
      and relations.

290. Hadwen, John G. How United Nations decisions are
      made. With Johan Kaufmann. 2d rev. ed. New
      York, Oceana Publications, 1962. 179p. (In-
      cludes bibliography)

      A description of the machinery and procedures of
      the United Nations for considering economic ques-
      tions. Illustrated case studies are included.

291. Hübler, Bernard. Die majistraturen des völkerrecht-

lichen verkehrs (gesandtschafts-und konsularrecht)
und die exterritorialität.   Zum gebraucht für
vorlesungen über völkerrecht und politik ... Berlin,
Puttkammer & Mülbrecht, 1900.   108p.

A general treatise on exterritoriality as well as
diplomatic and consular practice among nations.

292.   Ikle, Fred Charles.   How nations negotiate.   New
York, Praeger, 1967.   272p.   ("Bibliographical
note": p. 256-264)

An authoritative and analytical account of the
complicated process of international negotiation and
its relationship to diplomatic and consular practice.

293.   Irizarry y Puente, J.   Traité sur les fonctions internationales des consuls.   Paris, A. Pedone, 1937.
484p.   (Bibliographical footnotes)

An extensive and scholarly work on the function
of international consuls.

294.   Joy, Charles Turner   How Communists negotiate.
New York, Macmillan, 1955.   178p.

Admiral Joy, who headed the United Nations delegation in the Korean armistice negotiations, ana-
lyzes on the basis of his experience the Communists' methods at the conference table and sets
forth the lessons they provide for diplomatic service.

295.   Kannes, Jolle.   Dissertatio juridica inauguralis, De
munere consulum mercaturae gratia in exteris
terris constitutorum.   Amstelodami, ex officina
S. de Grebber, 1826.   92p.

A short but concise discussion of diplomatic and
consular practice among nations.

296.   Kuhlmann, Richard von.   Die diplomaten.   Berlin,
R. Hobbing, 1937.   171p.

Agreeable chapters on the lives of several modern
diplomats and various aspects of the diplomatic
career by a former Minister of Foreign Affairs in
Germany.

297. Labeyrie-Menahem, C. Des institutions specialisées, problèmes juridiques et diplomatiques de l'administration internationale. Paris, A. Pedone, 1953. 168p. (Bibliography: p. 163-164)

A monograph on the principal problems of international and domestic law, diplomacy and administration created by the rapid development of the specialized agencies and institutions in the international field.

298. Lall, Anand. Modern international negotiation; principles and practice. New York Columbia University Press, 1966. 404p. (Notes: p. 355-383)

A discussion of the modern means of negotiations which include conferences, commissions, inquiries, mediatory and conciliatory efforts (bilateral and unilateral) which occur mostly within the framework of the United Nations.

299 Larrainzar, Frederico. Los consulados. Mexico, Impr. del commercio, de N. Chavez, 1874. 158p.

A curt treatment of diplomatic and consular practice.

300. Leroy, Paul August. Des consulats, des legations et des ambassades; étude d'histoire et de droit. 2d ed. Paris, A. Marescq, 1876. 247p.

One of the more general treatises on consular practice with emphasis on the role of diplomatic officials.

301. Lion Depetre, Jose. Derecho diplomatico. Mexico, M. Porua, 1952. 309p.

A treatise on diplomatic and consular service in various nations.

302. Lisboa, Henrique Carlos Ribeiro. Les fonctions diplomatiques en temps de paix. Santiago de Chile, Imprenta franco-chilona, 1908. 274p.

A brief study of diplomatic activities of consular officials during relatively peaceful times.

303.   Mably, Gabriel Bonnot de.   Des principes des neg-
        ociations, pour servir d'introduction au Droit
        public de l'Europe, fonde sur les traités.   New
        ed. rev. and corrected.   LaHaie, 1767.   291p.

        An historical treatment of European politics and
        diplomacy during the eighteenth century and prior.
        Also deals with diplomatic and consular service.

304.   McKenna, Joseph Charles.   Diplomatic protest in
        foreign policy; analysis and case studies.   Chicago,
        Loyola University Press, 1962.   222p.   (Bibliog-
        raphy: p. 205-214)

        A study concerned with the effectiveness of diplo-
        matic protest as a device in international rela-
        tions.

305.   Madiedo, Manuel Maris.   Tratado de derecho de
        jentes, internacional, diplomatico i consular ...
        Bogota, Tip. de N. Ponton, 1874.   549p.

        Although basically a work on international law and
        relations, this work contains a good deal of infor-
        mation on diplomatic and consular practice among
        nations.

306.   Makowski, Julian.   O konsulach i konsulatach.   War-
        szawa, Nakl. F. Hoesicka, 1918.   48p.
        (Zrodia: p. 47-48)

        A brief historical overview of diplomatic and con-
        sular service in general.

307.   Maresca, Adolfo.   Le missione diplomatica.   Milano,
        Giuffre, 1959.   356p.   (Includes bibliography)

        This is an excellent study on the function of diplo-
        matic and consular service in the modern world.

308.   Markel, Erich H.   Die Entwicklund der diplomatschen
        Rang stufen.   Erlangen, 1951.   100p.   (Bibliog-
        raphy: p. 5-8)

        A brief overview of diplomatic and consular service
        history.

309.   Martens, Fedor Fedorovich.   Das consularwesen und
        die consular jurisdiction im Orient.   Mit ergan-
        zungen des autors ubers von H. Skerst.   Berlin,
        Weidmannsche buchhandlung, 1874.   594p.

        A more or less comparative study of diplomatic
        and consular jurisdiction in the Far East.

310.   Meisel, August Heinrich.   Cours de style diplomati-
        que.   Paris, J. P. Aillaud, 1826.   2v.

        A stylistic treatment of diplomatic and consular
        practice.

311.   Merillat, Herbert Christian Laing, ed.   Legal ad-
        visers and foreign affairs.   Dobbs Ferry, N.Y.,
        Published for the American Society of International
        Law by Oceana Publications, 1964.   162p.
        (Bibliographical footnotes)

        Summarizes a discussion, held under the auspices
        of the American Society of International Law, of the
        actual and potential roles and functions of foreign
        affairs legal advisers.

312.   Miltitz, Alexandre de.   Manuel des consuls.   Londres
        & Berlin, A. Asher, 1837-41.   2v. in 5.

        Primarily a manual of procedures and practices
        for consuls in general.

313.   Moore, John Bassett.   Asylum in legations and con-
        sulates and in vessels.   New York, Ginn, 1892.
        37, 197-231, 397-418.   (Reprinted from the
        Political Science Quarterly, vol. VII, nos. 1, 2
        and 3)

        A noted expert looks at the subject of asylum
        within the scope of diplomatic and consular ser-
        vice.

314.   Morse, Alexander Porter.   The so-called right of
        asylum in legations.   A consideration of recent
        international incidents.   Washington?, D. C.,
        1892.   5p.

        A very brief overview of the right of asylum in the

study of diplomacy and international law.

315.   Morton, Charles.   Les privileges et immunités diplo-
       matiques; étude théorique suivie d'un bref exposé
       des usages de la Suisse dans ce domain.   Lausanne,
       Imprimerie la Concorde, 1927.   176p.   (Bibliog-
       raphy: p. 5-8)

       A brief study of diplomatic privileges and immun-
       ities as practiced by the Swiss.

316.   Murray, Eustace Clare Grenville.   Droits et devoirs
       des envoyés diplomatiques.   Documents recueillis
       et arrangés.   Londres, R. Bentley, 1853.   234p.

       A compilation of documents relating to diplomatic
       and consular service.

317.   _____.   Embassies and foreign courts.   A history
       of diplomacy.   London, New York, G. Routledge,
       1855.   360p.

       A short but useful study on a phase of diplomatic
       and consular practice.

318.   Nava, Santi.   Corso di diritto di legazione e Conso-
       lare.   Firenze, Editrice universitaria, 1956.
       171p.   (Contains bibliographies)

       A general treatise on diplomatic and consular ser-
       vice.

319.   _____.   Sistema della diplomazia.   Padova, CEDAM,
       1950.   256p.

       A study of the formation and development of the
       art of diplomacy: the changing function of the
       ambassador, the diplomatic community and the
       decline of diplomatic immunity.

320.   Norton, Henry Kettridge.   Foreign office organiza-
       tion: a comparison of the organization of the Brit-
       ish, French, German and Italian foreign offices
       with that of the Department of State of the United
       States of America.   Philadelphia, American Acad-
       emy of Political and Social Science, 1929.   83p.
       (Supplement to Vol. CXLII of the Annals)

A comparative treatment of the British, French, German and Italian diplomatic structures with that of the United States. Interesting but now very dated.

321.   Nostrand, Howard Lee.   The cultural attache; field organizer and intellectual leader in six areas of cooperation between peoples.   New Haven, 1947? 45p.   (The Hazen pamphlets, no. 17)

A brief study of cultural diplomacy and the diplomat.

322.   Odier, Pierre Gabriel.   Des privileges et immunités des agents diplomatiques en pays de Chrétienté. Paris, A. Rousseau, 1890.   467p.

A precise and detailed study of diplomatic immunities and privileges within the framework of international law.

323.   Ormesson, Waldimir.   Enfances diplomatiques: Saint-Petersbourg-Copenhague-Lisbonne-Athenes-Bruxelles ...   Paris, Hachette, 1932.   256p.

An interesting discussion of the diplomatic activities of courtiers in regal courts.

324.   Patau, Paul.   De la situation comparée des agents diplomatiques et consulaires.   Toulouse, C. Dirion, 1910.   215p.   (Bibliography: p. 5-9)

A study of the functions of diplomatic agents in particular and diplomatic and consular service in general.

325.   Perrenoud, Georges.   Régime des privileges et immunités des missions diplomatiques étrangères et des organisations internationales en Suisse. Lausanne, F. Rouge, 1949.   253p.   (Bibliography: p. 245-248)

A basic discussion of the role of diplomatic and consular service in international affairs.

326.   Politis, Nicolas Socrate.   La convention consulaire grecoturque, et l'arbitrage des ambassadeurs des

grandes puissances à Constantinople du 2 avril
1901 ... Paris, A. Pedone, 1903.   195p.

A good discussion of Greco-Turkish consular
jurisdiction set within the framework of their
foreign policies.

327.   Pradier-Fodere, Paul Louis Ernest.   Cours de droit
diplomatique à l'usage des agents politiques du
ministere des affaires étrangères des états
européens et americains.   2d ed.   Paris, A.
Pedone, 1899.   2v.

A massive work on diplomatic practice with
emphasis upon the legal aspects.

328.   Ravndal, Gabriel Bie.   Origin of the capitulations
and of the consular institution.   Washington, 1921.
112p.   (Bibliographical footnotes)

A documented treatment of this important subject.

329.   Rayneli, Ernesto T.   Derecho diplomatico moderno.
Buenos Aires, J. Sajouane, 1914.   349p.

A study of diplomatic and consular service in
international affairs.

330.   Rouzier, Raoul.   Missions diplomatiques et consulaires.   Port-au-Prince, Haiti, Imprimerie de
l'état, 1942?+   v. 1+

A general treatise on diplomatic and consular service within the framework of international law and
relations.

331.′ Salles, Georges.   L'institution des consulats: son
origine, son developpement au Moyen-âges chez
les differents peuples.   Paris, E. Leroux, 1898.
104p.

A general history of diplomatic and consular practice among nations.

332.   Satow, Sir Ernest Mason.   A guide to diplomatic
practice. 3d ed. , rev. by H. Ritchie   New York,
Longmans, Green, 1932.   519p.   (Bibliography:

p. 496-501)

A scholarly and exhaustive treatment. It is packed
with documents and other illustrative material:
specimen copies of letters of credence, full powers,
instruction, extracts from notes, quotations from
diplomatic manuals etc.

333.   Scala, Arturo della. La scienza diplomatica. Roma,
       1950. 111p. (Bibliography: p. 90-111)

       A general treatise on diplomatic practice with
       emphasis upon Italian foreign relations.

334.   Sen, Biswanath. A diplomat's handbook of interna-
       tional law practice. The Hague, M. Nijhoff, 1965.
       522p. (Bibliography: p. 499-501)

       A basic manual of legal rules pertaining interna-
       tionally to diplomatic practice. Authoritatively
       written. It is particularly reliable for the expo-
       sition of the view on diplomatic practice held by
       the newer as well as the older established states.

335.   _____. International law relating to diplomatic
       practice. Delhi, Metropolitan Book Co., 1950.
       92p. (Bibliography: p. 85-87)

       A short treatise on the diplomatic and consular
       practice of nations within the framework of inter-
       national law.

336.   Sereni, Angelo Piero. La rappresentanza del
       diritto internazionale. Padova, A. Milani, 1936.
       455p. (Studi di diritto pubblico, diretti da
       Donato Donati ... 9)

       A work on international law and relations which
       also includes material on international arbitrations
       and ambassadors.

337.   Stieve, Friedrich. Diplomatie im Sprachgebrauch.
       Munchen, I. & S. Federmann, 195-.   184p.

       Within the scope of international law this work
       deals mainly with diplomatic and consular service.

338.   Strupp, Karl, ed.   Beitrage zur reform and kodif-
        ikation des volkerrechtlichen immunitatsrechts.
        Breslau, J. U. Kern, 1926.   84p.   (Bibliog-
        raphy: p. 18-21)

        A brief analysis of diplomatic and consular ser-
        vice and its role in the study of international
        politics.

339.   Szende, Julius.   Handbuch für diplomaten.   Wien, A.
        Holder, 1899.   266p.

        Intended to be a guide for diplomats in diplomatic
        practice and usuage.

340.   Ungerer, Werner.   Das diplomatische Asyl in deu-
        tschen Vertretungen Lateinamerikas.   Hamburg,
        1955.   108 leaves.   (Literatur zum Asylrecht:
        leaves, 106-108)

        Deals principally with the right of asylum along
        with the diplomatic and consular service of the
        Federal Republic of Germany and their South
        American foreign relations.

341.   United Nations Conference on Consular Relations,
        Vienna, 1963.   Convenzione de Vienna sulle
        relazioni consolari.   Padova, CEDAM, 1963.
        139p.   (Pubblicazioni della Societa italiana par
        l'organizzazione internazionale, Documenti, 15;
        Introduction in Italian; documents in English and
        French)

        A collection of documents on the codification of
        consular law.

342.   _____.   Official records.   New York, United Nations,
        1963+ v. 1+   (United Nations. Document. A/Conf.
        26/16)

        The official records of the conference.

343.   Ustor, Endre.   A diplomaciai kapscolatok joga.
        Budapest, Kozgazdasagi es Jogi Konyvkiado, 1965.
        566p.   (Table of contents in Hungarian, English,
        and Russian; Includes documents; Bibliography: p.
        525-529)

A detailed treatise on general and Hungarian diplomatic and consular service.

344. Vagts, Alfred. Defense and diplomacy; the soldier and the conduct of foreign relations. New York, King's Crown Press, 1956. 547p. (Bibliography: p. 533-547)

A study of the significant role of the military in the conduct of national and international policy.

345. Villagran Kramer, Francesco. L'asile diplomatique d'apres la pratique des Etats latino-americains. Bruxelles, Impr. Amibel, 1958. 188p. (Bibliography: p. 179-183)

A discussion of the Right of asylum in Latin American.

346. Warden, David Baillie. On the origin, nature progress and influence of consular establishments. Paris, Smith, 1913. 331p.

A detailed study on diplomatic and consular practice up to the 1st world war.

347. Wildner, Heinrich. Die Technik der Diplomatie; l'art de négocier. Wien, Springer, 1959. 342p. (Includes bibliography)

A broad work on the techniques of diplomacy and the functions of consular service in various nation states.

Domestic Agencies of Foreign Affairs Administration

In most nation states today the central agency which administrates foreign relations is the foreign office (though sometimes the title foreign ministry is used). The corresponding agency in the United States is called the Department of State because it originally had many, and still retains a few, domestic functions. The offices, although they had a modest beginning, have grown in size and complexity of structure and function throughout the last two centuries.

United States. In the United States the structure of

the department during the nineteenth century consisted of the
Secretary of State, a Chief Clerk, and a small group of
clerks who seem to have been first permanently assigned to
specified duties in 1818. The intervening years after the
turn of the century saw the first moves toward a more complex organizational pattern. Today this vast network of
functional areas includes economic affairs, international information and educational exchange, intelligence research
and international organization problems among other things.

      Great Britain. The British foreign office occupies
a position in the government corresponding closely to that
of the Department of State in the United States. Its functional areas of operations have been defined by the gradual
elaboration of offices which have separated out of one or
another of the functions originally vested in the office of the
Secretary of State, which had existed from the reign of
Henry III. Today the British foreign office is organized
into thirty-eight departments along with a corps of inspectors
and legal advisors. The achievement of interagency coordination in the British government requires somewhat less
artificial devices that in the United States because the cabinet
system is itself a co-ordinating mechanism which needs only
to be elaborated.

      France. In France the minister of foreign affairs,
like his British counterpart the foreign secretary, is a
political rather than a professional officer. Although the
french ministry is composed largely of career diplomats,
the main position of the president controls largely the direc-
tion of diplomatic events.

      Federal Republic of Germany. The German foreign
ministry was reestablished after World War II in September
of 1950. This ministry has been organized along conventional lines. Under the foreign minister is a Secretary of
State for foreign affairs, who with the help of a legal ad-
visor, press officer, and group of referents, directs the
office. Foreign policy has been controlled by the Chancellor, who uses the ministry less for policy consultation than
as an administrative group to carry out his instructions.

      U. S. S. R. In the Soviet Union the ministry of foreign
affairs is the administrative unit which carries out the di-
rectives of the Council of Ministers in matters of foreign
policy. Its personnel is interchangeable with diplomatic
agents, and officials of the ministry have from time to time

represented the U. S. S. R. in negotiations. The foreign minister, who directs the ministry, is usually a part member
of high, though not necessarily the highest, standing.

Africa

348.   McKay, Vernon, ed.   African diplomacy; studies in
       the determinants of foreign policy. New York,
       Published for the School of Advanced International
       Studies, Johns Hopkins University by Praeger,
       1966,   210p.

       A study in which authors from different academic
       disciplines concentrate on the economic, cultural,
       military, and political determinants of African
       diplomacy.

349.   Rosenthal, Eric.   South African diplomats abroad;
       the S. A. Department of External Affairs ...
       Bloemfontein, South African Institute of Interna-
       tional Affairs, 1949.   32p.

       Covers South African diplomatic and consular ser-
       vice as well as its general foreign relations.

Argentina

350.   Antokoletz, Daniel.   Manual diplomatico y consular
       (para uso de los aspirantes y funcionarios de
       ambas carreras). Buenos Aires, J. Roldán, 1928.
       2v.   (Bibliografia: v. 1, p. 4: v. 2, p.   7-8)

       A manual of usage and practice for Argentinean
       diplomatic and consular officials. Also deals with
       Argentinean foreign relations.

351.   Argentine Republic.   Ministerio de relaciones exter-
       iores y culto. Cuerpo consular extranjero.
       Buenos Aires, 1943+ v. 1+   (Irregular)

       Includes instructions and guidelines for Argentinean
       diplomatic and consular officials.

352.   Centeno, Francisco.   Digesto de relaciones exteriores,
       1810-1913 ... Buenos Aires, Est. grafico "Cen-
       tenario," 1913.   385p.

Along with a discussion of its foreign relations
this work includes a good deal of information on
Argentinean diplomatic and consular practice.

353.   Rodriguez Araya, Raúl. La diplomacia; evolución--
        profesionalidad-reglamentación. Rosario, Repúb-
        lica Argentina, Talleres gráficos Fenner, 1932.
        178p.   (Bibliography: p. 171-174)

        A well-documented historical and theoretical study
        of the art of Argentinean diplomatic practice by a
        distinguished Argentinean diplomat.

354.   Suárez, José León. Las embajadas en la diplomacia
        argentina (consideraciones históricas, constitucion-
        ales y diplomáticas). Buenos Aires, Talleres
        gráficos argentinos de L. J. Rosso y cia, 1918.
        154p.

        A general treatise on diplomatic and consular ser-
        vice.   Emphasis is placed on Argentinean practice.

Austria

355.   Austria. Bundeministerium für Auswärtige Angel-
        egenheiten.   Bundesministerium für Auswärtige
        Angelegenheiten, 1959-1962. Wein, 1962.   146p.

        Deals more specifically with Austrian foreign
        affairs administration.

356.   Austria. Bundeskanzleramt, Auswärtige Angelegen-
        heitem.   Verzeichnis der ausländischen Konsular-
        ämter. Wein, 1964+ v. 1+

        A series of volumes on Austrian diplomatic and
        consular practice.

357.   Malfatti di Monte Tretto, Josef.   Hanbuch desöster-
        reichisch-ungarischen konsularwesens, nebst einem
        anhange ... 2d ed. Wien, Manzsche buchhandlung,
        1904.   2v.

        A documented and systematic treatise on Austrian
        diplomatic and consular service.

358.   Piskur, Joseph.   Oesterreichs consularwesen ...
        Wien, G. Gerold's sohn, 1862.   374p.

        A general work covering most aspects of Austrian
        consular practice.

Belgium

359.   Arntz, Égide Rodolphe Nicolas.   Précis méthodique
        des Règlements consulaires de Belgique ... Brux-
        elles, Bruylant-Christophe, 1876.   88p.

        A brief work summarizing Belgian diplomatic and
        consular affairs.

360.   Belgium.   Ministère des affaires étrangères.   Annu-
        aire diplomatique et consulaire.   année 1930.
        Bruxelles, 1929+ v. 1+

        An annual handbook of information for Belgian
        diplomatic and consular officials.

361.   Dykmans, Gommaire Louis.   Législation et règle-
        ments consulaires belges.   Bruxelles Editions
        compatables, commerciales et financiers, 1952.
        203p.   (Bibliothèque générale des sciences éco-
        nomiques, 42)

        Deals with Belgian diplomatic and consular ser-
        vice with emphasis upon consular law and juris-
        diction.

362.   Garcia de la Véga, Désiré Francois Joseph de.
        Guide pratique des agents politiques du Ministère
        des affaires étrangères de Belgique, Cérémonial
        national et cérémonial de la cour.   4th ed. rev.
        and enl.   Paris, A. Fontemoing, 1899.   725p.

        A handbook for Belgian diplomatic and consular
        officials.

363.   Mees, Jules.   L'institution consulaire in Belgique
        depuis 1830 ... Renaix, Presses de J. Leherte-
        Courtin, 1908.   79p.

        Covers the diplomatic and consular service of

Belgium between the years 1830 and 1908.   Very
sketchy.

Brazil

364.   Carneiro de Mencoca Franco, Melchior, ed.   Consu-
        lar regulations of the empire of Brazil, and other
        legal dispositions and orders connected therewith;
        collected and published in English, for the use of
        the respective consular agents in countries of the
        same language.   London, T. Brettell, 1872.
        367p.

        Covers systematically the diplomatic and consular
        affairs and law of Brazil up to the date of publi-
        cation.   Deals also with Brazilian customs admin-
        istration and maritime law.

365.   Mello, Rubens de.   Tratado de direito diplomático.
        2d ed.   Rio de Janero, Livraria Classics Brasil-
        eira, 1949.   2v.   (Bibliography: v. 2, p. 357-
        370)

        An official Brazilian synthesis of current doctrine
        and practice.

366.   Silva, Geraldo Eulalio do Nascomento e. Manual de
        derecho consular.   Traducido del portugues pour
        Marta Casablanca, Rosarco, 1952.   208p.

        A manual for Brazilian diplomatic and consular
        personnel with emphasis on consular law.

Bulgaria

367.   Caleb, Raphael.   Die konsulargerichtsbarkeit in
        Bulgarien auf grund der capitulationen mit Türkei.
        Strassburg i. e. , Buchdr. C & J Goeller, 1903.
        109p.

        Although this work deals mainly with Bulgarian-
        Turkish foreign relations, it does contain a good
        deal of information concerning consular jurisdic-
        tion in both of these countries.

Canada

368. Cadieux, Marcel. The Canadian diplomat; an essay
      in definition. Translated by Archibald Day.
      Toronto, University of Toronto Press, 1963.
      113p.

      A brief but finely written treatise on Canadian
      diplomatic organization and practice.

369. Canada. Dept. of External Affairs. Canadian rep-
      resentatives abroad and representatives of other
      countries in Canada. Ottawa, E. Cloutier, 1947+
      v. 1+

      Includes some information on Canadian diplomatic
      and consular practice.

370. Eayrs, James. The art of the possible; government
      and foreign policy in Canada. Toronto, University
      of Toronto Press, 1961. 232p. (Includes bib-
      liography)

      This work gives a valuable analysis of the forma-
      tion of Canadian foreign policy and the place in
      it of various parts of the Canadian government.

371. Skilling, Harold Gordon. Canadian representation
      abroad, from agency to embassy. Toronto, The
      Ryerson Press, 1945. 359p. (Studies in inter-
      national affairs, no. 1)

      A sound, scholarly history of the growth of the
      Dominion's diplomatic relations with other countries.

Chile

372. Bustons, L. Emiliano, ed. Lejislación diplomática
      i consular de Chile. Santiago de Chile, Impr.
      "La Ilustracion," 1914. 375p.

      Includes information concerning consular law as
      applied in the diplomatic and consular service of
      Chile.

373.   Chile. Laws, statutes, etc. Servicio diplomático i
       consular: lejislación vijente en 1896. Santiago
       de Chile, Imprenta Meja, 1896.   992p.

       A detailed compilation of Chilean diplomatic legis-
       lation. Also this work is meant to be a handbook
       for diplomatic and consular officials of Chile.

374.   Fuenzalida Lamas, José Luis.   La institucion con-
       sular: conceptos generales y legislación chilena
       ... Santiago de Chile, 1948.   191p.   (Coleccion
       des estudios de derecho international publico.
       Sección: Servicio exterior del Estado, t. 1; Bib-
       liography: p. 187-191)

       A perceptive view of Chilean diplomatic and con-
       sular service.

375.   Guerra Araya, Jonas.   Prontuario de derecho consular
       chileno ... Santiago, Impr. Chile, 1948.   234p.
       (Colleccion de estudios de derecho internacional
       Sección Servicio exterior del Estado, t. 1; Fuentes:
       p. 213-215)

       A well-documented account of Chilean diplomatic
       and consular practice.

376.   Vera, Robustiano.   Manual para diplomáticos y
       consules.   Santiago de Chile, Imprenta, Galvez,
       1909.   402p.

       A handbook of procedures for the diplomatic and
       consular officials of Chile.

China

377.   Chao, Chin-yung.   Chinese diplomatic practice and
       treaty relations, 1842-1943, with special reference
       to the period of Ch'ing Dynasty ... Taipei, China
       Cultural Service, 1955.   65p.

       A systematic but short analysis of Chinese diplo-
       matic and consular service for the period covered.

378.   Hsü, Chung-yüeh.   China's entrance into the family
       of nations; the diplomatic phase, 1858-1880.

Cambridge, Harvard University Press, 1960.
255p.   (Harvard East Asian Studies, 5; Bibliography: p. i-xxxii)

A historical discussion of Chinese diplomatic and
consular service for the period covered.

379.   Liu, Pinghou C.   Chinese foreign affairs--organiza-
tion and control.   New York, Published under the
auspices of the Graduate School of New York
University, 1937.   27p.   (Bibliography: p. iii)

A pamphlet covering the structure and function of
the Chinese Ministry of Foreign Affairs and the
administration of China's foreign relations in the
1930's.

380.   Pergament, Mikhail Iaovlevich.   The diplomatic
quarter in Peking, its juristic nature.   Peking,
China bookseller ltd. , 1927.   133p.

A discussion of diplomatic practice in Chinese
foreign relations and its effect on international
politics.

381.   Swisher, Earl.   Chinese representation in the United
States.   Boulder, Colo. , University of Colorado
Press, 1967.   35p.   (University of Colorado,
studies, Series in history, no. 5; Bibliographical
footnotes)

Concentrates on U. S. -Chinese foreign relations but
includes material on diplomatic and consular service in both nations.

Colombia

382.   Calvo, Juan A.   Prontuario consular colombiano.
Leyes, decretos, circulares, convenciones, regla-
mentos y modelos de documentos y curadros.   2d
ed.   Bogotá, Imprenta nacional, 1938.   196p.

An overview of Colombian diplomatic practice and
procedure.   Includes many tables, forms and documents.

383.   Palau, Lisimaco. Guía para los cónsules colombianos
        ... 3d ed. Bogota, Impr. de Zalames, 1893.
        42p.

        A brief guide for Colombian diplomatic and con-
        sular officials.

384.   Perez-Sarimento, José Manuel. Manual diplomatico
        y consular colombiano. 5th ed. Bogotá, Talleres
        de ediciones Colombia, 1927. 406p.

        A detailed manual on diplomatic procedures for
        Colombian diplomats.

Congo

385.   Congo (Leopoldville Ministére des affaires étrangères.
        Almanach du corps diplomatiques. Léopoldville,
        1962+ v. 1+

        A handbook for Congalese diplomatic and consular
        officials.

Cuba

386.   Cortina, José Manuel. Estudios realizados para
        formular un Proyecto de ley organicando el ser-
        vicio diplomático y consular de la república de
        Cuba. La Habana, Imprenta Molina, 1938. 71p.

        A cursory discussion of the diplomatic relations
        of Cuba during the 1930's.

387.   Cuba. Servicio de Protocolo. Lista del cuerpo
        diplomático extranjero. La Habana, 1959+ v. 1+
        (Irregular)

        An irregular publication dealing in general with
        Cuban diplomatic and consular personnel.

388.   Torre y Reiné, Rapheal de la. Manual de derecho
        consular. Cubano ... Habana, A. Miranda, 1918.
        362p.

        A handbook of procedures for Cuban diplomatic and
        consular officials.

Dominican Republic

389.   Amiama Tió, Fernando A.   Las functiones consulares.
        2d ed. Ciudad Trujillo, Editora "Arte y Cine,"
        1952+   v. 1+

        A handbook for consular officials of the Dominican
        Republic coupled with a discussion of consular
        law.

390.   Llaverias, Federico.   Manual de derecho consular
        dominicano. Santo Domingo, R. D. , Impr. de
        J. R. vda. Garcia, 1925.   138p.

        A manual of consular law for diplomatic and con-
        sular officials.

Ecuador

391.   Montero Toro, Jose.   Práctica del derecho consular
        y comercial ecuatorian ... With Augusto Pérez
        Anda ... Quito, Tall. Gráf Nacionales, 1956.
        376p.

        A handbook for the diplomatic and consular offi-
        cials of Ecuador.

392.   Puig Vilazar, Carlos.   Derecho consular ecuatoriano.
        Guayaquil, Impr. de la Universidad, 1951.   384p.
        (Bibliography: p. 383-384)

        A documented and systematic treatise on the con-
        sular and general diplomatic practice of Ecuador.

France

393.   Aix-Marseille, Université d'Institut d'études juri-
        diques de Nice.   Centre de sciences politiques.
        Les Affaires Etrangères.   Paris, Presses univer-
        sitaires de France, 1959.   459p. (Its session,
        5)

        In this informative volume the authors describe
        the administration of foreign affairs in France and

the organization of French diplomacy.

394.   Almanach diplomatique & consulaire ... Paris, G.
       Ferrier, 1909+   v. 1+

       An expansive set of volumes which includes a
       large amount of information of French diplomatic
       and consular service.

395.   Baillou, Jean.   Les affaires étrangères.   With
       Pierre Pelletier.   Paris Presses universitaires de
       France, 1962.   378p.   (Bibliographical footnotes)

       A general treatment of French diplomacy and the
       function of the French Foreign Office.

396.   Boppe, Auguste.   Les introducteurs des ambassadeurs,
       1585-1900.   Paris, F. Alcan, 1901.   80p.

       A brief history of French diplomatic service focus-
       ing on the role of the ambassador.

397.   Born, Erhard.   Die grundzüge des französischen
       konsularrechts unter berücksichtigung des deutschen
       rechts ... Frieburg i. B. , Puchdr. von C. Strö
       cker, 1888.   61p.   (Bibliography: p. v-vii)

       A concise discussion on consular law with empha-
       sis upon the French practice.

398.   Bousquet, Georges.   Agents diplomatiques et consu-
       laires.   Paris, P. Dupont, 1883.   272p.   (Bib-
       liography: p. 271-272)

       A general treatise on French diplomatic and con-
       sular practice along with the detailed functions of
       diplomatic agents.

399.   Chevrey-Rameau, Paul.   Répertoire diplomatique et
       consulaire; indication, dans un ordre méthodique,
       des textes du droit français et du droit interna-
       tional positif qui doirent servir de règle de con-
       duite aux fonctionnaires et agents chargés de la
       surveillance de nos interèts a l'étranger.   Paris,
       L. Larose et Forcel, 1883.   395p.

400.   _____.   Supplement pour les années 1886-1887.

Paris, L. Larose et Forcel, 1888. 65, 637-761p.

Deals with French diplomatic and consular service. Includes the texts of many pertinent documents.

401. Cleroq, Alexandre John Henry de. Guide pratique des consultats, publié sous les auspices du Ministère des affaires étrangères. 5th ed. Paris, A. Pedone, 1898. 2v. (Bibliothèque internationale et diplomatique, I-II)

A practical guide on international law for French diplomatic officials. Also deals specifically with private international law.

402. Damiron, P. De l'incompétence des tribunaux francais dans les litiges concernant les agents diplomatiques. Paris, A. Michalon, 1908. 126p. (Bibliography: p. 7-8)

A treatise on the French legal system and its role with regard to diplomatic and consular practice.

403. Dischler, Ludwig. Der auswärtige Dienst Frankrechs ... Hamburg, Forschungsstelle für Volkerrecht und Auslandisches Offentliches Recht der Universität Hamburg, 1952. 2v. (Bibliography: v. 1, leaf, 170)

Covers French diplomatic practice including legislation affecting consular officials.

404. Dollot, René. Du secret diplomatique. New ed. rev. and enl. Paris, A. Pedone, 1946. 43p.

A brief analysis of French diplomatic practice.

405. Donnadieu, James. Les consuls de France. Paris, Recueil Sirey, 1928. 215p. (Bibliography: p. 205-212)

A basic treatment of French diplomatic and consular service.

406.   Flassan, Gaëtan de Raxis de.   Histoire générale et
       raisonnée de la diplomatie française ... 2d ed.
       Paris, chez Treutlel et Würtz, 1811.   7v.

       The most extensive and profusely documented dip-
       lomatic history of French foreign relations up to
       the early nineteenth century.

407.   Furniss, Edgar Stephenson.   The office of the Pre-
       mier in French foreign policy-making: an applica-
       tion of decision-making analysis.   Princeton, 1954.
       67p.   (Princeton University.   Organization Be-
       havior Section.   Foreign Policy Analysis Project.
       Foreign policy analysis series, no. 5; Bibliography:
       p. 65-67)

       A decision-making analysis of the Premier in the
       formulation of French foreign policy.

408.   Herbette, Louis.   Nos diplomates et notre diplomatie;
       étude sur le Ministère des affaires étrangères.
       Paris, 1874.   127p.

       An overview of the administration of French diplo-
       matic and consular affairs stressing the role of
       the Ministry of Foreign Affairs.

409.   Héritte, Louis Jean Paul.   Guide formulaire à l'usage
       des agents consulaires.   Paris, A. Pedone, 1900.
       340p.

       A guide or handbook for French diplomatic and con-
       sular officials outlining diplomatic usage and prac-
       tice.

410.   Lagét de Podio.   De la juridiction des consuls de
       France à l'étranger et des devoirs et obligations
       qu'ont à remplir ces fonctionnaires, ainsi que les
       armateurs, négocians, navigateurs.   Paris, Chez
       C. J. Trouvé, 1826.   400p.

       A primary source book on French consular juris-
       diction as well as its diplomatic and consular ser-
       vices in general.

411.   _____.   Nouvelle juridiction des consuls de France
       à l'étranger ... 2d ed.   Marseille, L'auteur,

1844. 2v. in 1.

The second and expanded edition of the above.

412. Laroche, Carlo. La diplomatie française. Paris,
Presses Universitaires de France, 1946. 127p.

A brief study of French diplomatic history and
practice.

413. Lehr, Ernest. Manuel théorique et pratique des
agents diplomatique et consulaires français et
étrangers. Paris, L. Larose et Forcel, 1888.
425p. (Bibliography: p. xi-xviii)

A scholarly treatment of French diplomatic and
consular service.

414. Levis Mireqoix, Emmanuael de. Le Ministère des
affaires étrangères; organisation de l'administration centrale et des services extérieurs (1793-
1932) ... Angers, Société anonyme des éditions
de l'ouest, 1934. 266p. (Sources consultées:
p. xiii)

A systematic and documented analysis of the
French Ministry of Foreign Affairs. Also deals
with French diplomatic and consular service in
general.

415. Marcas, Z. La diplomatie, les consulats et le
commerce français. Paris, 1890. 48p.

A short overview of French diplomatic and consular service.

416. Monnet, Raphael. Manuel diplomatique et consulaire;
aide-mémoire pratique des chancelleries. 3d ed.
Paris, Berger-Levrault, 1910. 730p.

An expanded and greatly detailed analysis of
French diplomatic and consular practice. Is useful for its coverage of consular law for the French
diplomat.

417. Morellil, L. J. A. de. Manuel des agents consulaires, français étrangers. Rev. ed. Paris,

Videcoq, 1853.   538p.   (Bibliography: p. iii)

An extensive work meant to guide French diplomatic agents with respect to consular law and
practice.

418.   Mousset, Albert.   La France vue de l'étranger; ou,
Le déclin de la diplomatie et le mythe de la prop-
agande.   Paris, L'Ile de France, 1926.   222p.

An account of French diplomacy and the role of
propaganda in the formulation of foreign policy.

419.   Noel, Léon.   Conseils à jeune français entrant dans
la diplomatie.   Paris, La Jeune Praque, 1948.
139p.

An overview of French diplomatic and consular
practice.

420.   Perrochel de Morainville, Marcel de.   Des consuls
négociants ... Paris, O. Henry, 1915.   102,
35p.

Deals specifically with the role of consuls in
French diplomatic practice.

421.   Pillaut, Julien.   Manuel de droit consulaire ...
Paris, Berger-Levraut, 1910.   281p.

A manual of consular law for French diplomatic
and consular agents.

422.   Pinheiro-Ferreira, Silvestre.   Observations sur le
Guide diplomatique de M. le Baron Ch. de
Martens.   Paris, Rey et Gravier, 1837.   190p.

A critical discussion of Martens and his guide to
diplomatic practice.

423.   Sallet, Richard.   Der diplomatische Dienst; seine
Geschicht und Organisation in Frankreich, Gross-
britannien und den Vereinigten Staaten.   Stuttgart,
Deutsche Verlags-Anstalt, 1953.   366p.

The history and organization of the foreign officer
and diplomatic services of France, Great Britain

and the United States from their origins to the present.

424.   Schlosser, Georges. Les actes diplomatiques con-
       sidérés comme actes de gouvernement. Paris,
       Les editions Domat-Montchvestein, F. Loviton,
       1933. 133p. (Bibliography: p. 131-133)

       A theoretical discussion of the role of diplomacy
       in the functions of government.

425.   Toubeau, Jean. Les institutes du droit consulaire
       ... 2d ed. Paris, N. Gosselin, 1700. 2v. in 1.

       Deals specifically with French diplomatic and
       consular service along with consular jurisdiction
       and commercial courts.

426.   Verdier, Abel Leonce. Manuel pratique des consulats.
       2d ed. Paris, 1957-58. 3v. (Bibliographical
       footnotes)

       A massive treatise on French diplomatic and con-
       sular practice. Basically a manual for french
       diplomatic servants.

Germany

427.   Brauer, Arthur von. Die deutschen justizgestze in
       ihrer anwendung auf die amtliche thätigkeit der
       konsuln und diplomatischen agenten und die kin-
       sulargerichtsbarkeit. Zum praktischen gebrauch
       zusammengestellt. Berlin, C. Heymann, 1879.
       195p.

       A handbook of German consular law and jurisdic-
       tion.

428.   Craig, Gordon Alexander. From Bismarck to Aden-
       aure: aspects of german statecraft. Rev. ed. New
       York, Harper & Row, 1965.

       An excellent treatise on the German diplomatic
       experience.

429.   Drehmann, Klaus. Ueber die geschichte der kon-

sulargerichts-barkeit des Deutschen reiches.   Lip-
pstadt, Westf. , Buchdruckerei Thiele, 1933.   55p.

An overview of German diplomatic and consular
service focusing upon consular jurisdiction and
exterritoriality.

430.   German (Democratic Republic, 1949-   ) Laws,
        statutes, etc. Gesandtschafts-und Konsularrecht
        und damit im Zusammenhang stehende gesetzliche
        Bestimmungen; Loseblatt-Textausgabe mit Anmer-
        kungen und Sach-register von Herbert Standke.
        Berlin, Deutscher Zentralverlag, 1960-   2v.
        (Loose-leaf)

        A loose-leaf publication dealing with diplomatic
        and consular service in East Germany.

431.   Kameke, Claus von.   Palais Beauharnais; Die Resi-
        denz des deutschen Botschafters in Paris.   Stutt-
        gart, Deutsche Verlags-Anstalt, 1968.   83p.

        A brief but sensitive account of the French phase
        of German diplomatic service.

432.   Kistemaker, Johannes.   Die deutschen konsulargerich-
        tsbezirke und ihre natur im strafrecht.   Munster
        i. W. , Druck der Aktien-gesellschaft für Verlag
        und druckerei "Der Westfale", 1904.   35p.
        (Bibliography: p. 7-8)

        Within the context of German diplomatic and con-
        sular practice this work discusses consular jur-
        isdiction and exterritoriality.

433.   Koch, August.   Das konsulatsgebührengesetz, mit
        erläuterungen und entscheidungen des Auswärtigen
        amts ... Berlin, Selbstverlag, 1914.   148p.

        Covers the entire scope of German diplomatic and
        consular service.

434.   König, Bernhard Woldemar von.   Handbuch des
        deutschen konsularwesens.   8th ed.   Berlin, D.
        Reimer (E. Vohsen) 1914.   928, 279p.   (Ab-
        kürzungen, p. xxi-xxii)

One of the most complete and documented treatises on German diplomatic and consular practice up to the date of publication.

435.   Kraske, Erich.   Handbuch des auswartigen Dienstes ... Tübingen, Mohr, 1957.   366p.

A close look at the diplomatic and consular service of the German Federal Republic.

436.   Kraus, Herbert.   Der auswärtige dienst Deutschen Reiches (diplomatie und konsularwesen) ... Verlag von G. Stilke, 1932.   1216p.

Along with the work by Konig this volume is a detailed survey of German diplomatic and consular practice up to the date of publication.

437.   Martens, Peter Christoph.   Das deutsche konsular-& kolonialrecht unter berücksichtigung der neusten gesetze und verordungen gemeinverstandilien ... Leipzig, L. Huberti, 1904?   122p.

Coupled with this overview of German diplomatic and consular service is a discussion of German colonial law and jurisprudence.

438.   Mendelssohn Bartholdy, Albrecht.   Diplomatie ... Berlin-Grunewald, W. Rothschild, 1927.   115p. (Bibliography: p. 16)

An address, with supplementary documents, in which a well known German authority discusses the pros and cons of diplomatic methods, old and new.

439.   Mensch, Friedrich August.   Manuel pratique de consulat: ouvrage consacré spécialement aux consuls de Prusse et des autres états formant le Zollverein.   Leipzig, F. A. Brockhaus, 1846.   xviii, 257p.

A nineteenth century handbook for German diplomatic and consular officials.

440.   Menzel, Viktor.   Deutsches gesantschaftswesen im mittelalter.   Hannover, Hahn, 1892.   259p.

A history of German foreign relations together
with a discussion of ambassadors, their role and
functions in international law and relations.

441.   Meyer, Herman.   Das politische schriftwesen in
       deutschen auswärtigen dienst; ein leitfaden zum
       verstandnis diplomatischer dokumente.   Tubingen,
       Mohr, 1920.   108p.

       A general treatise on the German foreign office
       and its role in diplomatic and consular affairs.

442.   Oberneck, Hermann.   Legalisation, freizü gigkeit
       vollstreckbarer urkunden, konsularisches notariat.
       With Leo Sternberg ... Berlin, C. Heymann,
       1927.   180p.   (Schriftuum: p. viii-ix)

       A work on legal instruments along with a general
       discussion of German diplomatic and consular
       practice.

443.   Peil, Willy.   Ersuchen um rechtshilfe im internation-
       alen verkehr, für die preussischen gerichte bear-
       veitet von landgerichtssekretar ... München, E.
       Rentsch, 1913.   130p.

       A brief work on private international law and
       German diplomatic and consular service.

444.   Riesser, Hand Eduard.   Haben die deutschen Diplo-
       maten versagt?   Eine Kritik an der Kritik von
       Bismarck bis heute.   Bonn, H. Bouvier, 1959.
       61p.

       A criticism of German diplomats from the time
       of Bismarck to the present.

445.   Rossteuscher, Philipp.   Die polizei der deutschen
       konsuln ... München, Schweitzer, 1907.   122p.
       (Bibliography: p. 5-6)

       A basic discussion of German diplomatic and con-
       sular practice with emphasis upon the problems of
       consular law.

446.   Trimborn, Peter.   Die rechliche stellung der deu-
       tschen konsuln in Bulgarien einst und jetzt ...

Traunstein, Buchdr. E. Leopoldseder, 1916.
70p. (Includes bibliography)

A short treatment of German diplomatic and consular service along with German-Bulgarian foreign
relations.

447.   Weiser, Walther.   Die deutsche konsulargerichtsbark-
        eit in zivilsachen; order, Die tätigkeit der deu-
        tschen konsulargerichte in burgerlichen recht-
        sstreitigkeiten.   Berlin, Puttkammer & Muhlbrecht,
        1912.   143p.   (Bibliography: p. vi-viii)

A discussion of German diplomatic and consular
practice with particular emphasis upon civil law
and procedure and its relation to German consular
jurisdiction.

448.   Zorn, Philipp Karl Ludwig.   Deutsches gesandtschafts-
        und konsularrecht auf der grundlage des allge-
        meinen volkerrechts.   Stuttgart, W. Kohlhammer,
        1920.   204p.

A wide ranging overview of German diplomatic and
consular service.

Ghana

449.   Ghana.   High Commissioner for the United Kingdom.
        Diplomatic staffs of Commonwealth and foreign
        missions in Accra, 1959-?   v. 1-

A series of volumes on diplomatic and consular
personnel in Ghana.

Great Britain

450.   Ashton-Gwatkin, Frank Trelawny Arthur.   The
        British Foreign Service; a discussion of the dev-
        elopment and function of the British Foreign Ser-
        vice.   Syracuse, N. Y. , Syracuse University Press,
        1950?   94p.   (Bibliography: p. 94)

The organization of the Foreign Office as it was
in the immediate post-war period is included.   The

book is particularly valuable for the background
it gives to the Eden-Bevin reforms of 1943, of
which the author was one of the principal initiators.
He also makes a strong plea for more efficiency
and representation in the Service.

451.   At the Court of St. James's.   London, Diplomatist
        Publications, 1954-   v. 1-   (Annual)

        A series of volumes covering diplomatic and con-
        sular practice in the United Kingdom.

452.   Beloff, Max.   New dimensions in foreign policy; a
        study in British administrative experience, 1947-
        1959.   New York, Macmillan, 1961.   208p.

        A perceptive study of the impact upon the admin-
        istration and political systems of independent states
        of the network of international organizations in
        whose work they are increasingly involved.

453.   Bindoff, Stanley Thomas.   British diplomatic repre-
        sentatives, 1789-1852.   With E. V. Malcolm
        Smith and C. K. Webster.   London, Office of the
        Roayl Historical Society, 1934.   216p.   (Royal
        Historical Society, Camden third series, v. 50)

        A broad treatment of British diplomatic and con-
        sular service from the latter half of the eighteenth
        century up to 1852.

454.   Bishop, Donald Gordon.   The administration of Brit-
        ish foreign relations.   Syracuse, N. Y. , Syracuse
        University Press, 1961.   410p.   (Bibliography:
        p. 383-394)

        A solid study of the governmental structure and
        operation by which British foreign policy is form-
        ulated and administered.   The treatment is largely
        topical.

455.   Bonham, Millege Louis.   The British consuls in the
        confederacy.   New York, Columbia University,
        Longmans, Green, 1911.   267p.   (Bibliography:
        p. 262-267)

        A scholarly treatise on the British diplomatic representatives and the Confederate States of America during the Civil War.

456.   Busk, Sir Douglas L.   The craft of diplomacy; how
        to run a diplomatic service.   New York, F. A.
        Praeger, 1967.   293p.   (Includes bibliographies)

        The author "describes the proper functioning of
        missions, the duties of embassy and consular
        officials, the structural and personnel problems
        that confront modern diplomatic services, and the
        human and material resources that are needed to
        meet the needs of national representation overseas.
        He gives a dictionary of diplomatic terms and
        functions, and appendixes on grades, personnel,
        and emolument, and on procedures for selecting
        recruits to the service.   Includes annotated bib-
        liography.

457.   Firth, Sir Charles Harding, comp.   Notes on the
        diplomatic relations of England and France 1603-
        1688; lists of ambassadors from England to France
        and from France to England.   Comp. with S. C.
        Lomas.   Oxford, B. H. Blackwell, 1906.   47p.

        A brief treatise on British-French diplomatic and
        consular practice focusing upon the role of am-
        bassadors.

458.   _____   ed.   Notes on the diplomatic relations of
        England and France ...   List of diplomatic repre-
        sentatives and agents, England and France, 1689-
        1763, contributed by L. G. Wickham Legg ...
        Oxford, B. H. Blackwell, 1909.   49p.

        A follow up on the first work covering the period
        1689-1763.

459.   _____ .   Notes on the diplomatic relations of England
        and Germany ...   List of diplomatic representatives
        and agents, England and North Germany, 1689-
        1727, contributed by J. F. Chance.   Oxford, B.
        H. Blackwell, 1907.   55p.

        A brief account of British-German diplomatic and
        consular service emphasizing the role of the am-
        bassador from 1689-1727.

460.   _____, ed.   Notes on the diplomatic relations of
            England with the north of Europe ... Lists of
            English diplomatic representatives and agents in
            Denmark, Sweden and Russia, and of those
            countries in England, 1689-1762, contributed by
            J. F. Chance.   Oxford, B. H. Blackwell, 1913.
            52p.

            A general overview of British-European diplomatic
            and consular service also giving special attention
            to ambassadors.

461.   Fynn, Robert.   British consuls abroad; their origin,
            rank and privileges, duties, jurisdiction and emo-
            lument.   London, E. Wilson, 1846.   328p.

            An excellent treatise on nineteenth century British
            diplomatic and consular service.

462.   Hall, William Edward.   A treatise on the foreign
            powers and jurisdiction of the British crown.
            Oxford, Clarendon Press, 1894.   304p.

            A provocative discussion of British consular juris-
            diction within the framework of international law
            and relations.

463.   Hertslet, Sir Edward.   Recollections of the old
            Foreign Office.   London, J. Murray, 1901.   275p.

            An interesting account of the early years of the
            British Foreign Office.

464.   Horn, David Bayne.   British diplomatic represent-
            atives, 1689-1789.   London, Offices of the Royal
            Historical Society, 1932.   178p.   (Royal His-
            torical Society Publication.   Camden third series,
            v. 46)

            A brief history of British diplomats and their
            activities from 1689-1789.

465.   _____.   The British diplomatic service, 1689-1789.
            Oxford, Clarendon Press, 1961.   324p.

            An enlargement of the above.   A well-documented
            account of British diplomatic practice for the time
            covered.

466.   Rendel, Sir George.   The sword and the olive; recol-
        lections of diplomacy and the Foreign Service,
        1913-1954.   London, J. Murray, 1957.   348p.

        These diplomatic memoirs deal chiefly with the
        Balkens and the Near East.   An insight in to
        British diplomatic and consular practice.

467.   Strang, William Strang.   The diplomatic career.
        London, A. Deutsch, 1962.   160p.

        Eight papers on the profession of the diplomatist,
        written by a distinguished authority who appreciates
        the pitfalls and rewards of a diplomatic career.

468.   _____.   The Foreign Office.   New York, Oxford
        University Press, 1955.   226p.

        An informative, if somewhat complacent, account
        of the present work of the major departments of
        the central government in Britain.

469.   Suck, Thomas.   Ueber die entwicklung der konsular,
        urisdiktion unter besonderer berücksichtigung
        Grossbritanniens.   Erlangen, Univ. -buchdruckerei.
        von E. T. Jacob, 1919.   65p.   (Bibliography:
        p. iv-vi)

        A treatise on British consular law and diplomatic
        practice.

470.   Tilley, Sir John Anthony Cecil.   The Foreign Office.
        With Stephen Gaselee.   New York, Putnam's,
        1933.   335p.   (Bibliography: p. 320-322)

        An authoritative history of the British Foreign
        Office.

471.   Tuson, E. W. A.   British consuls manual: being a
        practical guide for consuls, as well as for the
        merchants, shipowners, and master mariners,
        in all their consular transactions.   London, Long-
        man, 1856.   572p.

        A nineteenth century guide for British diplomatic
        officials and others.

472.   Willson, Beckles.   Friendly relations: a narrative
        of Britain's ministers and ambassadors to Amer-
        ica (1791-1930).   Boston, Little, Brown, 1934.
        350p.

        A somewhat popular treatment of Anglo-American
        relations by means of copious quotations from the
        dispatches of British diplomats in Washington.

473.   .   The Paris embassy; a narrative of Franco-
        British diplomatic relations 1814-1920.   London,
        T. F. Unwin, 1927.   368p.

        Sketches of Anglo-French relations from 1814-
        1920, based in part on the unpublished English
        correspondence.

474.   Young, Sir George.   Diplomacy old and new.   London,
        The Swathmore Press, 1921.   105p.

        Intended as a general introduction for the layman,
        this work, written by a former diplomat, criticizes
        the accepted system.

Guatemala

475.   Moreno, Laudelino.   Derecho consular guatemalteco.
        Guatemala, C. A.   Tipografía nacional, 1946.
        696p.   (Bibliography: p. 677-681)

        A well-documented treatment of Guatemalan con-
        sular law.

India

476.   Berkes, Ross North.   The diplomacy of India; Indian
        foreign policy in the United Nations.   With Mohin-
        der S. Bedi.   Stanford, Calif., Stanford University
        Press, 1958.   221p.

        Discusses India's role in the United Nations and
        its foreign policy in general.

Italy

477. Biondell, Giuseppe. Manuale teorico pratico del
      servizio consolare, ad uso degli uffici consolari,
      avvocati, notai e studi legali en geuere. Roma,
      1955. 555p.

      A general examination of Italian diplomatic and
      consular practice.

478. Fano, Alberto. Raccolta di norme per l'applicazione
      della tariffa consolare ... Nouva ed. ... Roma,
      Istituto poligrafico dello stato, Libreria, 1933.
      377p.

      An estimable discussion of Italian diplomatic and
      consular service.

479. Ferrara, Francesco. Manuale di diritto consolare.
      Padova, A. Milani, 1936. 365p. (Bibliography:
      p. 49-53)

      A manual of diplomatic practice for Italian consuls
      and other diplomatic officials. Places emphasis
      upon consular law.

480. Fink, Samuel Miles. Rights of Italian consular
      officers in American courts. New York, Printed
      by Appellate Press Corp. , 1953. 18p.

      A brief discussion of the consular rights of Italian
      diplomatic officials.

481. Gorrini, Giacomo, ed. Legislazione marittima-
      consolare vigenete al 10 dicembre 1897 ... Torino,
      Fratell Bocca; Roma, Tip. del Ministero degli
      affair esteri, 1898. 840p. (Biblioteca di legis-
      lazione diplomatica e consolare, vol. I)

      Includes a detailed discussion on Maritime law
      along with Italian diplomatic and consular service
      and law.

482. Testa, Luigi. Le voci del servizio diplomatico-
      consolare italino e straniero. 3d ed. Roma,
      Fratelli Treves, 1912. 734p.

An extensive discussion of diplomatic and consular
service with emphasis upon Italian practice and
consular law.

483. Zampaglione, Gerardo. Manuale di diritto consolare.
      Roma, Casa ed. Stamperia nazionale, 1958.
      1749p. (Bibliography: p. xliv-xlvi)

      An extensive and well-documented study of Italian
      diplomatic and consular practice.

Japan

484. Sekiguchi, Nobara K. The first Japanese ambassadors
      to America. Los Angeles, Society for East-West
      Synthesis, 1960?   42p.

      A brief pamphlet discussing the important initia-
      tion of diplomatic relations between these two
      nations.

485. Senga, Tsurutaro. Gestaltung und kritik der heutigen
      konsulargerichtsbarkeit in Japan. Berlin, R. L.
      Prager, 1897.   160p.

      A specific treatise on consular jurisdiction in
      Japan and its effect on her foreign policy.

486. Takeuchi, Tatsuji. War and diplomacy in the Japan-
      ese empire. Garden City, N. Y. , Doubleday,
      Doran, 1935.   505p.   (Bibliography: p. 485-
      489)

      This is a scholarly and thoroughly documented
      analysis of the Japanese constitutional system and
      the technique of Japanese diplomacy.

Mexico

487. López Romero, Adolfo. Comercio y servicio exter-
      ior mexicanos ... Mexico, 1957.   116p.   (In-
      cludes bibliography)

      A general discussion of Mexican foreign economic
      relations along with information on diplomatic and
      consular affairs.

488.   Mexico.   Direccion general de comercio exterior y
        del servicio consular.   Directorio consular de
        Mexico.   México, 1932+   v. 1+   (Irregular)

        A series of volumes covering diplomatic and con-
        sular service in Mexico.   Intended as a handbook
        for diplomatic officials and includes documents.

Netherlands

489.   Joekes, Adolf Marcus.   Schets van de bevoegdheden
        der nederlandsche consuls.   Leiden, E. I. Jko,
        1911.   203p.   (Litteratur: p. 12-14)

        Deals with diplomatic and consular service in the
        Netherlands particularly with the functions of
        consuls.

490.   Wertheim, Jacobus.   Manuel à l'usage des consuls
        des pays-bas.   Amsterdam, Binger, 1861.   3v.

        An extensive manual of diplomatic practice and
        procedures for the consular personnel of the
        Netherlands.

Panama

491.   Panama (Republic) Ministerio de relaciones exteriors.
        Guïa consular.   Panamá, Imp. nacional, 1944+
        v. 1+

        A series of manuals for the consular officials of
        Panama.

492.   _____.   Guïa diplomática.   Panamá, R. P. , 1944+
        v. 1+

        A more general set of volumes covering diplomatic
        procedures for all Panamanian diplomatic officials.

Peru

493.   Garcia Salazar, Arturo.   Guïa practica para los
        diplomáticos y cónsules peruanos.   Lima, Tip.

americana, 1918.   2v.

A detailed handbook for Peruvian diplomatic and
consular agents.

494.   Pérez de Cuéllar, Javier. Manual de derecho diplomático. Lima, Ediciones Peruanas, 1964.
178p.   (Bibliography: p. 177-178)

A short treatise covering all phases of Peruvian
diplomatic practice.

495.   Ugarteche, Pedro. Formación del diplomático peruano. Lima, Villanueve, 1955.   111p.

Essays and proposals concerning diplomatic training and measures to improve the Peruvian diplomatic service.

496.   _____. Valija de un diplomático peruano.   Buenos
Aires, Editorial Américalee, 1965.   140p.
(Bibliographical footnotes)

A collection of general essays on Peruvian diplomatic and consular service.

Portugal

497.   Martins, Armando. Direito consular internacional.
Lisboa, Imprensa Nacional de Lisboa, 1961.
456p.

An extensive and documented analysis of Portugese
diplomatic and consular service.

498.   Wildik, Pedro Affonso de Figueiredu. Bibliotheda
consular. Lisboa, Imprensa nacional, 1877-78.
2v.

An extended bibliographical treatise on Portugese
diplomatic and consular practice.   (See also section
on retrospective bibliographies)

Salvador

499.   Ramirez Pena, Abraham.   Cartilla consular.   San
        Salvador, Imprenta nacional, 1916.   369p.

        An outline of general practice within the diplomatic
        and consular service of Salvador.

Sardinia

500.   Magnone, Francesco.   Manuel des officiers consu-
        laires sardes et étrangers.   Marseille, VeCamoin,
        1847.   2v.

        A general handbook and manual for the diplomatic
        and consular officials of the Kingdom of Sardinia.

South America

501.   Albertini, Luis Eugenio.   Derecho diplomatico en sus
        aplicaciones especiales á las repúblicas sud-ameri-
        canas, seguido de un apéndice conteniendo las
        principales leyes, decretos y reglamentos de las
        repúblicas Argentina, de Chile, del Ecuador, Perú
        y Estados Unidos de Colombia.   Paris, C. Bouret,
        1909.   422p.

        A concentrated study of South American diplomacy
        and diplomatic practice.

502.   Barceló, Simón, comp.   Manual diplomático y consu-
        lar hispano-americano.   Barcelona, Tipografía de
        la casa editorial Maucci, 1909.   463p.

        A study of diplomatic and consular service in
        Spanish America with an attempt to treat the sub-
        ject of diplomacy in general terms.

503.   Suárez, José León.   Diplomacia universitaria ameri-
        cana.   Argentina en el Brasil; ciclo de conferen-
        cial: Derecho internacional, politica international,
        historia diplomática.   Buenos Aires, Imprenta
        Escoffiel, Caracciolo y cia, 1918.   616p.

An extensive treatment of Latin American foreign
relations and diplomacy. Specifically deals with
relations between Argentina and Brazil.

Soviet Union

504.   Aspaturian, Vernon V.   The Union Republics in
       Soviet diplomacy, a study of Soviet federalism in
       the service of Soviet foreign policy.   Genève, E.
       Droz, 1960.   228p.   (Publications de l'Institut
       universitaire de hautes études internationales, no.
       36)

       A monograph on the use by the Soviet state of its
       multi-national composition and juridical structure
       as instruments of foreign policy.

505.   Barghoorn, Frederick Charles.   The Soviet cultural
       offensive; the role of cultural diplomacy in Soviet
       foreign policy.   Princeton, N.J., Princeton
       University Press, 1960.   353p.

       A discussion of the background, purpose and im-
       pressive organization of Soviet cultural diplomacy
       as an important facet of foreign policy.

506.   Fedorov, L.   Diplomat i konsul.   Moscow, Mezhdun-
       arodnye otnosheniia, 1965.   167p.

       A broad discussion of Russian diplomatic practice.

507.   Heyking, Al´fons Al´fonsovich.   A practical guide
       for Russian consular officers and private persons
       having relations with Russia.   London, Eyre and
       Spottiswoode, 1904.   298p.

       A special handbook dealing with Russian diplomatic
       and consular service.

508.   Kovalev, An.   Azbuka diplomatii.   Moscow, Mezhdun-
       arodnye otnosheniia, 1965.   161p.   (Bibliographi-
       cal footnotes)

       An overview of Russian diplomatic practice and
       consular service.

509.   Kulyk, Ivan Iulianovych.   Zapiski konsula.   Moscow,
        Sovetskii pisatel, 1964.   238p.

        A little more detailed account of Russian diplomatic
        and consular service than the above.

510.   Thayer, Charles Wheeler.   Diplomat.   New York,
        Harper, 1959.   299p.   (Includes bibliography)

        A somewhat rambling and anecdotal work, but
        containing much informative and witty discussion
        of diplomatic practice at the working level.   Con-
        tains some useful insights into Russian diplomatic
        practice.

Spain

511.   Bernal de O'Reilly, Antonio.   Practica consular de
        España; formulario de cancillerias consulares y
        coleccion de decretos, reales ordenes y documentos
        diversos.   Havre, Impr. de A. Lemale, 1864.
        206, 292p.

        Articulates the development and practice of Spain's
        diplomatic and consular service.   Also serves as
        a handbook for consular law for Spanish diplomatic
        officials.

512.   Castro y Casaleiz, Antonio de.   Guia practica del
        diplomático Español.   2d ed.   Madrid, F. Fernan-
        dez, 1886.   2v.

        A plenary discussion of nineteenth century Spanish
        diplomatic and consular service along with Spain's
        foreign policy.

513.   Embajada española; an anonymous contemporary
        Spanish guide to diplomatic procedure in the last
        quarter of the seventeenth century, translated and
        edited by the Rev. H. J. Chaytoe.   London, Camden
        Society, 1926.   46p.   (Camden miscellany, v. 14,
        no. 2)

        Historical account of Spanish diplomacy in the
        seventeenth century.   Spanish text and English
        translation on opposite pages.

514.   Iturriage y Codes, Félix de. <u>Formularios consulares.</u>
        Madrid, Imp. del Ministerio <u>de Asuntos Exteriores,</u>
        1951- v. 1-

        A treatise on the international operation of the
        Spanish diplomatic service.

515.   Letamendi, Agustin de. <u>Tratado de jurisprudencia</u>
        <u>diplomático-consular, y manual prático para la</u>
        <u>carrea de estado.</u> Madrid, Impr. de Repulles,
        <u>1843.   258p.</u>

        A short but documented treatise on Spanish diplo-
        matic and consular service.

516.   Maluquer y Salvador, Miguel. <u>Derecho consular</u>
        <u>español.</u> Madrid, Hijos de Reus, 1899.   899p.

516A.   _____. <u>Apendice. Anos 1900-1901.</u> Madrid, Hijos
        <u>de Reus, 1901.   167p.</u>

516B.   _____. <u>Apendice. Anos 1902-1907.</u> Madrid, Hijos
        <u>de Reus, 1907.   150p.</u>

        A general treatise with supplements on Spanish
        consular law as well as diplomatic and consular
        service.

517.   Toda y Güell, Eduardo. <u>Derecho consular de España.</u>
        Madrid, El Progresso <u>editorial, 1889.   407p.</u>

        An extensive treatise on Spanish diplomatic and
        consular practice with emphasis placed on its legal
        aspects.

Switzerland

518.   Greisler, Karl. <u>Das Statut des schweizerischen dip-</u>
        <u>lomatischen personals.</u> Münsingen, 1949.   <u>118p.</u>
        (Bibliography: p. 5-6)

        A broad treatment of Swiss diplomatic and consular
        service.

519.   Marchand, Marcel G. <u>Die Konsulargerichtsbarkeit</u>
        <u>unter besonder Berücksichtigung der schweizeris-</u>

chen Konsularjurisdiktion in China.   Bern, 1947.
112p.   (Bibliography: p. 110-112)

Covers Swiss diplomatic and consular service as
applied in China. Deals more specifically with
Swiss consular jurisdiction in that country.

520.   Redard, Albert. Die diplomatischen Vertretuggen
        unter besonder Berücksichtigung der schweizeris-
        chen.   Paris, Lungern, 1948.   171p.   (Bibliog-
        raphy: p. vi-xiii)

        Covers diplomatic and consular service in general
        but emphasizes Swiss practice.

United Arab Republic

521.   Moussa, Farag. Le service diplomatique des États
        arabes.   Genève, 1960.   124p.   (Etudes et
        travaux de l'Institut universitaire de hautes études
        internationales, no. 1)

        A general study of Arabian diplomatic practice.

United States

522.   American Assembly.   The representation of the United
        States abroad.   Edited by Vincent M. Barnett, Jr.
        Rev. ed. New York, Praeger, 1965.   251p.

        A collection of essays dealing with effective organ-
        ization and staffing of U. S. representatives in
        foreign countries.

523.   American Foreign Service Association.   Committee
        on Career Principles.   Toward a modern diplo-
        macy; a report to the American Foreign Service
        Association.   Washington, 1968.   185p.   (Bibliog-
        raphical footnotes)

        A major study outlining the career opportunities
        available.

524.   Bailey, Thomas Andrew.   The art of diplomacy; the
        American experience.   New York, Appleton-Century-

Crofts, 1968.   303p.   (Bibliography: p. 289-298)

A manual of diplomatic practice in which the author attempts to set forth his views of how diplomacy should be carried out.

525.   Barnes, William. The Foreign Service of the United States; origins, development and functions. With John H. Morgan. Washington, Historical Office, Bureau of Public Affairs, Dept. of State, 1961. 430p.

This work is chiefly a history of the Foreign Service from its origins to the present. A final chapter provides a brief description of the Foreign Service today.

526.   Barron, Bryton. Inside the State Department; a candid appraisal of the bureaucracy. New York, Comet Press Books, 1956.   178p.

A rather critical and angry appraisal of the State Dept. Covers the problems raised by the Hiss case and others.

527.   Bates, Lindell Theodore. Unauthorized diplomatic intercourse by American citizens with foreign powers as a criminal offence under the laws of the United States. New York, the author, 1915.   16p

A brief study of unauthorized individuals who violate international rules of conduct in dealing with foreign nations.

528.   Beaulac, Willar Leon. Career diplomat: a career in the Foreign Service of the United States. New York, Macmillan, 1964.   199p.

A systematic treatment of the U.S. diplomatic service. His approach is temperate, judicious, and practical.

529.   Beichman, Arnold. The other State Department: the United States Mission to the United Nations; its role in the making of foreign policy. New York, Basic Books, 1968. 221p.   (Includes biblio-

graphical references)

A crisply written account of the structure, activities and main personalities of the U.S. mission
to the U.N.

530.   Bemis, Samuel Flagg. The diplomacy of the Amer-
       ican revolution. New York, Appleton-Century,
       1935.   293p.   (Bibliographical note: p. 265-273)

       An excellent account by a noted American diplo-
       matic historian.

531.   Berding, Andrew Henry Thomas. The making of
       foreign policy. Washington, Potomac Books, 1966.
       94p.   (Bibliography: p. 91-92)

       A very brief outline of the foreign policy making
       process in the U.S.

532.   Childs, James Rives. American foreign service.
       New York, Holt, 1948.   261p.

       A most useful and readable survey of the organ-
       ization and functions of the U.S. diplomatic ser-
       vice, in particular as affected by the Foreign Ser-
       vice Act of 1946.

533.   Committee on Foreign Affairs Personnel. Personnel
       for the new diplomacy, report. Washington,
       Carnegie Endowment for International Peace, 1962.
       161p.

       A frank discussion of problems facing the modern
       diplomat in terms of personnel and staffing diffi-
       culties.

534.   DeConde, Alexander. The American Secretary of
       State; an interpretation. New York, Praeger,
       1962.   182p.   (Includes bibliography)

       A brief biography of the office of Secretary of
       State--its responsibilities, influence and vulner-
       abilities in the American political system.

535.   Delaney, Robert Finley. Your future in the Foreign
       Service. New York, Richards Rosen Press, 1961.

158p.   (Careers in depth, 9)

An outline of the opportunities for a foreign service career.

536.   Elder, Robert Ellsworth.   Overseas representation
         and services for Federal domestic agencies.   New
         York, Carnegie Endowment for International Peace,
         1965.   106p.   (Foreign affairs personnel study,
         no. 2)

         This study concerns the overseas interests of fed-
         eral domestic agencies and the means by which
         they are or might be staffed.

537.   Elliot, Jonathan, comp.   The American diplomatic
         code embracing a collection of treaties and con-
         ventions between the U.S. and foreign powers:
         from 1778 to 1834.   With an abstract of important
         judicial decisions, on points connected with our
         foreign relations.   Also, a concise diplomatic
         manual, containing a summary of the law of Na-
         tions, from the works of Wicquefort, Martens,
         Kent, Vattel, Ward Story etc. Washington, Printed
         by J. Elliot, jun. , 1834.   2v.

         Not consulted.

538.   Foster, John Watson.   The practice of diplomacy as
         illustrated in the foreign relations of the United
         States.   Boston, Houghton Mifflin, 1906.   400p.
         (Bibliography: p. 383-388)

         The author discusses in an informative manner the
         utility of the diplomatic service, the duties of dip-
         lomats and their rank, qualifications, the consular
         service, the negotiation and framing of treatise,
         arbitrations and international claims.

539.   Gauss, Clarence Edward.   A notarial manual for
         consular officers.   Washington, Govt. Print. Off.,
         1921.   84p.   (Bibliographical footnotes)

         A handbook on notarial practice for U.S. diplomatic
         and consular officials.

540.   Gerberding, William P.   United States foreign policy;
        perspectives and analysis.   New York, McGraw-
        Hill, 1966.   383p.   (Includes bibliography)

        A basic discussion of the formulation of foreign
        policy and its administration.

541.   Griffin, Eldon.   Clippers and consuls; American con-
        sular and commercial relations with eastern Asia,
        1845-1860.   Ann Arbor, Mich. , Edwards Brothers,
        1938.   533p.   (Bibliography: p. 457-500)

        A scholarly work on U. S. diplomatic and consular
        relations in Asia.   The style is somewhat spotty
        in places.

542.   Harr, John E.   The anatomy of the Foreign Service;
        a statistical profile.   New York, Carnegie Endow-
        ment for International Peace, 1965.   89p.
        (Foreign affairs personnel study no. 4; Bibliog-
        raphy: p. 89; Bibliographical footnotes)

        A statistical study of foreign service operations
        and development.

543.   _____ .   The development of careers in the Foreign
        Service.   New York, Carnegie Endwment for Inter-
        national Peace, 1964.   104p.   (Foreign affairs
        personnel study, no. 3; Bibliographical footnotes)

        A hard hitting analysis of developing proper goals
        within the personnel system of the U. S. Foreign
        Service.

544.   _____ .   The professional diplomat.   Princeton, N. J. ,
        Princeton University Press, 1969.   404p.
        (Bibliography: p. 387-396)

        A systematic treatise on the challenge of Foreign
        Service work and the sociology of its organization.
        Well documented and outlined.

545.   Hart, Albert Bushnell.   The foundations of American
        foreign policy, with a working bibliography.   New
        York, Macmillan, 1901.   307p.

        A general study with a good bibliography.

546.   Haviland, Henry Field.   The formulation and admin-
        istration of United States foreign policy.   With
        the collaboration of Robert E. Asher, and others.
        Washington, Brookings Institution, 1960.   191p.

        A well-written analysis of the formulation and ad-
        ministration of U. S. foreign policy.

547.   Henshaw, Joshua Sidney.   A manual for United States
        consuls; embracing their rights, duties, liabilities,
        and emoluments.   New York, J. C. Riker, 1849.
        252p.

        A nineteenth century handbook for U. S. diplomatic
        and consular officials.

548.   Hinckley, Frank Erastus.   American consular juris-
        diction in the Orient.   Washington, D. C.   W. H.
        Lowdermilk, 1906.   283p.

        A provocative treatment of U. S. involvement diplo-
        matically in Asia.

549.   Ilchman, Warren Frederick.   Professional diplomacy
        in the United States, 1779-1939; a study in admin-
        istrative history.   Chicago, University of Chicago
        Press, 1961.   254p.   (Bibliography: p. 244-248)

        This study in administrative history traces the
        development of professional diplomatic service in
        the United States since its founding.

550.   Jones, Arthur Griffith.   The evolution of personnel
        systems for U. S. foreign affairs; a history of re-
        form efforts.   Washington, Carnegie Endowment
        for International Peace, 1965.   136p.   (Foreign
        affairs personnel study no. 1; Bibliographical foot-
        notes)

        A discussion of past studies of American personnel
        systems in the field of foreign affairs.

551.   Jones, Chester Lloyd.   The consular service of the
        United States, its history and activities.   Philadel-
        phia, Published for the University, 1906.   126p.
        (Publications of the University of Pennsylvania.
        Series in political economy and public law, no.

18; includes bibliography)

A scholarly monograph dealing with the subjects
of Legislative history, organization, rights and
duties of consuls etc.

552.   Lay, Tracy Hollingsworth.   The foreign service of
the United States.   New York, Prentice-Hall, 1928.
438p.   (Includes bibliography)

A standard treatise on the U. S. foreign service by
a man with much experience in consular posts.

553.   McCamy, James Lucian.   Conduct of the new diplomacy.   New York, Harper and Row, 1964.   303p.
(Bibliography: p. 287-295)

An analysis of how the American government executive is organized to carry out the new diplomacy--
the way the nation makes and augments foreign
policy-and how well the mechanism is working.

554.   Neal, Harry Edward.   Your career in foreign service.
New York, J. Messiner, 1965.   191p.

This work presents a picture of the various fields
of opportunities open for young Americans who are
interested in working abroad.

555.   Paullin, Charles Oscar.   Diplomatic negotiations of
American Naval Officers, 1778-1882.   Baltimore,
The Johns Hopkins Press, 1912.   380p.

This work is authoritative and contains valuable
footnotes with references to original sources and
correspondence that indicate the wide range of the
author's research and authority.

556.   Plischke, Elmer.   Conduct of American diplomacy.
3d ed.   Princeton, N. J. , Van Nostrand, 1967.
677p.   (Bibliography: p. 625-642)

This book emphasizes the principles, procedures,
and governmental machinery involved in the conduct
of foreign relations.

557.   Rappaport, Armin, ed.   Sources in American diplo-

macy.   New York, Macmillan, 1966.   367p.

A collection of essays on American foreign relations.

558.   Sapin, Burton M.   The making of United States foreign
       policy.   Washington, Brookings Institution, 1966.
       415p.   (Bibliographical footnotes)

       A scholarly description of the structure and func-
       tioning of the machinery that formulates and applies
       U. S. foreign policy along with a critical analysis.

559.   Savell, Max.   The origins of American diplomacy:
       the international history of Angloamerica, 1492-
       1763.   With the assistance of Margaret Anne
       Fisher.   New York, Macmillan, 1967.   624p.
       (Bibliography: p. 555-598)

       A well-documented discussion and analysis of
       American colonial diplomacy.

560.   Schuyler, Eugene.   American diplomacy and the
       furtherance of commerce.   New York, Scribner's
       sons, 1895.   469p.

       A systematic analysis of U. S. consular relations
       focusing on navigation rights up to the latter half
       of the nineteenth century.

561.   Scidmore, George Hawthorne.   Outline lectures on the
       history, organization, jurisdiction and practice of
       the ministerial and consular courts of the United
       States and Japan.   Tokio, Igirisu horitsu gakko,
       1887.   245p.   (Includes bibliography)

       Deals more specifically with consular law, courts
       and consular practices in the foreign relations of
       these two countries.

562.   Seward, George Frederick.   The United States consu-
       lates in China.   A letter with inclosures of the
       consul-general in China to the Secretary of State.
       Washington? Printed for private circulation, 1867.
       74p.

       An overview of U. S. diplomatic relations with
       China.

563.   Shaw, Gardiner Howland.   The State Department and
        its foreign service in wartime.   Washington, U. S.
        Govt. Print. Off. , 1943.   12p.

        A brief look at U. S. consular and diplomatic ser-
        vice during the Second World War.

564.   Simpson, Smith.   Anatomy of the State Department.
        Boston, Houghton Mifflin, 1967.   285p.   (Biblio-
        graphical references included in "Notes" p. 249-
        268)

        A sobering indictment of the bungling bureaucrats
        responsible for U. S. foreign policy and diplomacy.

565.   _____.   Resources and needs of American diplomacy.
        Special editor of this volume: Smith Simpson.
        Philadelphia, American Academy of Political and
        Social Science, 1968.   250p.   (Annals v. 380:
        Bibliographical footnotes)

        A group of informative essays by specialists on
        the administration of and problems involved in
        American diplomacy.

566.   Snow, Freeman.   Treaties and topics in American
        diplomacy.   Boston, The Boston Book Co. , 1894.
        515p.

        This is an account of American involvement, pri-
        marily in Latin America, our treaties and consular
        practices in these countries.

567.   Steiner, Zara S.   Present problems of the Foreign
        Service.   Princeton, N. J. , Center of International
        Studies, Princeton University, 1961.   57p.
        (Princeton University Center of International
        studies, Policy memorandum no. 23)

        A detailed analysis of many problem areas in the
        development of an effective foreign service system.

468.   _____.   The State Department and the Foreign Ser-
        vice: the Wriston report--four years later.   Princeton,
        N. J. ,   Center of International Studies.
        Princeton University, 1958.   57p.   (Princeton
        University.   Center of International Studies.   Mem-

orandum, no. 16)

A discussion of the reorganization of the State
Department.

569.   Stock, Leo Francis, ed. Consular relations between
        the United States and the Papal states; instructions
        and despatches. Washington, D. C. , American
        Catholic Historical Association, 1945.   467p.
        (Bibliographical footnotes)

        A detailed diplomatic history.

570.   Stuart, Graham Henry. American diplomatic and
        consular practice. 2d ed. New York, Appleton-
        Century-Crofts, 1952.   477p.   (Bibliography:
        p. 453-466)

        A useful survey of the machinery through which
        the foreign relations of the United States are con-
        ducted: based largely on postwar material.

571.   Terrell, John Upton. The United States Department
        of State; a story of diplomats, embassies, and
        foreign policy. New York, Duell, Sloan and Pearce,
        1964.   121p.

        A brief look at the State Dept. and its functions.
        Lack of detail limits the use of this work.

572.   Thompson, Kenneth W. American diplomacy and
        emergent patterns. New York, New York Univ-
        ersity Press, 1962.   273p.   (Includes Bibliog-
        raphy)

        The author makes a philosophical and historical
        survey of the American purpose and the ways and
        means of American diplomacy, where its origins
        life, and how it appears to be evolving.

573.   U. S. Congress. Senate. Committee on Government
        Operations. The Secretary of State and the Am-
        bassador; Jackson Sub-committee papers on the
        conduct of American foreign policy, edited by
        Henry M. Jackson. New York, Praeger, 1964.
        203p.

This series of papers presents the gamit of information on how modern ambassadors should function.

574.   U. S. Dept. of State.   Foreign relations of the United States.   Diplomatic papers ... Washington, 1861-
v. 1-   (annual)

Contains the texts of diplomatic communications, exchanges of notes, reports, Presidents' annual messages to Congress, and other official papers relating to the foreign relations and diplomacy of the United States.

575.   Van Dyne, Frederick.   Our foreign service; the "A. B. C. " of American diplomacy.   Rochester, N. Y. , the Lawyer's cooperative Publishing Company, 1909   316p.   (Bibliography: p. 195-205)

A survey of the diplomatic and consular service by the American consul at Kingston, Jamaica.   An appendix is added containing important regulations governing examinations, appointments and promotions, forms and present members of the foreign service.

576.   Villard, Henry Serrano.   Affairs of State.   New York, Crowell, 1965.   254p.

A veteran career diplomat gives a basic picture of the history of the U. S. Foreign Service and details its scope of current operations.   He stresses the obstacles hindering the efficiency and quality of our diplomatic efforts.

577.   Walther, Regis.   Orientations and behavioral styles of Foreign Service officers.   New York, Carnegie Endowment for International Peace, 1965.   52p. (Foreign affairs personnel study, no. 5)

A behavioral study of the qualifications and development of persons holding diplomatic posts.

578.   Waters, Maurice.   The ad hoc diplomat; a study in municipal and international law.   The Hague, M. Nijhoff, 1963.   233p.   (Bibliography: p. 222-230)

An enlightening study of those persons engaged in diplomatic activity other than career diplomats.

579. Weintal, Edward. Facing the brink; an intimate study of crisis diplomacy. With Charles Bartlett. New York, Scribner, 1967. 248p.

The authors examine the methods and the men guiding U. S. foreign policy circa World War II.

580. Westerfield, Bradford. The instruments of America's foreign policy. New York, Crowell, 1963. 538p. (Includes bibliography)

This work is a fair and knowledgeable summary and analysis of the way in which American foreign policy has functioned in the past generation.

581. Willson, Beckles. America's ambassadors to England (1785-1929) A narrative of Anglo-American diplomatic relations. New York, Stokes, 1929. 497p.

A survey of Anglo-American relations along the line marked out in the author's earlier books.

582. _____. America's ambassadors to France (1777-1927) A narrative of Franco-American diplomatic relations. New York, Stokes, 1928. 433p.

An illuminating series of pictures of American representatives, using the embassy archives to some extent.

583. Wriston, Henry Merritt. Diplomacy in a democracy. New York, Harper, 1956. 115p.

This work develops the theme that a sound professional diplomatic corps is neither impeded, on the one hand, nor guaranteed, on the other, by the fact of diplomacy. Wriston challenges a number of prevalent views on the workings of diplomacy in a democratic society. On the whole his findings are optimistic though certainly not complacent.

584. _____. Executive agents in American foreign relations. Baltimore, The Johns Hopkins Press, 1929. 874p.

A scholarly study of the constitutional position of executive agents, followed by a survey of different types of diplomatic agents, their status and activities.   A valuable contribution to the literature.

Foreign Service Administration

The first part of this chapter dealt with the broader aspects of foreign affairs administration viz diplomatic and consular service in general and the various agencies of individual countries. This part is concerned with the more specific administrative divisions and functions of diplomatic affairs.

Classification of Agents

The apparatus for diplomatic affairs had its origin shrouded in antiquity, but attained its first modern form during the Renaissance when the Italian city-states began the custom of appointing permanent ambassadors. Diplomatic procedures were more fully developed during the rise of the nation-state system and became stabilized at the Peace of Westphalia in 1648. They were brought up to date at the conference of Aix-la-Chappelle in 1818, and the most recent amendments were made at a multilateral conference in Vienna in 1961.

Currently diplomats are classified by means of a rank system that is accepted by all states. Heads of missions constitute one major classification. The highest ranking mission heads are ambassadors, papal nuncios, and papal legates. Below this group are, in order, envoys extraordinary and ministers plenipotentiary, ministers resident, and chargés d'affaires (ad hoc, entitre, or ad interim). An ad hoc or entitre chargé is assigned as such by his government if such a government for its own reasons does not wish to designate a head of mission. An ad interim chargé substitutes for the mission chief during the latter's temporary absence.

A chief is in charge of each mission. His second in command usually carries the title of counselor of embassy

or some similar title.   Below this level are first, second,
and third secretaries of embassy and a variety of special
officials covering a range of duties.   (e. g. cultural and
press officers, military and labour attachés, and the like). [10]

585.   Hill, David Jayne.   "The classification of diplomatic
        agents," American Journal of International Law,
        XXI (1927), 737-742.

        An excellent discussion on the development and
        problems of rank in the diplomatic profession.

586.   Whang, P. K.   "Matter of elevating diplomatic rank,"
        China World Review, LXXIII (June 1, 1935), 20.

        A brief article on the advances in diplomatic
        rank in China.

Functions of Agents

        Diplomatic duties of agents usually fall under four
headings: representation, negotiation, reporting, and protection.   Representation not only includes conveying diplomatic messages to a government, but also the function of
acting as spokesman, interpreter, and symbol of one's
country at occasions official and private, ceremonial and
informal, and cultivating friendship and understanding through
such contacts.

        The function of negotiation, of course, includes the
process of reaching, through exchange of views, conversation
or formal conference, agreements which can be expressed
in precise terms, generally written, as international agreements which the governments legally obligate themselves to
observe.   Treaties are the most formal of international
political agreements, the texts of which are carefully worked
out by the process of negotiations.   Others may be termed
conventions (usually administrative or technical matters),
protocols, acts, general acts, final acts (of conferences),
statutes, declarations, arrangements, accords, concordats,
modi vivendi (usually informal or temporary).

        The reporting function involves the preparation of
detailed information and data about the country to which
the diplomats are accredited, with interpretative analysis

designed to clarify policies, attitudes, and probable reactions
of government leaders, organized groups, and the general
public. It is important to realize that since this information
is intended to guide the diplomat's government in determining its policy, it is imperative that it be comprehensive and
accurate.

Protection of nationals and their interests is usually
thought of as the responsibility of consuls at the administrative levels and of diplomats at the policy level; however,
such a separation of functions is rarely practicable. The
duties of diplomats necessarily overlap those of consuls,
who are concerned principally with commercial relations
and protection of the interest of nationals.

Ambassadors. A classic and oft-repeated definition
of an ambassador states that he was "an honest man sent to
lie abroad for the good of his country". This statement
expresses the essence of the chicanery and deception indul-
ged in by states in the conduct of their foreign relations at
the time modern diplomacy was developing. The office or
rank of ambassador has had a colorful and tempestuous
history from antiquity to the present era. An ambassador
today has a complex task to perform which not only entails
a vast amount of administrative activity but ceremonial and
social duties as well. [11]

587.   Achenwall, Gottfried.   De transitv et admissione
        legati ex pacto repetendis ... Gottingae, Litteris
        Io. Christ. Lvd. Schvlzii, 1748.   xviiip.

        Covers briefly the functions of ambassadors.

588.   Adair, Edward Robert.   The exterritoriality of am-
        bassadors in the sixteenth and seventeenth cent-
        uries. New York, Longmans, Green, 1929.   282p.

        A study of the relationship of exterritoriality and
        the functions of ambassadors during the sixteenth
        and seventeenth centuries.

589.   Bijnkershoek, Cornelis van.   De foro legatorum
        liber singularis, a monograph on the jurisdiction
        over ambassadors in both civil and criminal cases
        ... A photographic reproduction of the text of
        1744, Opera minora, v. 4, with an English trans-

lation by Gordon J. Laing... Oxford, Clarendon
Press, 1946. 135p. (The Classics of international law, no. 21)

A general treatment of the judicial functions of
ambassadors.

590.   Bragaccia, Gasparo.   L'Ambasciatore... Padova, F.
       Bolzetta, 1626.   675p.

       An early and extensive volume on the role and
       functions of ambassadors in international relations.

591.   Caraffa, Carlo Maria.   El embaxador politico-
       christiano.   Tr. from the Spanish by Monso Man-
       iqve.   Palemo, T. Romolo, 1691.   300p.

       A historical sketch of the evolution of ambassadors
       and their role in the main stream of diplomacy.

592.   Carlino, Paolo.   Genesi e fondamento delle immunitá
       diplomatiche.   Roma, Athenaeum, 1915.   215p.
       (Bibliographical footnotes)

       This essay covers the role of the ambassador
       within the international sphere.   Also deals with
       diplomatic and consular service in general.

593.   Embassies and ambassadors in Rome; articles by
       Roberto Paribeni and others.   Milano, Roma,
       Bestetti & Tumminelli, 1927.

       A collection of articles covering various aspects
       of Roman history including diplomatic relations
       and especially the role of ambassadors.

594.   Gentili, Alberico.   De legationibva libri tres.   New
       York, Oxford University Press, 1924.   2v.
       (The Classics of international law, no. 12)

       One of the classics in the field of international
       law covering the role of ambassadors and their
       legal framework.

595.   Grabař, Vladimir Emmanuilovich, ed.   De legatis
       et legatonibus tractatus varil.   Dorpati Livonorum,
       Mattieseniano, 1905.   250p.

A treatise on the functions and role of ambassadors in the diplomacy of nations.

596.   Guesalaga, Alejandro. Agentes diplomáticos: la ex-
       territorialidad--de los privilejois é inmunidades--
       de sus functiones y de sus deberes. Berlin, 1893.
       238p.

       Discusses exterritoriality and ambassadors with-
       in the framework of diplomatic privileges and
       immunities.

597.   Hothorn, Carl. Die völkerrechtliche sonderstellung
       des gesanden, ein beitrag zur theorie des gesand-
       tschaftsrechts. Breslau, Kern, 1928.   106p.
       (Bibliography: p. 98-106)

       An overview on ambassadors and exterritoriality.

598.   Hotman, Jean. The ambassador. London, Shawe,
       1603.   154p.

       Discusses the emergence of the ambassadorial
       function and its role in diplomacy.

599.   Jusserand, Jean Adrien Antoine Jules. The school
       for ambassadors, and other essays. New York,
       Putnam's, 1925.   355p.

       The lead essay in this work is an excellent dis-
       course on the development of the ambassadorial
       role in diplomacy. The rest of the essays have
       little or no relevance to diplomacy.

600.   LaMothe le Vager, Felix de. Legatva, seu Delega-
       tione, egatorvmqve priuilegiia, officio ac munere
       libellus. Hanoviae, G. Antonium, 1596.   3v.
       in 1.

       An extensive Latin work on the origins and devel-
       opment of ambassadors.

601.   Mirot, Leon. Les Ambassades anglaises pendant la
       guerre de cent ans; catalogue chronologique (1327-
       1450) Paris, A. Picard, 1900.   104p.

       A chronological discussion on ambassadors during

the late medieval period.

602. Moser, Johann Jakob. Beytrage zu dem neuesten
europaischen gesantschafftsrecht. Frankfurt am
Mayn, Verrentrapp, Sohn und Wenner, 1781.
312p.

This work deals with the functions of ambassadors
and covers most other aspects of diplomacy.

603. Ozanam, Charles. L'immunité civile de juridiction
des agents diplomatiques. Paris, A. Pedone,
1912. 210p. (Index bibliographique: p. 191-
194; Bibliographical footnotes)

A well-written and documented work on ambassadors, diplomatic and consular service and exterritoriality.

604. Pacassi, Johann Baptist. Einleitung in die sammtlichen gesandschaftsrechte. Wein, Gedruckt bey
J. T. edlen fon Trattnern, 1777. 308p.

An early work on the origins and development of
the ambassadorial function in diplomacy.

605. Paschal, Carlo. Legatus. Amstelodami, apud L.
Elzevirium, 1645. 543p.

An early treatment on ambassadors and their
importance to the development of diplomatic practice.

606. Queller, Donald E. The office of ambassador in the
Middle Ages. Princeton, N. J. , Princeton University Press, 1967. 251p. (Bibliography: p.
229-247)

A scholarly and well-documented account of the
ambassador's office during the period covered.

607. Roca, Juan Antonio Vera. El anbaxador. Seuilla,
Francisco le Lyra, 1620. 3v. in 1.

An extensive treatise on the role of ambassadors
in seventeenth century European politics.

608.   _____. Le parfait ambassadeur.   Leide, T. Haak,
        1709.   2v.

        An enlargement of the author's earlier work
        listed above dealing more with structures and
        functions.

609.   Roederer, Jean.   De l'application des immunités
        de l'ambassadeur au personnel de l'ambassade.
        Paris, L. Larose, 1904.

        A brief but important discussion of the functions
        of ambassadors within the diplomatic and consular
        world.

610.   Roijen, Isaac Antoine.   De fictie der exterritoriali-
        teit.   Opmerkingen naar aanleiding van de vraag:
        zijn van de boedels van de Nederlandsche gezan-
        ten successierechten verschuldigd?   Groningen, J.
        B. Huber, 1885.   107p.   (Stellingen: p. 93-
        107)

        Discusses a variety of topics including exterritori-
        ality, inheritance and succession in the Nether-
        lands, ambassadorial and diplomatic practice in
        general.

611.   Snouckaert van Schauburg, Albert Carel.   Dissertatio
        inauguralis, juris gentium, De legatis rebusque,
        ab his agendis.   Trajecti ad Rhenum, ex offic.
        Joh. Alteer, 1827.   204p

        Deals with the role of ambassadors in diplomatic
        practice.

612.   Traité des ambassades et des ambassadeurs.   Rot-
        terdam, J. Hofhout, 1726.   180p.

        A brief look at the role of ambassadors in the
        framework of international relations.

613.   U. S. Dept. of State.   The American ambassador.
        Washington, U. S. Govt. Print. Off. , 1957.   22p.

        A brief outline of the role and functions of Amer-
        ican ambassadors.

614.   Wicqueford, Abraham.   The ambassador and his
       functions.   Translated by John Digby.   London,
       B. Lintoll, 1716.   570, 28p.

       An interesting and informative early account of
       ambassadors in the perspective of the Holy Roman
       Empire and its constitutional law.

615.   Zouche, Richard.   Punishment of Ambassadors who
       transgress the laws of countries where they re-
       side; founded upon the judgment of Hugo Grotius.
       (Dissertation) Written originally in Latin, done
       into English by D. J.   London, 1717.   122p.

       A classic discussion of the origins and nature of
       the ambassadorial function in diplomacy.

       Consuls, Consular Law and Jurisdiction.   Nominally
a consul is an official appointed by, or with the authority
of, a government to reside in some foreign country, to
care for the commercial interest of the citizens of the
appointing government, and to protect its seamen.   Consular
service as a whole represents the combined consular
officers of a nation state.   It includes various ranks, such
as in the United States, consuls general, consuls, vice-
consuls and consular agents.   Generally consular officials
are members of the foreign service of the state they represent; however, they differ in a technical sense from the
diplomatic service.   At times the term consul is used in
a very broad sense to include consular officers regardless
of grade or classification, and at other times a narrow definition of the term is employed to include only officers of
a particular rank.   Consuls can be divided into two broad
classifications: consules missi who are professional consuls
and always subjects or citizens of the sending state, and
consules electi, who may or may not be citizens of the
sending state.   The general law of nations does not dis-
tinguish their status.

       Consular jurisdiction is different from the mutually
enjoyed exterritorial right and privileges extended by all
civilized states to foreign diplomats who are lawfully within
their borders.   Since consuls are not diplomatic officers,
they cannot claim as a right the immunity from civil and
criminal jurisdiction of local authorities generally accorded
to diplomatic officers.   What privileges and immunities

they do enjoy with respect to their exemption from local
jurisdiction rest entirely upon treaties, reciprocity, courtesy,
national laws and regulations, and the official policy pro-
nounced by the receiving state. [12]

616.   Bodin, Albert.   Des immunités consulaires dans
        les pays de chrétienté.   Bordeaux, Imprimerie
        Y. Cadoret, 1897.   144p.   (Bibliography: p.
        139-141)

        This is a short treatise dealing with the activities
        of consuls and their functions.

617.   Bouffanais, Pierre.   Les consuls en temps de
        guerres et de troubles.   Paris, Domat-Montchres-
        tien, 1933.   252p   (Bibliography: p. 241-248)

        A pioneer study covering civil as well as inter-
        national wars based on a wide examination of the
        historical precedents.

618.   Bulmerincq, August von.   Consularrecht.   Hamburg,
        J. F. Richter, 1887.   113p.

        A concise treatment of consular law particularly
        applicable to continental Europe.

619.   Candioti, Alberto Maria.   Historia de la institución
        consular en la antigüedad y en la e dad media
        ... con documentos justificativos, muchos de
        ellos inédito.   Madrid, Buenos Aires, Editora
        internacional, 1925-   v. 1-   (Bibliography: v. 1,
        p. 764-801)

        An extensive and well-documented series on the
        historical development of consular institutions and
        diplomatic and consular service in general.

620.   Contuzzi, Francesco Paola.   La istituzione dei con-
        solate ed il diritto internazionale europeo nella
        sua applicabilita in Oriente.   Napoli, E. Anfossi,
        1885.   711p.

        An extensive treatment on the functions of consuls
        and consular jurisdication.

621. Elias, Hugo. Competenze e attribuzioni dei con-
      soli. Milano, IDOS, 1953.   166p   (Bibliog-
      raphy; p. 165-166)

      A provocative discussion of consular functions
      and law.

622. Farley, Philip Faulkner. Rights of foreign consuls
      in the United States. New York, 1931.   60p.

      A brief treatise on consular jurisdiction and law.

623. Gence, Émile. De la répression des crimes commés
      par les Français dans les Echelles du Levant.
      Paris, V. Giard & E. Briere, 1906.   118p.
      (Bibliography: p. i-ii)

      An overview of French consular jurisdiction in
      the Orient during the early twentieth century.

624. Guillén, Fedro. Derecho consular. Mexico, 1949.
      54p.

      A brief work on consular law.

625. Hardy, Michael James Langley. Modern diplomatic
      law. New York, Oceana Publications, 1968.
      150p

      A short but effective treatment on diplomatic
      law and its applications.

626. Hernández-Bretón, Armando. Atribuciones i per-
      rogativas de los cònsules. Munich, BOTS, 1947.
      155 leaves.   (Bibliography; leaves 153-155)

      A mimeographed monograph on consular law and
      practice.

627. Hunziker, Arthur. Die konsularische eheschliessung
      ihre grundlagen und ihre stellung im schweizer-
      sichen recht. Zürich, Buchdruckerei Fluntern,
      1945.   171p.   (Bibliography: p. 5-8)

      Deals with marriage law in Switzerland and its
      relationship to consular jurisdiction.

628.   Ketchkitch, Dragolioub.   Les mariages diplomatiques
       ou consulaires et leurs effets internationaux.
       Paris, P. Bouset, 1931.   243p.   (Index Bibliog-
       raphiques; p. i-x)

       An interesting work on marriage law and its rela-
       tionship with diplomatic and consular law.   Also
       treats the subjects of private international law and
       comparative law.

629.   Larrive, Georges.   Les privilèges des consuls dans
       les pays d"Occident.   Paris, L. Boyer, 1901
       125p.   (Bibliography: p. 5-6)

       A good overview of the functions of consuls and
       consular practice.

630.   Lawrence, William Beach.   Études sur la jurisdiction
       consulaire en pays chrétiens et en pays non chrétiens,
       et sur l'extradition.   Leipzig, F. A. Brockhaus,
       1880.   569p

       An excellent discussion of consular jursidiction
       and extradition.

631.   Lee, Luke Tsung-Chou.   Consular law and practice.
       New York, Praeger, 1961.   431p.   (The Library
       of world affairs, no. 50; Recent consular treaties:
       p. 336-340)

       A systematic and analytical treatment of modern
       consular functions and position.   Intended for the
       serious student or consular officer.

632.   Lippmann, Karl.   Die konsular jurisdiktion im Orient.
       Ihre historische entwicklung von den fruhesten
       zeiten bis zur gegenwart.   Leipzig, Veit, 1898.
       192p.

       An overview of the jurisdiction of consuls in the
       Orient and commercial problems in the late nine-
       teenth century.

633.   Ludwig, Ernest.   Consular treaty rights and com-
       ments on the "most favored nation" clause.   Akron,
       Ohio, the New Werner company, 1913.   239p.

The most extensive treatise on the relationship of
the "most favored nation" clause and consular jurisdiction.

634.   Meunier, Georges. Le rôle maritime du consul en
       temps de guerre, essai historique et juridique.
       Paris, A. Pedone, 1944.   134p.   (Bibliography:
       p. 127-131)

       A treatise on the functions of consuls within the
       framework of international and maritime law.
       Also describes French diplomatic consular service.

635.   Nowery, James Shaw, comp. Consular requirements
       for exporters and shippers to all ports of the
       world, including exact copies of all forms of con-
       sular invoices, with some hints as to drawing out
       of bills of lading. 2d ed.   London, New York,
       Pitman, 1921.   157p.

       A handy but now out of date guide for consular
       officials.

636.   Pagès, Ferdinand Joseph Hélie. De l'infériorité
       sociale des affranchis à Rome et des moyens de
       la relever ... De la condition des Français en
       Orient. Paris, H. Jouve, 1886.   280p.

       A treatise on French consular jurisdiction in the
       Levant and Asia.

637.   Piggott, Sir Francis Taylor. Exterritoriality; the
       law relating to consular jurisdiction and to resi-
       dence in oriental countries.   London, 1892.
       303p.

       An excellent treatise on the relation of exterri-
       toriality and consular jurisdiction.

638.   Puente, Julius Irizarry. The foreign consul; his
       juridical status in the United States.   Chicago,
       B. J. Smith, 1926.   157p.   (Bibliography: p.
       ix-xii)

       A good discussion of consuls and consular juris-
       diction in the United States.

639. _____. Traité sur les fonctions internationales des
consuls. Traduit par C. Schlegel. Paris, Editions. A. Pedone, 1937. 484p. (Bibliographical
footnotes)

An enlarged treatment of the author's book published in 1926 and translated into French.

640. Ravaut-Bignon, Robert. Du droit de police des consuls dans les pays horschrétiente. Paris, A.
Rousseau, 1905. 152p.

A provocative treatise on consular jurisdiction and
police power in foreign nations.

641. Rey Francis. La protection diplomatique et consulaire dans les échelles du Levant et de Barbaric, avec des documents inédits tirés des
Archives du Ministère des affaires étrangères.
Paris, L. Larose, 1899. 552p. (Bibliography:
p. xvi)

With the French relations in the Barbary States
as its focus this work deals with various aspects
of consular jurisdiction.

642. Roman, Edmond. Rapports des consuls avec la
marine marchande. Paris, A. Leclerc, 1906.
224p. (Bibliography: p. 219-220)

A wide ranging discussion of consuls and consular
jurisdiction in foreign relations.

643. Rosa Rullo, Gabriel de. Code-memorial international & maritime des consulats. Napes, F.
Sorrentino, 1902- v. 1-

A series of volumes dealing with consular law in
particular and diplomatic and consular service in
general.

644. Sperduti, Guiseppe. La competenza dei consoli nelle
controversie maritime. Milano, A. Diuffre 1940.
57p. (Bibliographical footnotes)

An overview of consular jurisdiction in foreign nations.

645.   Stewart, Irvin.   Consular privileges and immunities.
       New York, Columbia University Press, 1926.
       216p.   (Bibliography: p. 202-210)

       A thorough and scholarly treatment of this im-
       portant subject.

646.   Stowell, Ellery Cory.   Le consul; fonctions, immu-
       nités, organisation, exequatur; essai d'exposé
       systématique.   Paris, A. Pedone, 1909.   353p.
       (Bibliography: p. 319-345)

       An excellent work on the functions of consuls in
       particular and diplomatic and consular practice in
       general.   Includes a good working bibliography.

647.   _____ .   Consular cases and opinions, from the
       decisions of the English and American courts and
       the opinions of the attorneys general.   Washing-
       ton, D. C., J. Byrne, 1909.   811p.

       A collection of cases.   Of special value is the
       digest of opinions of the U. S. Attorneys general
       in important questions.

648.   Syz, Raymond.   Konsularische Privilegen insbesondere
       der ausländischen Konsuln in der Schweiz.   Zur-
       ich, Schultess, 1947.   98p.   (Bibliography: p.
       95-97)

       A brief analysis of consular functions in modern
       nations.

649.   Verge Jacques.   Des consuls dans les pays d'Oc-
       cident.   Paris, Société anonyme de publications
       périodiques, 1903.   144p.   (Bibliographical
       footnotes)

       A discussion of French consuls and consular jur-
       isdiction in the western world.

650.   Westphal, Harald.   Die Konsulargestzgebung im
       deutschen und ausländischen Recht.   Hamburg,
       1957.   203p.

       A treatise on consular law and its difficulties.

651.   Zimmer, Rudolf. Die jurisdiktionsverhältinisse der
       fremdländischen konsuln in Deutschland, insbeson-
       dere auf grund der vom deutschen reiche abges-
       chlossen en konsular-und handelsverträge.   Greif-
       swand, Druck von F. W. Kunike, 1897.   41p.
       (Bibliography: p. 5-9)

       A general discussion of consular jurisdiction with
       emphasis upon German practice and thought.

                    Privileges and Immunities of Agents

            In order that the conduct of foreign relations by
       governments be handled in an effective manner, it has long
       been recognized that diplomatic, and to a lesser degree
       their consular agents, should be accorded special privileges
       and immunities in the countries to which they are accredited.
       These rights are mostly defined by international law.   They
       most likely had their origins in the representative character
       of ambassadors and ministers, which led rulers to consider
       molestations of their agents as a personal affront to them-
       selves and to demand for them rights equivalent to those
       which they would themselves enjoy if they visited another
       country. [13]

            A diplomat's special position results not from the
       extension of the territorial jurisdiction of the sending state
       into the receiving state, but rather from a grant by the
       receiving state of a personal exemption from its normal
       territorial jurisdiction to the extent that usage has estab-
       lished this as necessary to facilitate international relations.
       Privileges and immunities accorded to diplomats is not
       absolute, but related to the agent's duties and dependent
       upon his good faith and respect for the rights of the re-
       ceiving state in discharging them.

            Any state reserves the right to declare a diplomat
       who violates trust persona non grata and have him expelled.
       However, the government demanding expulsion still has a
       legal obligation during a diplomat's period of accreditation
       to protect his person from injury, obstruction, detention,
       or indignity, and to guarantee his immunity from criminal
       or civil suit or compulsion to appear as a witness.

            Diplomats as well as consuls are exempt from the
       taxes of the receiving state.   They may also import any
       articles for personal or office use which are not prohibited

by law without payment of customs duties. Diplomats are
obliged, even though they have these privileges, to practice
proper conduct. Chiefs of missions usually will not tolerate
improper conduct by members of their staffs. Abuse will
usually be terminated by discipling offenders as soon as
attention is drawn to their misconduct by the receiving
state, and such action sometimes terminates foreign service
careers. 14

652.   Azud, Ján. Diplomatické imunity a výsady; Bratis-
        lava Vydavate stvo Slovenskej akadémie vied,
        1959.   122p.   (Bibliographical footnotes)

        A summary of information on diplomatic privileges
        and immunities in the English and Russian lang-
        uages.

653.   Bastid, Suzanne (Basdevant). Les fonctionnaires
        internationaux. Paris, Librairie du Recueil Sirey,
        Société anonyme, 1931.   335p   (Bibliography:
        p. 327-331)

        A systematic treatise on international officials and
        employees coupled with a discussion of diplomatic
        privileges and immunities.

654.   Bejaoui, Mohammed. Fonction publique interna-
        tionale et influences nationales. New York, Prae-
        ger, 1958.   674p.   (Bibliography: p. 625-664)

        A scholarly examination of the functions, respon-
        sibilities and operations of the secretariats and
        staffs of the U. N. and related organizations.

655.   Crosswell, Carol McCormick. Protection of interna-
        tional personnel abroad; law and practice affecting
        the privileges and immunities of international or-
        ganization. New York, Oceana Publications,
        1952.   198p.

        A study of the law and practice relating to the
        privileges and immunities of international organ-
        izations and their functionaries.

656.   Deak, Francis. Classification, immunites and priv-
        ileges of diplomatic agents. Cambridge, Mass. ,

1927.   89 leaves.

A paper in the Harvard University library giving
a general overview of the classification in the
privileges and immunities accorded diplomatic
agents in foreign countries.

657.   Dinstein, Yoram.   Consular immunity from judicial
process, with particular reference to Israel.
Jerusalem, Institute for Legislative Research and
Comparative Law, 1966.   89p.   (Jerusalem.
Hebrew University, Institute for Legislative Re-
search and Comparative Law, Publication, 12;
Includes bibliographical references)

Briefly treats the complexities of diplomatic privileges and immunities in modern nations.

658.   Eyzaguirre, Jaime.   Privilegios diplomáticos; sín-
thesis téorica y de legislación comparada.   Santiago, Prensas de la Universidad de Chile, 1932.
118p.

A brief but useful summary containing many illustrations from recent history, particularly in Latin
America.

659.   Hershey, Amos Shartle.   Diplomatic agents and immunities.   Washington, U.S. Govt. Print. Off.,
1919.   218p.

A general treatise on diplomatic privileges and
immunities in the international arena.

660.   Hill, William Martin.   Immunities and privileges of
international officials, the experience of the League
of Nations.   Washington, Carnegie Endowment for
International Peace, 1947.   281p.   (C.E.I.P.
Division of International Law.   Studies in the Administration of International Law and Organization,
no. 8; Bibliographical footnotes)

A careful legal study, based on League practice.

661.   Jenks, Clarence Wilfred.   International immunities.
New York, Oceana Publications, 1961.   175p.
(Bibliography: p. 173-174)

This is an examination of the functions of international immunities, about which the author holds:
"In the present state of development of world organizations they are an essential device for the
purpose of bridling unilateral and sometimes irre-
sponsible control by particular governments of
the activities of international organizations."

662.   Katakazi, Konstantin Gavrilovich.   Un incident diplo-
        matique.   Lettre au chef justice S. Chase.   Paris,
        Amyot, 1872.   80p.

        A letter on the subject of diplomatic privileges
        and immunities in the foreign relations between
        the United States and Russia.

663.   Kauffmann, Siegmand.   Die immunität der nicht-
        diplomaten; ein beitrag zur kodification des völ-
        kerrechts.   Leipzig, R. Noske, 1932.   159p.
        (Bibliography: p. xi-xvii)

        Contains information concerning the problems of
        diplomatic agents and the privileges and immuni-
        ties accorded them.

664.   Kebedgy, Michel Stavro.   Die diplomatischen pri-
        vilegien.   Akademischer vortrag gehalten im
        bernischen Grossratssaal (1900).   Bern, Buch-
        druckerei Buchler, 1901.   48p.

        A brief overview of the ramifications of privileges
        and immunities in diplomatic practice.

665.   King, John Kerry.   International administrative juris-
        diction, with special reference to the domestic
        laws and practices of the United States of Amer-
        ica.   Brussels, International Institute of Admin-
        istrative Sciences, 1952?   228p.   (Bibliography:
        p. 224-225)

        This work deals specifically with the diplomatic
        privileges and immunities of the United Nations
        as well as other international organizations.

666.   Leval, Gaston de.   De la protection diplomatique
        des nationaux à l'étranger.   Bruxelles, E. Bruy-
        lant, 1907.   188p.

An analysis of the privileges and immunities of foreign nationals working and traveling abroad.

667.   Mantovani, Mario.   Agenti diplomatici di cittaden-anza italiana presso il sommo pontefice nel Trat-tato lateranense.   Roma, G. Bardi, 1934.

Deals with the diplomatic relations of the Catholic church and the Concordat of 1929. Also contains much information concerning diplomatic privileges and immunities.

668.   Miele, Mario.   L'immunità giurisdizionale degli organi stranieri.   Pisa, P. Mariotti, 1947. 230p.   (Bibliographical footnotes)

An introspective look at diplomatic privileges and immunities with an orientation toward Italian prac-tice.

669.   .   Privilèges et immunités des fonctionnaires internationaux; avec le texte des conventions inter-nationalesen vigueur.   Milano, A. Giuffré, 1958. 210p.

A fair discussion of the problems related to diplo-matic privileges and immunities.

670.   Ogdon, Montell.   Juridical basis of diplomatic im-munity; a study in the origin, growth and purpose of the law.   Washington, D. C. , J. Byrne, 1936. 254p.   (Bibliography: p. 225-243)

A good, thorough study in English of the theo-retical basis of diplomatic immunities.

671.   Pantzer, Robert Franz Hannibal.   Neuere fortbil-dungen im system der völkerrechtlichen exem-tionen.   Berlin, W. Pilz, 1908.   52p.

A brief summary on exterritoriality, the problem of war in international law and diplomatic privi-leges and immunities.

672.   Pareja Paz Soldán, José.   Las inmunidades consul-ares.   Su aplicación en el Perú.   LaHabana, Talleres tipográficos de Carasa, 1940.   31p.

Within the structure of Peruvian diplomatic and consular service. This brief work discusses diplomatic privileges and immunities.

673. Reiff, Henry. Diplomatic and consular privileges, immunities, and practice. Cairo, Ettemad Press, 1954. 290p. (Bibliography: p. 278-281)

An extended study of international practice concerning diplomatic privileges and immunities.

674. Rustom, Souheil. Les conditions d'admission aux privilèges et immunités diplomatiques pour les chefs et les autres membres des missions diplomatiques: étude comparée de la pratique des états. Genève, 1957. 150p. (Bibliography: p. 141-144)

A good discussion on diplomatic privileges and immunities in international affairs.

675. Saboia de Medeiros, Fernando. A legislacao estrangeira sôbre i sencao de direltos advaneiros em geral e para automóveis, em favor los diplomatas e cônsules. Rio de Janeiro, Imprensa nacional, 1938. 122p.

A basic discussion of diplomatic privileges and immunities and their relationship to tariff law.

676. Secretan, Jacques. Les immunités diplomatiques des représentants des états membres et des agents de la Société des nations. Lausanne, Genève, Librairie Payot, 1928. 120p. (Bibliography: p. 114-118)

A short general treatise on the problems surrounding diplomatic privileges and immunities.

677. Sinner, Uda de. L'immunité judiciaire civile des agents diplomatiques étrangers. Lausanne, 1906. 345p. (Bibliography: p. 335-339)

An incisive treatise on the function of civil law on diplomatic privileges and immunities.

678. United Nations Conference on Diplomatic Intercourse

and Immunities, Vienna, 1961. Convenzione di
Vienna sulle relazione diplomatiche. Padova,
CEDAM, 1961. 69p. (Società italiana per'l'
organizzazione internazionale. Pubblicazioni:
Documenti, 13)

A collection of documents on diplomatic privileges
and immunities.

679.   . Official records. Geneva, 1962-   v. 1-
        (Bibliographical footnotes)

The official records of this important conference.

680.   United Nations Conference on Diplomatic Intercourse
        and Immunities, Vienna, 1961.   Delegation from
        the United States.   Vienna convention on diplo-
        matic relations, together with the optional protocol
        concerning the compulsory settlement of disputes.
        Washington, U. S. Govt. Print. Off. , 1963.   85p.

An important report of a conference on this timely
topic.

681.   Wilson, Clifton E.   Cold war diplomacy; the impact
        of international conflicts on diplomatic communica-
        tion and travel.   Tucson, University of Arizona
        Press, 1966.   67p.   (Arizona. University.
        Institute of Governmental Research.   International
        studies, no. 1; Bibliographical footnotes)

A study of the impact of international conflict
on diplomatic communications and travel in the
era of the cold war.

682.   . Diplomatic privileges and immunities.
        Tucson, University of Arizona Press, 1967.
        300p.   (Bibliography: p. 281-284)

An extensive and detailed account of modern practice with respect to the privileges and immunities
of diplomatic officials.

683.   Yeh, Sao-liang.   Les privilèges et immunités des
        agents diplomatiques à l'egard des états tiers.
        Paris, Editions Jel, 1938.   156p.   (Biblio-
        graphie: p. 145-151)

A hard hitting discussion of diplomatic privileges
and immunities. This work is particularly concerned with the problem of immunities during times
of belligerency.

Diplomatic Protection

The exclusive jurisdiction of a state within its own
borders is checked by certain rights of protection accorded
by international law to the status of an alien therein. The
bond of nationality which unites a person to his own state
is the basis for extension of both control and protection
over him in foreign lands. His status is evidenced by his
passport. From the viewpoint of domestic law, the citizen
may not ordinarily demand protection from his home state,
as of legal right; but from the viewpoint of international
law, his state may afford protection to him if it wishes.
The extent of this protection and the procedure to be followed are regulated by international law. [15]

684. Battaglini Giovanni. La protezione diplomatica delle
società. Padova, CEDAM, 1957. 354p.
(Bibliographical footnotes)

A well-documented treatment on diplomatic protection not only of officials but foreign nationals
as well.

685. Bertschy, Ruth. Die Schutzmacht im Völkerrecht;
ihre richtliche und praktische Bedeutung. Freiburg
in der Schweiz, 1952. 114p. (Bibliography:
p. 111-114)

A short treatise on diplomatic protection.

686. Borchard, Edwin Montefiore. The diplomatic protection of citizens abroad; or, The law of international claims. New York, The Banks Law Publishing Co., 1928. 988p. (Bibliography: p.
xxvii-xxxviii)

This is a detailed treatment of the legal aspects
of alien rights in various countries and consular
practice with regard to these rights.

687. Doehring, Karl. Die Pflicht des Staates zur Gewäh-
      rung diplomatischen Schutzes; deutsches Recht
      und Rechtsvergleichung. Köln, Citleymann, 1959.
      127p. (Includes bibliography)

      An excellent treatise on the responsibilities of
      states to extend diplomatic protection to their
      nationals.

688. Dunn, Frederick Sherwood. The diplomatic protec-
      tion of Americans in Mexico. New York, Colum-
      bia University Press, 1933. 439p.

      This excellent study covers the period since 1825
      and is based on the study of the documents.

689. _____. The protection of nationals; a study in the
      application of international law. Baltimore, the
      Johns Hopkins Press, 1937. 228p.

      A scholarly and detailed study of the problems of
      protecting nationals of another state. Particularly
      valuable for its treatment of the function of diplo-
      mats in this area.

690. Eroğlu, Hamza. La représentation internationale
      en vue de protéger les intérets des belligérants.
      Neuchâtel, 1949. 160p. (Bibliography: p. 153-
      155)

      Covers the rights of belligerents in being accorded
      diplomatic protection during times of conflict.

691. Escher, Alfred. Der schutz der staatsangehörigen
      im ausland durch fremde gesandtschaften und kon-
      sulate. Aarau, H. R. Sauerländer, 1929. 100,
      lp. (Bibliography: p. 99-101)

      A rather cursory treatment on the protection ac-
      corded to diplomatic and consular officials.

692. Franklin, William McHenry. Protection of foreign
      interests; a study in diplomatic and consular prac-
      tice. New York, Greenwood Press, 1969. 328p.
      (Bibliographical footnotes)

      A detailed examination of diplomatic protection
      particularly with respect to consular practice.

693.   Janner, Antonio.   La puissance protectrice en droit
        international d'après les expériences faites par
        la Suisse pendant la seconde guerre mondiale.
        Tr. de l'allemand par P. Monney.   Basel, Helbing
        & Lichttenhahn, 1948.   79p.

        A brief introspection of Swiss foreign relations
        and their practice of protection accorded diplo-
        mats.

694.   Klay, Andor.   Daring diplomacy; the case of the
        first American ultimatum.   Minneapolis, Univ-
        ersity of Minnesota Press, 1957.   246p.
        (Sources and references: p. 237-240)

        A scholarly and interesting monograph on an im-
        portant technique used in diplomatic practice.

695.   Maag, Jakob.   Der konsularische und diplomatische
        schutz des Auslandschweizers.   Zürich, Juris-
        Verlag, 1953.   114p.   (Bibliography: p. ix-xiv)

        Deals with the diplomatic protection of Swiss na-
        tionals and the laws of foreign nations.

696.   Pittard, Edmond.   La protection des nationaux à
        l'étranger.   Genève, Impr. W. Kundlig & fils,
        1896.   352p.   (Bibliography: p. 345-347)

        Diplomatic protection is analyzed within the frame-
        work of international law.

697.   al-Shawi, Khalid A.   The role of the corporate entity
        in international law.   Ann Arbor, Mich. , Over-
        beck Co. , 1957.   133p.

        A treatise on foreign corporations, particularly
        those in the Netherlands.   Also deals in part
        with persons in international law and diplomatic
        protection.

698.   Villaseñor, Victor Manuel.   La nacionalidad de las
        sociedades y la protección diplomatica de los
        intereses extranjeros en México.   México, Tallera
        linotipográficos El Modelo, 1930.   137p.

        An overview on citizenship in general and in

Mexico in particular.   Deals also with corpora-
tion and diplomatic protection.

V

The Language of Diplomacy

Throughout the history of diplomatic relations the
use of language has played an interesting and important
role. This role, according to Nicolson, may be thought of
in three senses. The first refers to the actual language
used by diplomatists in their conversation or correspondence
with each other. A second sense means those technical
phrases which, in the course of history, have become tra-
ditionally part of ordinary diplomatic vocabulary. In its
most common use diplomatic language is used to describe
that guarded under-statement which enables diplomatists
and ministers to say sharp things to each other without be-
coming provocative or impolite.

Since diplomacy involves the application of intelligence
and tact to accomplish its purposes, language becomes an
indispensible tool in this process. Within this context words,
terms and phrases assume measureable values much like
that of money. For example, if a diplomatic official of
high rank informs the government to which he is accredited
that his own government "cannot remain indifferent" to some
major internation dispute, he is really implying that his
government will undoubtedly intervene in the dispute. By
the same token other phrases have specific meanings. If
a diplomat in a speech or communication indicates that his
government "views with concern" or "views with grave concern" he in effect means that this is a matter on which his
government intends to adopt a strong line. The disregard
by a government of this warning may cause the diplomat to
voice a stronger position while maintaining a courteous and
conciliatory posture. If he states that "in such an event
my government would feel bound carefully to reconsider its
position", he is indicating that the present state of friendliness is about to end. Further, if he says "my government feels obliged to tender grave reservations concerning
..." he is, in fact, saying "my government will not allow
...". If a severance of relations is being considered then
the diplomat may say "in that event my government will be

obliged to consider its own interests" or "to claim a free
hand. " If the diplomat warns a foreign government that
a specific action on its part will be regarded "as an unfriendly act" he is, in reality, issuing a threat of war. If
he further indicates "he must decline to be responsible for
the consequences" this means that he is about to provoke
an incident which will eventually lead to war. A polite demand for a reply on a certain day at a specific time in a
diplomatic communication is considered an ultimatum. [16]

Needless to say this system of communication has
both advantages and disadvantages. Its chief advantage is
that as a means of communication stern meanings may be
conveyed in an atmosphere of calm which aids clear understanding of the implications involved. On the other hand,
the public or the diplomatist may not be fully aware of the
value of the terms which may lead to misunderstanding and
confusion as to the intended meaning. Careful reading of
diplomatic messages from foreign governments is always a
delicate and difficult task.

The use of language in the practice of diplomacy has
had an interesting background. It was common up to the
eighteenth century for diplomats to correspond and speak in
Latin. During the eighteenth century the French made re-
peated attempts to have their language substituted for Latin.
Most other nations were reluctant to change; however, by
the middle of the eighteenth century the French language
had firmly established itself, in all but name, as the official
language of diplomacy. At the conclusion of the First World
War English finally was given equality of rights with French
in diplomatic intercourse. [17]

699.   Czechloslovak Republic.   Ministerstuo zahranicnich
        veci.   Diplomaticka korespondence.   V. Praze,
        194-?   2v.

        An extensive work on the language of diplomacy.

700.   Gaselee, Sir Stephen.   The language of diplomacy.
        Cambridge, Eng. , Bowes & Bowes, 1939.   75p.

        A systematic and well designed treatise on the use
        of specialized language in the history of diplomacy.

701.   Liu, Chên-p'êng, ed.   Practical diplomatic corres-

pondence. N. P. , Chung Hwa Book Co. , 1964. 210p.

Deals mainly with diplomatic documents but also includes a discussion on diplomatic language. Written in Chinese, English and French.

702. Marwick, Lawrence. A handbook of diplomatic Hebrew; Hebrew-English and English-Hebrew volcabularies, abbreviations, bilingual list of international organizations. Washington, Davelle Publishers, 1957. 59,60p.

A rather brief dictionary of diplomatic terminology in the Hebrew and English languages.

703. Ostrower, Alexander. Language, law, and diplomacy; a study of linguistic diversity in official international relations and international law. Philadelphia, University of Pennsylvania Press, 1965. 2v. (Bibliography: v. 2, p. 825-903)

Vol. 1 contains a review of official linguistic practices from the beginning of political society to the present. Vol. 2 deals with constitutional law, resolutions of international bodies, and questions of international law.

704. Reuter, Paul, ed. Traités et documents diplomatiques. With Andŕe Gros. Paris, Presses universitaires de France, 1960. 500p. (Includes bibliographies)

A general collection of treaties; however, it includes an extensive discussion on diplomatic language.

705. Romiguière, Henriette. Le français dans les relations diplomatiques. Berkeley, Calif. , University of California Press, 1926. 340p.

An extensive treatment of the difficulties arising out of the languages used by diplomats. Particularly the French language.

706. Scott, James Brown. Le français, langue diplomatique moderne. Étude critique de conciliation

<u>internationale</u>.   Paris, A. Pedone, 1924.   330p.

A study of diplomatic language with emphasis upon
French usage.

A Glossary of Diplomatic Terms[18]

ACCESSION.   Refers to a clause in a treaty under which
        Powers who were not represented at the negotiations
        and who did not sign the original treaty can "accede"
        to it later.

ACCORD.   Matters of general international interest which
        are not of sufficient importance to justify a formal
        treaty or convention are oft times arranged by means
        of an accord or agreement.

ACTE FINAL.   A formal summary of the proceedings of a
        conference or congress.   Such statements enumerate
        the treaties signed as the result of the conference,
        and often contain certain expressions of opinion, or
        agreed comments on the subjects discussed.   See
        also <u>Proces Verbal Final.</u>

AD REFERENDUM.   A principle related to the negotiation
        of treaties which holds that the agreement is subject
        to formal approval by the governments of the signa-
        tories.

ADJUDICATION.   A judicial means of settling disputes
        peacefully where an impartial court arrives at a
        decision in law and equity and both parties are bound
        by the decision.

AGRÉATION.   A process of consultation where governments
        come to some agreement regarding the appointment
        of a particular person to act as the diplomatic agent
        of a sending government in a receiving country.

AGRÉMENT.   The resulting agreement from the process of
        agréation.

AIDE-MÉMOIRE.   A concise, factual diplomatic communi-
        cation bearing no signature.   Simply a memorandum.

ALTERNAT.   Refers to the practice of signing treaties in

which the position of the signature (the preferred
position, etc.) varies respectively in the copies they
retain.

AMBASSADOR.   Many times this term has been used interchangeably with emissary or envoy.   Specifically, an
ambassador is the chief of a diplomatic mission of
embassy rank who is accredited by a head of state
to a foreign government or international organization
such as the United Nations.

ARBITRATION.   The settlement of a dispute by an arbitral
agent chosen by the parties who are bound by the
accommodation reached.

ASYLUM.   The providing of sanctuary or refuge for a person or persons to protect them from mistreatment
or harm.   Asylum may be within an establishment
in a foreign country or within the boundaries of a
foreign state.

ATTACHÉ.   Generally, a technical expert on the diplomatic
staff of his country in a foreign nation.   This includes
persons in such areas as agriculture, commerce, or
military personnel who have specific functions.

BAG, THE.   The case or container of written diplomatic
communications which are carried by couriers.

BELLIGERENT RIGHTS.   This expression is one which concerns international law rather than diplomatic practice.   It refers to certain rights which accrue to a
belligerent such as blockage of coasts and ports etc.

BILATERAL.   An indication that treaties and other agreements have two signatories.   Also applies to international conferences at which representatives of two
governments participate.

BIPARTITE.   Refers to diplomatic agreements or treaties
that have two corresponding parts or comments, one
for each of the two signatories.

CAPITULATION.   An act or instrument of surrender during
periods of hostility such as cessation of hostilities,
armistice or official surrender.

CAREER AMBASSADOR.   This is the highest position in the
    Foreign Service to which an officer has arrived
    through the ranks where his duties are comparable
    to those of ambassador and ministers.   Refers to a
    career rank and not an assigned title.

CAREER DIPLOMAT.   A professional diplomatic officer
    not appointed from outside the service.

CAREER MINISTER.   The Foreign Service rank immediately
    below that of career ambassador.

CASUS BELLI.   An event or set of circumstances which
    is the cause of war, or is used to justify a nation's
    entry into hostilities.

CASUS FOEDERIS.   The act or event provided for in a
    treaty of alliance which makes it officially operative.

CHANCELLERIES.   This expression denotes the actual office
    of a head of a diplomatic mission, viz. his first,
    second, and third secretaries, plus the attendant
    clerks.   It is also used to designate the premises in
    which they exercise their functions.

CHARGÉ D'AFFAIRES.   The diplomatic rank under ambas-
    sador and minister.   He is the chief of diplomatic
    mission accredited by the sending government to the
    Ministry of Foreign Affairs of the receiving govern-
    ment.   He also serves as temporary or provisional
    diplomatic representative during the absence of the
    ambassador, or in the interim pending the appoint-
    ment of a new chief of mission.

CHIEF OF STATE.   The top agent or representative of a
    country in its diplomatic relations with other nations.

COLLECTIVE SECURITY.   A concept of mutual commit-
    ment by a group of nations to guarantee the security
    of one another against foreign intervention or agres-
    sion.

COMMISSION.   An official document that certifies appoint-
    ment to the Foreign Service or to a diplomatic or
    consular assignment, which is signed by the Presi-
    dent or some official designated by him.   A com-
    mission may also denote a diplomatic delegation sent

on a special assignment, usually to a conference to negotiate a treaty or agreement.

COMPROMIS D'ARBITRAGE. An agreement or special understanding, often in the form of a treaty, to submit a
particular dispute to international arbitration or adjudication, specifying the nature and organization of
the arbitral agency or court, the issue to be decided,
and sometimes, the principles to be applied in decid-
ing the award.

COMPULSORY JURISDICTION. A legal principle in which a
court may bring before it the side not initiating the
action which, if it fails to appear, forfeits the case.

CONCILIATION. A means of settling disputes peacefully
where the parties submit the dispute to an agency or
commission, which either simply files a report on the
facts at issue, or, if so authorized by the parties,
proceeds to make specific recommendations for the
resolution of the controversy, based upon equity and
mutual compromise. The parties to the dispute are
not bound in advance to accept the report or the rec-
comendations.

CONCLAVE. An international conference which holds its
meetings or negotiations in secret.

CONCORDAT. An international treaty or agreement between
the Papacy and secular nations, concerning the interests of the Roman Catholic Church and ecclesiastical
matters.

CONFERENCE DIPLOMACY. The conduct of diplomatic
negotiations multilaterally which involves some form
of conferencing in ad hoc meetings, regularized conferences, or sessions of deliberative agencies of
international organizations.

CONGRESS. A type of international meeting. Formerly
it was a top level gathering for major peace settle-
ments; however, currently the term is limited to
the semi-public meeting or technical or administrative meetings concerned with non-political matters,
particularly in inter-American meetings.

CONSUL. A Foreign Service officer who heads a consulate

and performs consular as distinct from diplomatic
functions.

CONSULAR CONVENTION.   An agreement or treaty among
governments which provides for the establishment and
administration of consular relations; not simply
custom or usage.

CONSULATE.   A foreign mission which deals with commercial relations between nations.   These are usually
established in major ports, industrial or transportation centers.

CONTINGENCY PLANNING.   An advance plan of policy or
course of action to be taken if certain contingencies
should occur.

CONTINGENT FUND.   A special emergency fund at the dis-
posal of the President which may be used for diplomatic purposes without giving a full account of its
use.

CONVENTION.   A term used interchangeably with treaty.
It is generally restricted in meaning to multipartite
treaties that deal with cultural, commercial, and
consular affairs, or treatment of governmental, administrative, any legal matters, rather than political
issues.

CORPS DIPLOMATIQUE.   The diplomatic body in any capital
which is composed of the diplomatic staffs of the
several mission, including the attachés.

COUNSELLOR.   Refers to the senior secretary at an embassy (and in exceptional cases at a legation).

COUNTRY TEAM.   A group of officers stationed in a
foreign nation representing the Dept. of State and
other agencies, who are amalgamated into a cooperative team to assist the ambassador in an advisory
capacity coordinating U.S. policy, programs and
action in that nation.

COUP D'ÉTAT.   A violent change in government usually
overthrowing a previous regime.

COURIER.   A diplomatic messenger who personally conveys

a communication to and from Washington to the States and foreign countries.

COURTESY RESIGNATION.   The formal, automatic resignation filed by every U. S. ambassador and minister when a new President takes office, which he may accept or reject as the case may be.

CREDENTIALS.   An official signed document of an appointed ambassador or minister by his head of state authorizing him to function in his appointive capacity. Until he has formally presented his letters he is not officially recognized.

DECLARATION.   A statement of policy concerning the conduct of international affairs by a government or two governments on a principle of international law as mutually understood.   This statement may or may not be in the form of a formal treaty.

DÉMARCHE.   A French term meaning to make representations which may range from proposals to threats.

DÉTENTE.   In simple terms this expression means a relaxation of tension

DIPLOMACY.   The art and practice of conducting negotiations between nations with skill and tact in order to avoid arousing hostility.

DIPLOMATIC ILLNESS.   At times it is convenient for a diplomat or a negotiator to absent himself from some ceremony or meeting.   In order not to cause undue offense, he pleads illness.   In cases where this malady is a feigned pretext it is called "diplomatic."

DIPLOMATIC MISSION.   The agency which provides representation and negotiation which is distinct from consular services.   This agency may be an embassy or legation of a special group concerned with some particular and temporary diplomatic assignment.

DOLLAR DIPLOMACY.   A term arising out of U. S. policy in the Caribbean area and Asia where financial and commercial interests were promoted.

DOYEN.   The highest ranking diplomat in a capital.   This

position is gained by holding the highest diplomatic
rung in a country for the longest time.

EMBASSY.   A body or organization of diplomatic representatives headed by an ambassador.   This term has also
been used in reference to the residence and offices of
an ambassador.

EMISSARY.   A diplomatic agent sent upon a mission as a
representative of a nation.

EN CLAIR.   Diplomatic communications written not in code
but ordinary language.   Such messages are sent when
it is intended that the local government should read
the message with little difficulty.

ENTENTE.   A cordial understanding or a similarity of views
and interests between certain countries and an identity
of policy upon certain issues.

ENVOY.   A minister plenipotentiary or diplomatic agent
accredited to a foreign government who ranks between
an ambassador and a minister resident.   An envoy
is also any person designated to represent one government in its intercourse with another.

EXCELLENCY.   A title usually accorded ambassadors, vice-
roys and governors-general in Great Britain.   In
foreign countries it is extended to Cabinet Ministers
and all those of a certain age and standing whom it
is desired to please.

EXECUTIVE AGREEMENT.   An understanding between two
nations to establish, alter, or terminate mutual
rights and other reciprocal obligations.   In the U.S.
it refers to an understanding that does not require
the consent of the Senate under the formal treaty
making procedure of the Constitution.

EXEQUATUR.   The official document issued by a nation to
a foreign consul which authorizes him to function in
his official capacity.

EXTERRITORIALITY.   The legal principle which recognizes
that a diplomat, along with his family and suite,
staff, residence, and archives, lies outside the legal
jurisdiction of the country to which he is accredited.
See also Extraterritoriality.

EXTRADITION. The surrender of an alleged criminal usually
     under the provisions of a treaty or statute by one
     state or other authority to another having jurisdiction
     to try the charge.

EXTRAORDINARY. In the beginnings of diplomacy there
     existed a distinction between "ordinary" or resident
     ambassadors, and "extraordinary" ambassadors sent
     on special missions. This led to invidious distinc-
     tions, and now all ambassadors are called "extra-
     ordinary. "

EXTRATERRITORIALITY. A principle which exempts one
     from the appliaction or jurisdiction of local law or
     tribunals. See also Exterritoriality.

FIN DE NON RECEVOIR. A diplomatic expression which is
     used to describe the practice of rejecting an official
     complaint without examining its merits.

FINAL ACT. The final, comprehensive, and inclusive
     written review of an international conference which
     includes its activities and texts of the agreements
     concluded.

FOREIGN SERVICE OFFICER. The career officer who is
     selected on the basis of an examination and appointed
     by the President with approval of the Senate to carry
     out diplomatic or consular duties for the United
     States.

FOREIGN SERVICE RESERVE OFFICER. A career officer
     with non-permanent status, who is appointed on a
     non-continuing basis to file immediate staffing needs,
     often to provide specialists in the Foreign Service
     who are not normally acquired through ordinary re-
     cruitment.

FOREIGN SERVICE STAFF. This includes personnel, other
     than Foreign Service and Reserve Officers, who per-
     form administrative, fiscal, managerial, and clerical
     services in diplomatic missions abroad.

FULL POWERS. A Presidentially signed official document
     that authorizes a diplomatic agent to represent, neg-
     otiate, and sign a treaty or agreement for the United
     States. Full powers also may be used in other

official documents, such as a letter of credence or
"letters patent." With respect to a negotiating conference, the full power is delivered or exchanged
with conferees.

GENERAL ACT. A summary of the conclusions of a conference or detailed regulations derived from certain
principles embodied in a treaty.

GOOD OFFICER. Refers to a means of settling disuptes
peacefully by means of a third party attempting,
through suggestion or advice, to induce disputants
to join in attempting to negotiate their disagreement
and resolve their differences. See also Mediation.

GUARANTEE, TREATIES OF. Certain treaties contain
clauses under which the signatories guarantee their
execution and maintenance.

HEAD OF GOVERNMENT. The Chief executive of a national
government so designated. He may be called a Prime
Minister, Premier, Chancellor or President.

HOT LINE. The special communications system established
between the Soviet Union and the United States which
provides both countries with a direct and constantly
available electronic teletype facility. It is not a
telephone circuit between the White House and the
Kremlin.

INTERNUNCIO. Refers to a Papal diplomatic representative
who is accredited to a government, and has ministerial rank.

INVIOLABILITY. An international legal principle which holds
a diplomat exempt from restraint, personal or legal
injury, to his premises, his archives, and his communications.

LAISSER PASSER. A letter of recommendation issued by
an embassy of a country to a diplomatic official
which directs customs authorities not to examine his
luggage.

LEGATION. A diplomatic mission in a foreign country of
the second highest rank, headed by a minister. This
term may also be used to refer to the official residence and office of a diplomatic minister at the seat

of a foreign government.

LETTER OF CREDENCE. With respect to U. S. practice
this term refers to the official signed Presidential
document which is addressed and formally presented
to the head of a receiving government or to an international organization. This document identifies an
emissary, indicates the object of his mission, and
authorizes him to represent the U. S. government.

LETTER OF RECALL. The official and signed Presidential
document which recalls a particular envoy and terminates his participation in the mission on which he was
engaged.

LETTERS PATENT. An official document issued to a special agent in lieu of a letter of credence, which often
contains full powers. This term may also refer to
the documentation given a consul by his government
which verifies his appointment and authorizes him to
perform his duties.

MEDIATION. A means of settling international disputes by
a third party intervening to promote reconciliation,
settlement, or compromise.

MÉMOIRE. Varying types of memoranda which differ from
notes in that they begin with no formal introduction
and need not be signed.

MINISTER. A diplomatic representative ranking below an
ambassador and usually accredited to states of less
importance.

MISE EN DEMEARE. The definition of intentions or a curt
"take it or leave it" demand made by one government
to another.

MODUS VIVENDI. A feasible arrangement or practical compromise of a provisional nature pending a more permanent undertaking for settling a dispute or resolving
a problem.

MOST-FAVORED-NATION CLAUSE. A principle which is
more commonly applied in commercial, trade, and
consular treaties that provides that contracting states
reciprocally enjoy the commercial or consular advan-

tages of the state that is accorded the greatest benefits, so that further benefits granted to a third country
by either party are automatically extended to the other
party having the most-favored-nation relations with
the granting state.

MULTILATERAL.   A treaty or other international agreement
participated in by more than two states or parties.

MULTIPARTITE.   Refers to treaties and agreements having
more than two signatories, with commitments involv-
ing more than two parties.

NON-SELF-EXECUTING TREATY OR AGREEMENT.   A
treaty or international agreement that is not enforceable automatically on the basis of its stated stipulations, but requires legislation or formal executive
regulations to implement and render it executable.

NOTE VERBALE.   An impersonal and unsigned written diplomatic communication drafted in the third person.

NUNCIO.   A papal legate of ambassadorial rank permanently
accredited to a civil government.

OPTIONAL CLAUSE;   A special stipulation contained in the
Statute of the International Court of Justice which
allows members, as a voluntary option, to accept
ipso facto and without special agreement the compulsory adjudication of certain types of legal disputes.
In a case where one subscribing state brings suit
against another the court may compel the latter to
appear or forfeit the case.

OVERSEAS MISSION.   A very general term which covers
ordinary diplomatic and consular missions.   (e.g.
embassies, legations, and consulates) regularized
missions to international organizations, and temporary special diplomatic missions which take emissaries
to a foreign territory.

PACT.   The more popular title given for important treaties,
usually creating significant commitments concerned
with peace-keeping, collective security, or with
establishing an alliance such as NATO or the Warsaw
Pact.

PAPAL LEGATE.   A papal diplomatic representative of
ambassadorial rank.   See also Nuncio.

PARLIAMENTARY DIPLOMACY.   This term refers to the
conduct of diplomatic relations in the multilateral
forum-either the ad hoc or the regularized international conference, or the agency of an international
organization--with decision-making handled by a formal system of voting.

PERSONA GRATA.   A diplomatic official or agent who is
personally acceptable to the government of a foreign
country to which he is accredited.

PERSONA NON GRATA.   A diplomatic official or agent who
is not acceptable to the government of a foreign nation
at the time of appointment or while serving in his
appointment.

PERSONAL REPRESENTATIVE.   See Presidential agent.

PLACEMENT.   The science of seating diplomatic guests in
such a manner as to avoid enraging them.

PRECEDENCE.   Refers to the order of relative ranking
or priority of governmental leaders and diplomats for
purposes of status, reception, seating, speaking, and
otherwise participating in diplomatic affairs.

PRENDRE ACTE.   A diplomatic expression which means
"I shall take note of this and bring it up against you
in the future."

PRESIDENTIAL AGENT, EMISSARY, OR ENVOY.   A particular or special diplomatic emissary, appointed and
assigned by the President without Senate confirmation,
to a special mission, usually of an ad hoc nature.
As a Presidential agent he is often directly responsible to him.

PROCÈS VERBAL.   An official written record of the minutes of an international conference or other international meeting.

PROTOCOL.   A term with a number of uses.   When used
to denote a written document it means the same as
Proces Verbal.   It is also used to denote proper

international deportment such as formal procedures, etiquette, and precedence in ceremonies of state and diplomatic relations.

RAISON D'ÉTAT.   Refers to the diplomatic and political theory under which the interests of the state assume precedence over all private morality.

RAPPORTEUR.   The spokesman of a committee or sub-committee of a conference who makes a report on some specific matter to the main conference.

RATIFICATION.   The process of approving formally a treaty by a nation.

REBUS SIC STANTIBUS.   A Latin expression meaning "things remaining the same." With regard to diplomacy it applies to the termination of a treaty, in as much as, under certain limited conditions, the obligations of a treaty are deemed to terminate by virtue of a vital change in the circumstances or conditions under which the treaty was concluded.

RECOGNITION.   The formal process of acknowledging a new state's existence within the family of nations or a new government in an existing state.

RESERVATION (to treaty).   A formal stipulation in a treaty with respect to its text which specifies such inter-pretations, limitation, or qualification-but not actual treaty text amendment-that a government makes a formal part of its ratification.   As an example re-servation may be initiated by the Senate or the Presi-dent and are embodied in the ratification instrument.

RIGHT OF LEGATION.   Refers to the legal right of a nation to engage in diplomacy.   To send and receive diplo-matic agents for such purposes.

SAFE CONDUCT.   The authorization given to a diplomatic envoy which grants him permission to pass unmoles-ted into, out of, or through the territory of a bel-ligerent state during time of hostilities or of a country involved in revolution or civil disorder.

SANCTIONS.   Penalties enacted against a party or nation for a breach of a law or international agreement.

SECRET AGENT.   See Presidential Agent.

SELF-EXECUTING TREATY OR AGREEMENT.   A treaty
or agreement that is enforceable automatically on
promulgation on the basis of its stipulation, and does
not require implementing legislation or regulations.

SHIRTSLEEVE DIPLOMACY.   Refers to diplomatic negotiations conducted in a direct, blunt and often brusque
manner, which avoids delicate treatment, diplomatic
finesse, and protocol.

SPECIAL DIPLOMATIC AGENT OR REPRESENTATIVE.   See
Presidential Agent.

SPECIAL MISSION.   A non-traditional mission, which is
accredited to and provides representation in an international organization or to an international conference,
to the government or leaders of a country to which
a nation is not yet ready to engage in normal official
relations or for some other special purpose, such as
the mission of a Presidential special emissary.

SPONSION.   Refers to a diplomatic agent's commitment or
agreement when he is not properly authorized or
commissioned to do so.   In such cases the agent has
exceeded his authority and the commitment or agreement is voidable if not automatically null and void.

STATE VISIT.   The formal visit by a Chief of State to a
foreign country, upon invitation.   This term also
refers to visits of others as well including heads of
governments and leaders above the ministerial level.

STATUS QUO.   Refers to the existing state of affairs.
Status quo ante bellum means the condition or state
of affairs prior to a war.

SUMMIT DIPLOMACY.   Diplomatic relations or negotiations
at the Chief-of-State or a head of government level,
or Presidential personal diplomacy.

TREATY.   A contract in writing, between two or more
states formally signed by representatives duly authorized and usually ratified by the law-making authority of the states involved.

ULTIMATUM.   Usually refers to the last word before negotiations are broken off.   It most likely takes the
form of a written intimation that unless a satisfac-
tory reply is received by a certain hour on a certain
date certain consequences will follow.

UNDER FLYING SEAL.   A diplomatic communication sent
by an ambassador to his government by way of a
second ambassador who reads it on its way through.

UNFRIENDLY ACT.   A warning by a nation to other nations
that certain actions on their part might lead to war.

UNILATERAL DECLARATION.   On occasion a leading nation
will seek to establish its rights or policy by a declaration or principle which is communicated to other
nations for their information and guidance.

VENUE.   The signification of the place where a conference
or meeting is held.   The term is used mostly in
journalistic parlence and is considered by professional
diplomats as rather vulgar.

VOEUX.   The addition to a treaty of certain recommendations
for future good conduct.   These have no binding force
upon the signatories.

WHITE PAPER.   A report issued by a Foreign Office or the
Dept. of State which contains a collection of selected
documents and attempts to present a case or justify
a policy or action.

WRISTIONIZATION.   The process of integrating the officer
personnel of the Dept. of State and the Foreign Service.   "De-Wristionization" refers to subsequent
undoing of certain aspects of such amalgamation.

VI

Selected Reference and Auxiliary Sources

In the sections prior to this one we have cited and annotated a number of monographs, pamphlets and articles. Reference sources differ from these in that they do not present information in a sequence intended to invite continuous reading, but are designed to impart separate information conveniently arranged for intermittent consultation. In general, reference works are distinguished from others in that they are meant to be referred to for specific information.

There is a wide variety of reference works directly or indirectly related to the art and practice of diplomacy. Accompanying reference sources are auxiliary works which contain valuable information on a broad range of subjects which are not technically reference material. The works cited below are suggestive of the types of reference and auxiliary information which a researcher might be seeking.

Abstracts and Digests.

Works of this nature give a brief summary of the contents of a book, article or other material. They generally do not contain any critical evaluation of the material they abstract or digest. Their express purpose is to describe the important or essential features of the material they are dealing with as a whole.

707.   Arms control & disarmament. v. 1+ winter 1964/65+ Washington, For sale by the Superintendent of Documents, U. S. Govt. Print. Off. , 1964/65+ v. 1+ (Quarterly; Compiled by Arms Control and Disarmament Bibliography Section, Library of Congress)

Abstracts and annotates a great number of period-

icals, books, monographs, selected government
publications of the U.S. and some other countries.
An excellent source for materials on diplomacy.

708.   Background on world politics.
        See
        International Studies quarterly.

709.   California. University, Berkeley. Bureau of Inter-
        national Relations. International relations digest
        of periodical literature. Berkeley, 1950-   v. 1-

        A digest of articles found in scholarly journals
        relating to international relations. Current publi-
        cation in doubt.

710.   Current abstracts of the Soviet press. New York,
        Joint Committee on Slavic studies. 1968-   v. 1-

        Augments Current digest of the Soviet press.

711.   Current digest of the Soviet press. Washington,
        Joint Committee on Slavic Studies, 1949-   v. 1-
        (Weekly)

        A condensation of news items taken from Pravda,
        Izvestia, and other Soviet newspapers, magazines
        and literary publications on a weekly basis.
        Arranged by subject, with a quarterly index.

712.   Current thought on peace and war. Oshkosh, Wis.,
        Wisconsin State University, 1962-   v. 1-

        A basic digest of literature and research in prog-
        ress on the problems of world order and conflict
        along with those of diplomacy and its ramifications.

713.   Deadline data on foreign affairs. New York, Dead-
        line data, 1956-   (Index cards)

        A good quick reference source on 5 x 8 cards
        which reports on the domestic and foreign as well
        as diplomatic affairs of every country in the world.
        Kept up to date by supplementary cards issued
        weekly.

714.   Hackworth, Green Haywood. Digest of international
        law. Washington, D.C., U.S. Govt. Print. Off.,

1940-44.   8v.

Follows, in general, the outline of Moore's Digest,
but does not duplicate its material.   According to
its compiler, "For the most part the Digest represents the position of the Government of the United
States on the subject discussed as revealed by the
voluminous records of the Dept. of State..."   Vol.
I. , Chapter I, is a general discussion of International law; Chapter II defines some terminology
frequently used.   The remainder of Vol. 1 and
the following ones through No. VII consider various
aspects of International Law.   Vol. VIII consists
of a General index and list of cases.

715.   International law reports; 1919-1922-   London, Long-
        mans, 1929-1938; Butterworths, 1938-   v. 1-
        (annual)

        A series of important volumes which give accurate
        digests of international law cases under broad sub-
        ject headings.

716.   International political science abstracts.   Paris,
        UNESCO, 1951-   v. 1-   (quarterly)

        A classified list of abstract articles from a world
        list of political science and related journals.

717.   International studies quarterly.   Detroit, Mich. ,
        Wayne State University, 1957-   (quarterly)

        Contains digests of approximately 100 articles
        dealing with the problems of world politics includ-
        ing diplomacy.

718.   Moore, John Bassett.   Digest of international law.
        Washington, U. S. Govt. Print. Off. , 1906-   8v.

        "A digest of international law as embodied in dip-
        lomatic discussions, treaties and other interna-
        tional agreements, international awards, the dec-
        isions of municipal courts, and writings of jurists,
        and especially in documents, published and unpub-
        lished, issued by presidents and secretaries of
        state of the United States, the opinions of the
        attorneys-general, and the decisions of courts,

federal and state." This work follows the same
plan as Wharton's Digest.

719.   Peace research abstracts journal. Clarkson, Ont.,
        Canadian Peace Research Institute, 1964-   v. 1-
        (monthly)

        A journal of abstracts on all phases of peace and
        its related issues. Also covers many aspects of
        international relations. Each issue has an author
        index, and a cumulative subject index is included
        in every third issue.

720.   Wharton, Francis, ed. A digest of international law
        of the United States. 2d ed. Washington, Govt.
        Print. Off., 1887. 3v.

        Contains "documents issued by presidents and
        secretaries of state, and... decisions of federal
        courts and opinions of attorneys-general." (Sub-
        title)

721.   Whiteman, Marjorie Millace. Digest of international
        law. Washington, U.S. Dept. of State: for sale
        by the Superintendent of Documents, U.S. Govt.
        Print. Off., 1963-   v. 1-

        This is the successor to Hackworth's Digest of
        international law, and treats public international
        law and related matters, especially for the past
        two decades.

Atlases.

        These are sources not usually considered important
in the study of diplomacy except in a limited way. Atlases
are sources which may picture or present information in
some other graphic manner.

722.   Hammond (C. S.) and Company, inc. Diplomat
        world atlas. Maplewood, N.J., 1961.   320p.

        A scaled down version of the Hammond Ambassa-
        dor World Atlas. It differs from the parent pub-
        lication in providing two separate indexes instead

of one comprehensive listing of cities, towns, etc.
and omits the tables of social and economic data
and illustrated geography and gazetteer of the world.
The maps are excellent, clearly delineated, up-to-
date and clear.

Bibliographies and Indexes - Current

A bibliography or index is a systematic listing of
materials for reference purposes. For diplomacy there are
only a few current sources of this type, and they vary widely
in terms of scope, purpose and design.

723.   Carnegie Endowment for International Peace. Library.
       Select bibliographies. Washington, D. C. , 1833-
       No. 1-

       A series of bibliographies on international relations
       of which No. 4 deals with diplomacy.

724.   Index to legal periodicals. New York, Published for
       the American Association of Law Libraries by
       H. W. Wilson, 1908- v. 1-

       Includes leading articles, notes, case comments,
       and book reviews in more than 275 English-language
       legal periodicals. Generally has many citations
       of articles dealing with diplomatic privileges and
       immunities.

725.   International bibliography of political science. Paris,
       UNESCO & Chicago, Aldine, 1953- v. 1-
       (annual)

       An extensive, although selective, annual classified
       bibliography which includes some 4,000 to 5,000
       items per year.

726.   International politics; a selective bibliography. Wash-
       ington, 1956- v. 1- (monthly)

       A selected list of articles from periodicals which
       are analyzed by the Library of the Dept. of State.

727.   Public affairs information service. Bulletin ...

annual cumulation. New York, 1915-   v. 1-

An extensive subject index in the field of the social
sciences. Includes citations of books, pamphlets,
government publications, reports of public and private agencies, yearbooks, and other useful materials
as well as articles from periodicals. Has a good
listing of items related to diplomacy.

728.   Royal Institute of International Affairs. Bibliography
of books dealing with international affairs. Bungay,
Suffolk, 1926-   No. 1-

Includes a large number of works related to diplomacy.

729.   Social sciences and humanities index ... formerly International index. New York, H. W. Wilson, 1907-
v. 1-

The best source for articles on diplomacy. Indexes
over 200 periodicals many of which deal with diplomatic subjects.

730.   U. S. Superintendent of Documents. Monthly catalog
of United States government publications. Washington, U. S. Govt. Print. Off. , 1895- v. 1-

A monthly subject listing with cumulative annual
index of publications issued by all branches of the
government, including both congressional and de-
partmental documents.

Bibliographies and Indexes - Retrospective.

The same may be said for this group of reference
sources as for the current ones except there are more of
them.   One major problem in this area has been the dearth
of bibliographic coverage given to diplomacy as a specific
area of study which, in a sense, is a raison d'être for this
work.

731.   Boehm, Eric H. , ed.   Bibliographies on international
relations and world affairs; an annotated directory.
Santa Barbara, Calif. , Clio Press, 1965.   33p.

(Bibliography and reference series, no. 2)

"This bibliography of bibliographies gives information on international relations. " It contains
listings of major English-language journals which
contain book reviews, bibliographies etc. Many of
the journals cited carry information relevant to
diplomacy.

732.   Brown, J. Cudd. Administration of United States
       foreign affairs; a bibliography. With Michael B.
       Rieg. University Park, Fred Lewis Pattee Li-
       brary, Pennsylvania State University, 1968.
       126 leaves.

       A classified bibliography with good coverage.

733.   DeConde, Alexander. New interpretations in Amer-
       ican foreign policy. Washington, Service Center
       for Teachers of History, 1957. 31p.

       A brief bibliography with good coverage.

734.   Degras, Jane (Tabrisky). Calendar of Soviet docu-
       ments on foreign policy, 1917-1941. London,
       and New York, Royal Institute of International
       Affairs, 1948. 248p.

       Chronological arrangement by periods and countries
       with reference to Russian and other sources.

735.   Douma, J. , comp. Bibliography on the International
       court including the Permanent court, 1918-1964.
       Leyden, A. W. Sijthoff, 1966. 387p. (Hague.
       Permanent court of international justice. The
       case law of the International court, V. 4-C)

       A detailed bibliography on the work of the Interna-
       tional Court. Contains many annotations.

736.   Essen, Jan Louis Frederik van. Immunities in inter-
       national law. With the collaboration of J. L. G.
       Tichelaar. Leyden, A. W. Sijthoff, 1955. 56p.
       (Selective bibliographies of the Library of the Peace
       Palace, 3)

       An extensive and partially annotated bibliography.

Includes many monographs, documents, articles, etc.

737.   Flynn, Alice H.   World understanding; a selected bibliography.   Dobbs Ferry, N. Y. , Published for the United Nations Association of the United States of America by Oceana Publications, 1965.   263p.

An annotated bibliographical guide of books concerning the U. N.   Arranged by subject with a list of publishers and author index.

738.   Foreign affairs bibliography; a selected and annotated list of books on international relations, 1919-1962.   New York, Harper, Russell & Russell, Bowker, etc.   4v.   published to date.

An extensive selected listing of monographs in English and in major Western European languages dealing with all aspects of international affairs.

739.   Grabař, Vladimir Emmanuilovich.   De legatorum jure tractatuum catalogus completus ab anno MDXXV usque ad annum MDCC.   Dorpati Livornorum, Mattiesnianis, 1918.   311p.   (Index auctorum atque tractaluum, p. 299-311)

A bibliography on the ambassadorial role in diplomacy.   Also treats in a more general fashion the spectrum of diplomatic and consular service as well as international law and relations.

740.   Gray, Richard A.   Serial bibliographies in the humanities and social sciences.   Compiled with the assistance of Dorothy Villmow.   Ann Arbor, Mich. , Pierian Press, 1969.   345p.

An extensive listing of periodicals carrying bibliography.   Includes relevant bibliography pertaining to diplomacy.

741.   Hart, Albert Bushnell.   Handbook of the history, diplomacy, and government of the United States, for class use.   Cambridge, Printed for the University (Harvard), 1903.   481p.

A basic syllabus and bibliography.   Useful for the

early period of U. S. diplomatic history.

742.   Harvard University. Law School. Library. Catalog
        of international law and relations. Edited by
        Margaret Moody. Cambridge, Mass. , 1965-67.
        20v.

        This is a book catalog in which is reproduced
        some 360,000 cards. It has a dictionary arrange-
        ment; full bibliographic information is given in the
        main entry. Subject and added entries have been
        shortened. Includes a large number of entries
        relating to diplomacy.

743.   Jameson, John Franklin. A provisional list of printed
        lists of ambassadors and other diplomatic repre-
        sentatives. Paris, Les Presses universitaires de
        France, 1928. 16p.

        A convenient record of printed lists of diplomats
        arranged by country. In some cases the record
        goes back to the middle ages.

744.   Martens, Karl. Guide diplomatique ... Bruxelles,
        Meline, Cans, et Companaque, 1838. 2v.

        The most extensive bibliographical work on diplo-
        macy covering the early period.

745.   _____. Manuel diplomatique; ou, Précis des droits
        et des fonctions des agents diplomatiques; suivi
        d'un recueil d'actes et d'offices politique. Paris,
        Treuttel et Würtz, 1822. 622p.

        Extensive bibliographic coverage of diplomacy es-
        pecially in the eighteenth century.

746.   Metron, inc. , New York. Universal Reference System.
        International affairs; an annotated and intensively
        indexed compilation of significant books, pamphlets,
        and articles, selected and processed by the Univer-
        sal Reference System, a computerized information-
        al retrieval service in the social and behavioral
        sciences. Prepared under the direction of Alfred
        De Grazia. New York, 1965. 1205p.

        An extensive listing on international relations in

general but is weak in the area of diplomacy.

747. Moore, Margaret Findlay. Two select bibliographies
      of mediaeval historical study. New York, B.
      Franklin, 1967. 185p. (Burt Franklin bibliog-
      raphy & reference series, no. 124)

      Contents. --Account of the classes in medieval
      history at the London School of Economics. --
      Bibliography on paleography & diplomatics. --Bib-
      liography of manorial and agrarian history.

748. Moussa, Farag. Diplomatie contemparaine; guide
      bibliographique. Genève, Centre européan de la
      Dotation Carnegie pour la paix internationale,
      1964. 199p.

      The most up-to-date bibliography available on the
      subject of diplomacy. Concentrates mostly on
      foreign works.

749. Plischke, Elmer. American diplomacy; a bibliography
      of bibliographies, autobiographies, and commen-
      taries. College Park, Bureau of Governmental
      Research, College of Business and Public Admin-
      istration, University of Maryland, 1957.   27p.

      A brief unannotated bibliography. Has good cover-
      age of twentieth century biographical and auto-
      biographical works on American diplomatic history.

750. _____ . American foreign relations; a bibliography
      of official sources. College Park, Bureau of
      Governmental Research, College of Business and
      Public Administration, University of Maryland,
      1966, c1955.   71p.

      An excellent brief bibliography of diplomatic source
      materials with very useful annotations.

751. Pogány, András H. Political science and international
      relations; books recommended for the use of
      American Catholic college and university libraries.
      Compiled with Hortenzia Lers Pogány. Metuchen,
      N. J. , Scarecrow Press, 1967.   387p. (Seton
      Hall University bibliographical series, v. 1)

Includes over 5,000 items only a few of which
pertain to diplomacy.

752.   Sass, Johann.   Die deutschen weissbücher zur
        auswärtigen politik, 1870-1914; geschichte und
        bibliographie.   Berlin und Leipzig, W. de Gruyter,
        1928.   224p.   (Bibliographical footnotes)

        A general retrospective bibliography of works on
        German foreign relations from 1870-1914.

753.   Strupp, Karl.   Bibliographie du droit des gens et
        des relations internationales.   Leyde (Holland)
        A. W. Sijthoff, 1938.   521p.

        An extensive bibliography with a fairly large num-
        ber of entries related to the art and practice of
        diplomacy.

754.   Temperley, Harold William Vazeille, ed.   A century
        of diplomatic blue books, 1814-1914; lists edited
        with historical introduction.   With Lillian M.
        Penson.   London, Cass, 1966.   600p.

        This volume provides in a methodological manner
        a list of the titles of foreign blue books from
        Castlereagh to Grey and adds the dates on which
        they were laid before parliament.   It serves as a
        complete bibliography of these papers.

755.   Thomas, Daniel H., ed.   Guide to the diplomatic
        archives of Western Europe.   Edited with Lynn
        M. Case.   Philadelphia, University of Pennsylvania
        Press, 1959.   389p.   (Includes bibliography)

        A welcome guide, by country, to the diplomatic
        archives of Western Europe.   Information includes
        the history of depositories, the arrangement and
        classification of the records, regulations and bib-
        liography.

756.   Ugarteche, Pedro.   Panorama de la literatura diplo-
        matica; de la edad media al siglo XX.   Zaragoza,
        Institutción "Fernando el Catolica," 1958.   179-
        193p.   (Separata de Cuadernos de historia deplo-
        mática, IV.)

A bibliographical essay on the literature of diplomacy from the middle ages to the twentieth century.

757.   U. S. Dept. of State. Library. <u>A list of books received at the library of the Department of State</u> ... With references to international treaties and articles on subjects relative to the law of nations and diplomacy in magazines received. Washington, 1886-87.   11v. in 1.

758.   _____. <u>A list of books, pamphlets</u>, Washington, Dept. of State, Bureau of rolls and library, 1893-1906.   32v. in 4.

      A good list of early U. S. diplomatic materials as gathered by the Dept. of State Library for the periods covered.

759.   U. S. Information Agency.   <u>International relations.</u> Washington, U. S. Information Agency, Information Centre Service, 1969.   45p.   (Its Subject bibliography no. 6/69)

      Includes some items of relevance to diplomacy.

760.   U. S. Library of Congress.   General Reference and Bibliography Division.   <u>A guide to bibliographic tools for research in foreign affairs</u>, compiled by Helen F. Conover.   2d ed.   With suppl. Washington, 1958.   145, 15p.

      A carefully selected and extremely well annotated bibliography which includes an index of authors and titles and a subject index.

761.   Vogel, Robert.   <u>A breviate of British diplomatic Blue Books, 1919-1939.</u>   Montreal, McGill University Press, 1963.   474p.

      Attempts to carry on the work of the Temperley volume by listing the titles of all Parliamentary papers, published between 1919 and 1939, directly related to British foreign policy.   Arranged in chronological order.   Includes a subject index.

762.   Wildik, Pedro Affonso de Figueiredu.   <u>Bibliotheca consular.</u>   Lisboa, Imprensa, nacional, 1877-78. 2v.

A bibliographical treatise on Portugese diplomatic
and consular service.

763.   Will, Georg Andreas.   Kleine Beiträge zur der dip-
       lomatik und deren Literatur.   Altdorf, im Mon-
       athischen Verlag, 1789.   8p.

       A short general bibliography on diplomacy.

Dictionaries.

       The primary purpose of these sources is to define
the meaning of words and phrases.   Anyone who has had
some acquaintance with diplomacy will recognize the importance of language and meaning in international negotiation.
There are a fair number of good dictionaries for diplomatic
terminology.

764.   Academie Diplomatic Internationale.   Dictionnaire
       diplomatique.   Paris, 1933-   v. 1-   4 vols. to
       date.   (Includes bibliographies)

       This monumental diplomatic reference collection
       contains biographies of outstanding statesmen and
       diplomats from the Middle Ages to the middle of
       the twentieth century.   Also has useful bibliog-
       raphies and chronological tables along with ex-
       tensive definitions.

765.   Bleiber, Fritz.   Handwörterbuch der Diplomatie und
       Aussenpolitik.   Barmstadt, C. W. Leske, 1959.
       280p.

       A general dictionary of words and phrases used
       in international law and relations.   Many terms
       used in diplomacy are included.

766.   Brinckmeier, Eduard.   Glossarium diplomaticum zur
       erläuterung schwieriger, einer diplomatischen,
       historischen, sachlicher.   Hamburg und Gotha,
       F. A. Perthes, 1850-63.   2v.

       Perhaps the most extensive glossary of terms used
       in diplomatic archives and the handling of official
       documents.

767.   Calvo, Carlos. Dictionnaire manuel de diplomatie
        et de droit international public et privé. Berlin,
        Puttkammer & Muhlbrecht, 1885.   475p.

        This dictionary includes terms used in international
        law and relations focusing particularly upon pri-
        vate international law.   Contains many diplomatic
        terms.

768.   Cussy, Ferdinand de Cornot. Dictionnaire, ou,
        Manuel-lexique du diplomate et du consul. Leip-
        zig, F. A. Brockhaus, 1846.   799p.

        An extensive coverage of terms and phrases used
        in diplomatic practice as well as international
        law and relations.

769.   Dictionnaire de la terminologie du droit internationale,
        publié sous le patronage de l'Union académique
        internationale.   Tables en anglais, espangnol,
        italien, allemand.   Paris, Sirey, 1960.   755p.

        A useful compilation of technical definitions of
        terms, their classification and their different
        meanings.   Terms included were selected from
        treaties, diplomatic correspondence, proceedings
        of diplomatic congresses etc.   Each definition is
        illustrated by one or more accurate quotations
        from the sources.

770.   Diplomaticheskii slovar'.   V trek tomakh.   Glavnaia
        redaktsiia A. A. Gromyko i dr. Moskva, Gos.
        Izd-vo Politicheskoi Lit-ry 1960-64.   3v.

        Basically a dictionary of modern diplomacy and
        international relations with emphasis upon Russia.
        Contains definitions of diplomatic terms and a
        considerable amount of biography.   Quite a num-
        ber of articles are on international conferences,
        treaties, diplomatic proceedings, and the foreign
        policies of different nations.   Some articles include
        bibliographies and v. 3 contains an index of sub-
        jects arranged by country.

771.   Gamboa, Melquiades Jereos.   Elements of diplomatic
        and consular practice; a glossary.   Quezon City,
        Philippines, Central Lawbook Pub. Co. ; distri-

buted by Central Book Supply, inc. , Manila, 1966.
489p.   (Bibliographical footnotes)

This helpful reference aid includes not only topics
relating to diplomatic and consular practice, but
also covers subjects pertaining to international
law and to the United Nations such as a diplomat
or consul may encounter in the course of his
career.

772.   Grosse, Helmut.   Europäisches Wörterbuch; das
        system der westlichen zusammenarbeit in Stich-
        worten.   With Gerhard Flak, and others.   Ashaf-
        fenburg, Panorama-Verlag, 1955.   60p.

        A brief but useful glossary of terms used in inter-
        national relations.

773.   Hajdu, Gyula, ed.   Diplomáciai és nemzetközi jogi
        lexika.   Budapest, Akadémiai Kiado, 1959.   567p.

        A detailed dictionary of terms used in the fields
        of international law and relations.   Includes many
        entries relating to diplomacy.

774.   al-Hamawi, Ma'mun.   Diplomatic terms; English
        Arabic.   Beirut, Khayats, 1966.   56, 21p.
        (Bibliographical footnotes)

        A brief list of diplomatic terms, definitions, most
        of which are in Arabic.   The terms themselves
        are in English.

775.   Hanesch, Günther.   Internationale Terminologie;
        Diplomatie, Vertrage, international Organisationen,
        Konferenzen.   International terminology; diplomacy,
        treaties, international organizations, conferences.
        Stuttgart, R. Müller Fremdsprachen-Verlag, 1954.
        180p.

        A polyglot glossary of some 1,121 terms arranged
        under subject headings.   Treats the most import-
        ant vocabulary from international politics and dip-
        lomacy.   Following the systematic sections are
        alphabetical indexes in each of the four languages.

776.   Hyamson, Albert Montefiore.   A dictionary of inter-

national affairs. Washington, Public Affairs
Press, American Council on Public Affairs, 1947.
352p.

This small encyclopedia is useful in spite of the
arbitrary selection of entries and its not always
accurate data. Geographical and political units
appear to constitute the major categories of items
treated.

777.   India (Republic) Central Hindi Directorate. List of
technical terms in Hindi: diplomacy. Delhi, Man-
ager of Publications, Govt. of India, 1962- v. 1-
(India, Republic, Ministry of Education Publication no. 552)

A series of volumes of Hindi legal as well as diplomatic terms and phrases.

778.   Mansoor, Menahem, ed. Legal and documentary
Arabic reader; with explanatory notes, exercises,
vocabularies and model answers. Leiden, E. J.
Brill, 1965. 2v.

An exhaustive Arabic legal dictionary which contains many entries relating to international law
and relations.

779.   Morellil, L. J. A. , de. Dictionnaire de chancelleries diplomatiques et consulaires... rédigé...
et completé au moyen de documents officiales.
Paris, J. Renouardg, 1855. 2v.

A good dictionary of terms and phrases used in
international law and relations. Includes many
diplomatic terms.

780.   Palomar, José Ignacio. Diccionario diplomatico
consular. Buenos Aires, Talleres gráficos
Cavalari y del Pozo, 1937- 2v.

An extensive Spanish dictionary covering the entire
field of international law and relations as well as
diplomatic and consular service.

781.   Pan American Union. Organization of American
States style manual; a guide to editorial practice,

with terminology related to the inter-American
system and to international organization. Washington, 1957-   1v.   (loose-leaf)

This work includes a polyglot listing of terms
used in international relations among which are
a number relating to the art and practice of diplomacy

782. Roland de Bussy, Théodore. Dictionnaire des consulats, exposé des devoirs, droits et fonctions
des consuls. Alger, 1854.   240p.

A dictionary of terms closely associated with
French diplomatic and consular service.

783. Strupp, Karl. Wörterbuch des Völkerrechts. New
2d ed. Edited by Hans-Jürgen Schlochauer and
Herbert Kruger.   Berlin, DeGruyter, 1960-64.
4v.

An excellent listing of words, terms and phrases
used in international law. One of the most extensive lists of diplomatic terms is included in this
work.

784. Theimer, Walter. An encyclopedia of modern world
politics. New York, Rinehart, 1950.   696p.

A survey of political terms, problems, treaties,
and catchwords of the contemporary world in an
alphabetical arrangement. Also includes short
political sketches of many countries with a few
biographical notes on important political figures.

785. Vasco, Miguel Antonio. Diccionario de derecho
internacional. Quito, Editorial del Ministerio
de Educación. 1963.   538p.

An extensive Spanish-language dictionary of terms
in international law and relations as well as diplomacy.

786. Wörterbuch der Aussenpolitik. (Hrsg. von Wolfgang
Kerff und Horst Seydewitz). Dusseldorf, Brücken-
Verlag, 1965.   751p.

An extensive German dictionary of terms used in international law and relations as well as diplomacy.

Directories and Biographical Information.

In the actual conduct of diplomacy factual information about people, organizations, places and things is useful in a great many ways. Directories are a convenient means to finding this type of information.

787.   Administration et diplomatie d'Afrique noire et de Madagascar.   Paris, Europe-Outremer, 1962- v. 1-   (annual)

A guide to the governments of 15 new African republics in the French community, includes standard organization and directory information for each country. Supplementary material gives directory information on African interstate organizations.

788.   Almanac of current world leaders.   Palo Alto, Calif., Stanford Scholastic Associates, 1957-   v. 1- (tri-annually; Publisher varies; Kept up to date by monthly pocket supplements)

A current listing of major government officials in a great many countries and other organizations and alliances.

789.   L'Annuaire des ministères.   Numéro spécial de Revue de l'administration française, 1945-   v. 1- (annual)

Contains listings of administrative officials including the diplomatic corps, etc. Title and frequency vary.

790.   Annuaire diplomatique et consulaire de la Républic Française.   Paris, Impr.   Nationale, 1858-1954. v. 1-   (annual)

Contains a historical listing of the ministers of foreign affairs since 1589, and directory informa-

tion on the diplomatic and consular service of
France. With biographical sketches. Title
varies. Current publication in doubt.

791. Australia. Dept. of External Affairs. <u>Diplomatic</u>
<u>list.</u> Camberra, 1966. 62p.

A register of all diplomatic and consular officials
for Australia in 1966.

792. Brazil. Departamento diplomatico e consular. Divisão consular. <u>Lista do corpo consular estrang-</u>
<u>erio.</u> Rio de Janeiro, 1937- v. 1-

A series of manuals and lists of diplomats for
Brazilian consular officials.

793. <u>The British imperial calendar and civil service list.</u>
London, 1809- v. 1-

A listing of administrative officials in the royal
households. Cabinet offices and public department,
ministries, commissions, etc. of England and
Wales, Scotland and Northern Ireland. Includes
name, official position, degrees, honors and
salary. Alphabetical index of names.

794. Canada. Dept. of External Affairs. <u>Canadian repre-</u>
<u>sentatives abroad and representatives of other</u>
<u>countries in Canada.</u> Ottawa, E. Cloutier, 1947-
v. 1-

A list of Canadian diplomatic representatives and
a list of foreign emissaries within Canada.

795. Ceylon. Ministry of External Affairs. <u>Diplomatic,</u>
<u>consular and other representation in Ceylon and</u>
<u>Ceylon representation abroad.</u> Colombo, 1955-
v. 1-

The basic register of Ceylonese diplomatic and
consular officials.

796. <u>Code diplomatique et consulaire; annuaire pour les</u>
<u>corps diplomatique et consulaire du monde entier.</u>
11th ed. Zurich, Code mondial, 1963? 760p.

A general world list of major diplomatic and consular officials.

797.   Colombia. Ministerio de relaciones exteriores.   Lista
        consular.   Bogotá, 1947-   v. 1-

        The basic list of Columbian diplomatic and con-
        sular officials.   Continues its Lista diplomática y
        consular.

798.   Council of Europe.   Secretariat.   List of local nota-
        bilities.   Strasbourg, 1957-   v. 1-

        A listing of diplomatic and consular officials pri-
        marily in Europe.

799.   Council on Foreign Relations.   American agencies
        interested in international affairs.   New York,
        Council on Foreign Relations, 1931-   5th ed.
        (1964) is the current volume.

        Directory of research and action groups in the
        United States working directly or indirectly in the
        many fields related to world politics and interna-
        tional affairs in general.

800.   The Diplomatic Press directory of Ghana including
        trade index and biographical section.   London,
        Diplomatic Press and Pub. Co. , 1959-   v. 1-

        Although basically an industrial and commercial
        directory for Ghana, it includes current lists of
        consular officials.   Items 801-808 are essentially
        similar and are not annotated.

801.   The Diplomatic Press directory of Jamaica including
        trade index and biographical section.   London,
        Diplomatic Press and Pub. Co. , 1962-   v. 1-

802.   The Diplomatic Press directory of the Federation of
        Nigeria including trade index and biographical
        section.   London, Diplomatic Press and Pub. Co. ,
        1960-   v. 1-

803.   The Diplomatic Press directory of the Republic of
        Cyprus including trade index and biographical sec-
        tion.   London, Diplomatic Press and Pub. Co. ,

804. The Diplomatic Press directory of the State of Sing-
      apore. London, Diplomatic Press and Pub. Co. ,
      1960-   v. 1 -

805. The Diplomatic Press Hong Kong trade directory,
      including classified trade index.   London, Diplo-
      matic Press and Pub. Co. , 1964-65-   v. 1 -

806. The Diplomatic Press trade directory of Malta.
      London, Diplomatic Press and Pub. Co. , 1965-
      v. 1 -

807. The Diplomatic Press trade directory of the Empire
      of Ethiopia, including classified trade index.
      London, Diplomatic Press and Pub. Co. , 1965-
      v. 1 -

808. The Diplomatic Press trade directory of Trinidad and
      Tobago, including alphabetical and classified trade
      index.   London, Diplomatic Press and Pub. Co. ,
      1963-64-   v. 1 -

809. The Diplomatic Service list.   London, H. M. Station-
      ery Off. , 1966-   v. 1 -   (annual)

      An official register of British diplomatic officials.
      Supersedes in part the Foreign Office list and the
      Commonwealth Relations Office Yearbook.

810. The Diplomat's annual.   London, 1950-   v. 1 -

      An annual register of both international and British
      diplomats.

811. The Diplomat's directory.   New Delhi, M. H. Samuel,
      1962? -

      A directory of Indian diplomatic officials.

812. The Foreign office list and diplomatic and consular
      yearbook.   London, Harrison, 1806-1966.   160v.
      (annual)

      Gives organization of the office, various diplomatic
      and consular lists, "Statement of services" with
      biographical notices of some length, obituaries,
      references to biographical notices in earlier vol-

umes, various chronological lists, etc.

813.   Germany (Federal Republic, 1949-   ) Auswärtiges
       Amt.   Liste des diplomatischen Korps in Bonn.
       Berlin, 1957-   v. 1-

       The basic register of diplomatic and consular
       officials of the German Federal Republic.

814.   Gt. Brit.   Foreign Office.   Alphabetical list of the
       foreign embassies and legations in London.   Lon-
       don, 1959-   v. 1-   (irregular)

       As the title implies this series is a listing of
       foreign embassies and legations in London.

815.   Iceland.   Utanríkisraouneytio.   Diplomatic list, in-
       cluding consuls of career accredited at Reykjavik
       and list of honorary consuls in Iceland.   Reykj-
       avik, 1942-   v. 1-

       The basic list of Icelandic diplomatic and consular
       officials.

816.   The International yearbook and statesman's who's
       who.   London, Burke's Peerage, 1953-1968-   v. 1-

       Combines information concerning political and
       economic conditions of the world with an interna-
       tional biographical directory which gives short
       sketches of about 10,000 persons of international
       import such as statesmen, diplomats, military
       leaders etc.

817.   Italy.   Ministero degli affari esteri.   Ambasciate
       elegazioni in Italia.   Roma, 1946-   v. 1-
       (irregular)

       The basic list of Italian diplomatic and consular
       officials and their ranks and place of service.

818.   Jordan.   Ministry of Foreign Affairs.   Diplomatic
       list.   Amman, Print. & Publication House, 1955-
       v. 1-

       The basic register of Jordanian diplomatic and
       consular officials.

819.   Kenya Colony and Protectorate.   Directory of Common-
       wealth commissioners and the consular corps.
       Nairobi?, 1959-   v. 1-

       The basic register of diplomatic and consular
       officials for the Colony of Kenya.

820.   Korea (Republic Ministry of Foreign Affairs.   Diplo-
       matic list.   Seoul, 1957-   v. 1-

       The basic register of diplomatic and consular
       officials for the Republic of Korea.

821.   New Zealand.   Dept. of External Affairs.   Diplomatic
       and consular representatives in Wellington.   Well-
       ington, 1955-   v. 1-

       The basic list of diplomatic and consular officials
       of New Zealand.

822.   Repertorium der diplomatischen Vertreter aller
       Länder seit dem Westfalischen Frieden (1648)
       Repertory of the diplomatic representatives of
       all countries since the Peace of Westphalia (1648)
       Veröffentlicht vom Internationalen Ausschuss für
       Geschichtswissenschaften.   Oldenburg i o. , G.
       Stalling, 1936-65.   3v.   (Includes bibliographies)

       Under each major country the representatives are
       listed by the country to which they were sent.
       For each man is given his name, his capacity,
       the duties of his mission, and the source of this
       information.   Each volume has a personal name
       and country index.

823.   Syria.   Ministére des affaires étrangères.   Liste
       de MM.   les membres du corps diplomatique à
       Damas.   Damas?, 1951-   v. 1-

       A basic register of Syrian diplomatic and consular
       officials.

824.   U. S. Dept. of State.   Biographic register.   Washing-
       ton, U. S. Govt.   Print. Of. , 1870-   v. 1-
       (annual but also irregular)

       A directory of personnel of the Dept. of State.

Includes education and career sketches of Foreign
Service officers.

825.   _____. Diplomatic list. Washington, U. S. Govt.
        Print. Off. , 1893-   v. 1-

A list of foreign diplomatic representatives in
Washington, arranged in order of precedence,
with addresses. Issued periodically.

826.   _____. Foreign consular offices in the United States.
        Washington, U. S. Govt. Print. Off. , 1932-
        v. 1-   (Quarterly, 1932-33; Semi-annual 1934-40;
        annual 1941-   )

Includes a complete and official listing of foreign
consular officers in the U. S. together with their
jurisdiction and personnel. Has an alphabetical
arrangement by country.

827.   _____. Foreign service list. Washington, U. S.
        Govt. Print. Off. , 1829-   v. 1-

A register of field staffs at all foreign posts of
the Dept. of State, U. S. Information Agency,
Agency for International Development, Peace
Corps and the Dept. of Agriculture. Includes
posts of assignment, categories and classification.
Published quarterly since 1955.

828.   _____. Key officers of foreign service posts; guide
        for businessmen. Washington, Dept. of State,
        Office of Operations, Division of Publishing Ser-
        vices. U. S. Govt. Print. Off. , 1964.   53p.

Includes economic data along with a listing of key
officers of embassies and consulate generals.
Compiled to aid American business interests in
foreign countries.

829.   _____. Register of the Department of State. Wash-
        ington, U. S. Govt. Print. Off. , 1869-19-   v. 1-
        (annual)

Provides background information on personnel of
the Department of State and the Foreign Service,
and of other federal agencies participating in the

field of foreign affairs.

830.   Venezuela.   Ministerio de Relaciones Exteriores.
       Cuerpo diplomático de Venezuela.   Caracas,
       1955-   v. 1-

       The basic register of diplomatic and consular
       officials for Venezuela.

831.   The World diplomatic directory and world diplomatic
       biography.   2d: 1951.

831A.   _____. World diplomatic directory Service.   Supple-
       ment, no. 1- London, 1956-   v. 1-

       First edition was divided into two parts each
       arranged alphabetically by country.   Part 1 gives
       the principal missions and consular offices abroad
       of each country including the U. N.   Part 2 includes
       brief biographical data for officers listed in the
       first part.   Supplements are issued at irregular
       intervals.

Guides to the Literature.

       A guide to the literature is a bibliographical source
which attempts to systematize and introduce the subject
matter of a discipline.   There has been no general guide
to the literature of diplomacy up to now although there are
several general or specialized ones of relevance.

832.   Aufricht, Hans.   Guide to League of Nations publi-
       cations; a bibliographical survey of the work of the
       League, 1920-1947.   New York, Columbia Univ-
       ersity Press, 1951.   682p.

       The most comprehensive bibliographical guide to
       the documents of the League and its autonomous
       affiliates.

833.   Bemis, Samuel Flagg.   Guide to the diplomatic his-
       tory of the United States, 1774-1921.   With Grace
       G. Griffin.   Washington, U. S. Govt. Print. Off. ,
       1935.   979p.

An important reference work containing both bibliographic data and remarks on the sources of information.

834.   Brock, Clifton.   The literature of political science:
        a guide for students, librarians and teachers.
        New York, Bowker, 1969.   232p.

        An excellent guide for students doing research in
        the field of political science generally.   However,
        it contains only a few items related to diplomacy.

835.   Burchfield, Laverne.   Student's guide to materials
        in political science.   New York, Holt, 1935.
        426p.

        The best guide to important source materials, bib-
        liographies and reference works of a retrospective
        nature.   Pages 223-265 deal with international law
        and diplomacy.

836.   Harmon, Robert Bartlett.   Political science: a bib-
        liographical guide to the literature.   New York,
        Scarecrow Press, 1965.   388p.

836A.   _____.   Supplement, 1968.   Metuchen, N. J., Scare-
        crow Press, 1968.   331p.

        Pages 268-269 of the first volume list books on
        diplomacy.   The 1968 supplement includes such
        works in the Chapter on International Politics.
        Generally this work is weak in this area.

837.   Mason, John Brown.   Research resources; annotated
        guide to the social sciences.   Santa Barbara,
        Calif., ABC-Clio, 1968-   v. 1-   (V. 1 Interna-
        tional relations & recent history; indexes, ab-
        stracts & periodicals)

        Lists a few reference works in the area of diplo-
        macy but has an excellent listing of periodicals
        in international relations, v. 1, pp. 37-103.

838.   Wynar, Lubomyr Romain.   Guide to reference mat-
        erials in political science; a selective bibliography.
        With the assistance of Linda Fystrom.   Rochester,
        N. Y., Libraries Unlimited, Inc., 1966-   v. 1-

(2 vols issued to date)

Volume II pages 15-80 deal with international relations. Includes many more reference items
relating to diplomacy than does Mason (837)

839.   Zawodny, Janusz Kazimirez.   Guide to the study of
        international relations.   San Francisco, Chandler
        Pub. Co. , 1966.   151p.

        Includes classified lists of bibliographies and bio-
        graphical works, scholarly journals, atlases,
        archives, collections of national libraries, etc.
        Many of the entries are annotated; some are not.
        Generally weak with respect to the area of diplo-
        macy.

Periodicals.

        Most of the journals dealing with foreign affairs con-
tain articles on diplomacy.   The listing below is a selection
of the more important of these scholarly journals.

840.   American consular bulletin.   New York, Washington
        D. C. , American Consular Association, 1922-24.
        6v.

        A periodical of general interest to U. S. diplomatic
        and consular officials.   Superseded by the Amer-
        ican Foreign Service Journal.

841.   The American journal of international law.   Washing-
        ton, D. C. , American Society of International Law,
        1907-   v. 1-   (quarterly)

        A quarterly journal devoted primarily to contemp-
        orary questions of international law and relations.
        Represents one of the better periodical sources
        for materials on diplomacy.   Includes book reviews
        and notes, and a section on official documents.
        The section titled Periodical Literature of Interna-
        Law listed articles from 60 to 85 journals from
        all over the world until it was discontinued in
        October of 1964.   Has a cumulated index every
        20 years.

842.   The American political science review.   Menasha,
        Wis., etc., American Political Science Associa-
        tion, 1906-   v. 1-   (quarterly)

        The most significant source for bibliography and on
        international relations and political science includ-
        ing diplomacy.

843.   Archives diplomatiques; recueil mensuel de diplomatie,
        d'histoire et droit international.   Paris, Amyot,
        1861-1914.   193v.   in 112.   (no more published)

        From 1861-1914, the Archives served as a deposi-
        tory for documents exchanged between all nations
        concerning matters of international affairs and
        politics.   During the more than fifty years of its
        existence, it published the full texts of more than
        100,000 documents and this comprises a detailed
        record of international affairs during the latter
        part of the nineteenth century and the pre-World
        War I years of the twentith century.

844.   Corps diplomatique; the journal of modern diplomacy.
        Washington, D. C., Pub. Co., 1946.   1v.   (no
        more published)

        A general periodical containing varied articles on
        the various aspects of diplomacy and international
        relations.

845.   Denver,   University.   Social Science Foundation.
        Monograph series in world affairs.   Denver.   1963-
        v. 1-

        An excellent set of monographs issued periodically
        covering many aspects of international relations
        including diplomacy.

846.   Diplomat.   Delhi, Diplomatic Publications, 1965-
        v. 1-   (monthly)

        An Indian journal on issues of world politics and
        diplomacy.

847.   Diplomatic bulletin.   London, Diplomatic Press and
        Pub. Co., 1946-   v. 1-   (semi-monthly)

Includes articles of interest to British diplomatic and consular personnel. Also includes matters on British foreign relations, and lists of arrivals and departures of foreign diplomats, consuls and commonwealth officials.

848. The Diplomatist. London, 1955?- v. 1- (monthly)

A general journal which includes articles on British diplomatic practice.

849. Les Documents politiques, diplomatiques et financiers; sommaire. Paris, 1920- v. 1- (monthly)

A periodical covering a wide area of international relations including a large number of valuable diplomatic documents.

850. Foreign affairs. New York, 1922- v. 1- (monthly)

An important source for American study of international affairs; each issue includes annotated bibliographies.

851. Foreign service journal. Washington, American Foreign Service Association, 1924- v. 1- (monthly)

Supersedes American consular bulletin. An unofficial publication depicting pictorially the office and personnel of the Foreign Service. It also provides a comprehensive collection of photographs of American embassy, legation, and consular buildings abroad.

852. International affairs. London, Royal Institute of International Affairs, 1922- v. 1- (quarterly)

An important journal, the British counterpart to Foreign Affairs. Includes an extensive book review section.

853. International studies. Bombay, New York, Asia Pub. House, 1959- v. 1- (quarterly)

Contains articles on international politics, economics, and law as well as on the political, economic

and social developments in all parts of the world.
Includes a section entitled "India and world affairs:
an annual bibliography. "

854.   Journal of conflict resolution: a quarterly for research
        related to war and peace.   Ann Arbor, Mich. ,
        Dept. of Journalism, University of Michigan, 1957-
        v. 1-   (quarterly)

        Offers a wide variety of articles on international
        conflicting issues.   Includes book reviews.

855.   Journal on international affairs.   New York, School
        of International Affairs, Columbia University, 1947-
        v. 1-   (semi-annual)

        Each issue concentrates on a central topic and
        contains articles written by scholars and statesmen.
        Also includes book reviews.

856.   Neue politische Literatur: Berichte über des interna-
        tionale Schrifttum.   Stuttgart, Ring-Verlag, 1956-
        v. 1-   (monthly)

        A journal of reviews of international political
        science literature.   Includes many items on diplo-
        macy and an annual author and subject index.

857.   Orbis.   Philadelphia, Foreign Policy Research Insti-
        tute, University of Pennsylvania, 1957-   v. 1-
        (quarterly)

        Contains articles on important issues in interna-
        tional relations.   With emphasis upon foreign policy
        and current events this journal is an excellent
        source for information on diplomacy.

858.   Revista de derecho internacional y ciencias diplo-
        máticas.   Rosario, Argentina, Instituto de
        Derecho Internacional, Facultad de Ciencias Eco-
        nómicas, Commerciales y Politicas, 1949-   v. 1-

        A general journal on international law and diplo-
        macy.

859.   Revista internacional y diplomática.   México, D. F. ,
        1950-   v. 1-   (monthly)

Contains scholarly articles on world politics and
diplomacy.

860. Revue française de science politique. Paris, Presses
      universitairies de France, 1951-   v. 1-   (quarterly)

      A large part of each issue is devoted to survey-
      ing current literature including diplomacy.

861. Revue d'histoire diplomatique; publiée par les soins
      de la Societé d'histoire diplomatique. Paris, E.
      Leroux, etc., 1887-19   v. 1-   (quarterly)

      Contains articles on international diplomatic rela-
      tions and history during the period from the mid-
      dle ages to modern times. Contributors have in-
      cluded eminent historians, as well as important
      statesmen from various countries, whose scholar-
      ship has been based to a great extent on newly
      discovered and declassified documents. There are
      also extensive book reviews written by authorities.

862. U N monthly chronicle. New York, United Nations,
      Office of Public Information, 1964-   v. 1-

      Supersedes UN review. Covers the U N and its
      related agencies in great detail. Includes record
      of the month, articles on major developments and
      activities, progress reports, trends in international
      affairs, and texts of important documents.

863. U. S. Dept. of State.   The Department of state bul-
      letin. Washington, U. S. Govt. Print. Office, 1939-
      v. 1-   (weekly)

      Includes articles explaining U. S. policy, speeches
      by officials, and documents such as treaties and
      executive agreements.

864. _____. Newsletter. Washington, 1961-   v. 1-
      (monthly)

      Includes a variety of information on departmental
      developments of interest to the personnel of the
      Dept. of State.

865. World politics; a quarterly journal of international

relations.   Princeton, Center for International
Studies; Princeton University Press, 1948-   v. 1-

Articles contained in this journal are of a scholarly and general nature on the basic problems of
international relations and international organization.   Review articles are exceptionally worth-
while.

Yearbooks.

The most distinctive feature of a yearbook is its
annual appearance.   There are a number of these that have
relevance to diplomacy and provide factual and up to date
information on modern international affairs.

866.   Académie diplomatique internationale.   Séances et
          travaux.   Paris, 1927?-1941.   13v.

          An annual which included the activities of the
          Académie along with articles on various aspects
          of international relations including diplomacy.

867.   Almanach de Gotha; annuaire généalogique, diplo-
          matique et statistique.   Gotha, J. Perthes, 1763-
          v. 1-   (annual)

          A standard handbook in which coverage varies.
          Contains general information about governmental
          organization, diplomatic and consular represent-
          atives.

868.   Annuaire diplomatique.   Genève, 1952-   v. 1-
          (annual)

          An annual review of world diplomatic efforts by
          country.

869.   Annuaire français de droit international.   Paris,
          Centre national de la recherche scientifique,
          1955-   v. 1-

          Along with articles on current legal and interna-
          tional relations questions, this excellent annual
          includes a chronology, critical book reviews and

a systematic bibliography of works in international
law published during the year.

870.   Anuario hispano-luso-americano de derecho interna-
       cional. Zaragoza, El Noticiero, 1959-   v. 1-

       Primarily a large collection of essays, articles,
       by Latin American scholars in international law
       and relations.

871.   Anuario juridico interamericano. Inter-American
       juridical yearbook... Annuaire juridique inter-
       Americane. Washington, Pan American Union,
       1948-   v. 1-

       A publication of the Pan American Union which
       includes essays, documents, bibliographies, etc.
       in international law and organization.

872.   Anuario uruguayo de derecho internacional. Mont-
       evideo, 1966-   v. 1-

       Articles on international law are included in this
       work by Uruguayan scholars. Includes texts of
       international documents and documented articles.

873.   Asociación Francisco de Vitoria. Anuario. Madrid.
       Imprenta La Rafa, etc. , 1929-   v. 1-

       This yearbook covers the fields of Spanish law,
       law in general as well as international law. In-
       cludes a large assortment of diplomatic documents.

874.   Asociación Guatemalteca de Derecho Internacional.
       Revista. Guatemala, 1954-   v. 1-   (annual)

       A Guatemalan yearbook of international law and
       relations. Includes articles, reviews, bibliog-
       raphies and documents.

875.   The Australian yearbook of international law. Sydney,
       Butterworths, 1965-   v. 1-

       A collection of essays, documents and bibliographies
       on the law of nations written largely by Australian
       scholars.

876.   The British yearbook of international law.   London,
        New York, Oxford, University Press, 1920/21-
        v. 1-

        A useful annual volume of original essays, notes
        and book reviews.   There is an index to volumes
        I-XXXVI, compiled by J. G. Colle (1963)   150p.

877.   The Canadian yearbook of international law.   Annuaire
        canadien de droit international.   Vancouver, Pub-
        lications Centre, University of British Columbia,
        1963-   v. 1-

        Includes essays on current questions of internation-
        al law.   Also has a section of notes and comments,
        book reviews and an index.   In French and English.

878.   Czechoslovak yearbook of international law.   Hlídka
        mezinárodního prava.   London, Published under the
        auspices of the Czechoslovak branch of the Interna-
        tional Law Association, 1942-   v. 1-

        Published in the English language this collection
        includes articles, notes on cases, notes on meet-
        ings, along with book reviews and documents.

879.   The Diplomatic yearbook.   New York, Funk & Wag-
        nalls in association with United Nations World,
        1950-   v. 1-

        Compiled by the editors of the United Nations
        World.   Includes sections on diplomatic practices
        and procedures and lists for the various persons
        in the diplomatic service throughout the world.
        Only one issue published?

880.   Grotius; annuaire international.   La Haye, M. Nij-
        hoff, 1913-   v. 1-

        Contains scholarly articles, documents and bib-
        liographies.

881.   The Indian yearbook of international affairs.   Madras,
        1952-   v. 1-   (irregular)

        A collection of articles on international law and
        international relations published annually from
        1952-1959; irregularly since 1960.

882.   Institute of International Law.   Annuaire de l'Institut
        de droit international.   Ed. nouv, abrégée.   Brux-
        elles, Impr. Lesigne, 1928-31.   7v.

        The annual of the Institute of International Law
        containing the activities of the diplomats and dis-
        cussions of many diplomatic functions for the
        period covered.

883.   Die Internationale Politik.   München, R. Oldenbourg,
        1955-   v. 1-   (annual)

        A basic survey of international relations with sub-
        stantial appendices of current literature, notes,
        and documents.   This is a scholarly, reliable
        source of information prepared by specialists.

884.   Jahrbuch des völkerrechts.   München & Humbolt,
        1913-26.

        A group of volumes, no longer published, with
        articles and documents on various phases of inter-
        national law.

885.   Jahrbuch für internationales Recht.   Göttingen, Van-
        denhoick & Ruprecht, 1948-   v. 1-

        Title varies.   A german yearbook of international
        law containing articles, documents, book reviews
        and bibliographies.

886.   The Japanese annual of international law.   Tokyo,
        Japan Branch of the International Law Association,
        1957-   no. 1-

        A collection of essays on international law.

887.   The Jewish yearbook of international law.   Jerusalem,
        R. Mass, 1948-   v. 1-

        Includes writings of Jewish scholars on the legal
        aspects of international relations.

888.   Jus gentium; annuario italiano di dritto internazionale.
        Napoli, S. A. E. N. , Società anonima editrice Napo-
        letana, 1938-   v. 1-

This is a collection of essays by scholars on a
wide variety of topices in international law and
relations.

889.   Rocznik prawa miedzynarodowego.   Warszawa, 1949-
        v. 1-

        A polish yearbook of international law with articles
        on its various aspects.

890.   Schweizerisches Jahrbuch für internationales Recht.
        Annuaire suisse de droit international.   Zürich,
        Polygraphischer Verlag, 1944-   v. 1-

        Each volume has two main sections which include
        documents of international organizations and im-
        portant articles on aspects of international law.
        Published in French and German.

891.   Sovetskii exhegodnik mezhdunarodnogo prava.   Soviet
        yearbook of international law.   Moskva; Soviet.
        Assot. Mezhd. Prava.   Akademia Nauk SSSR,
        1959-   v. 1-   (annual)

        Each volume includes scholarly articles, book re-
        views, reports and bibliographies.   The primary
        articles have a summary in English.

892.   The Statesman's yearbook; a statistical and historical
        annual of the states of the world.   Rev. after of-
        ficial returns.   New York, St. Martin's Press,
        1864-   v. 1-

        This work is a concise and reliable manual of des-
        criptive and statistical information about govern-
        ments of the world.   Includes lists of diplomatic
        representatives.

893.   Survey of International affairs.   Published under the
        auspices of the British Institute of International
        Affairs.   London, New York, Oxford University
        Press, 1925-   v. 1-

        An outstanding series reviewing events of interna-
        tional importance throughout the world.   Subject
        coverage varies and contents consist of detailed
        factual statements, documented with references.

894. _____. Consolidated index to the Survey of international affairs, 1920-1938; and Documents on international affairs, 1925-1938; compiled by E. M. P.
Ditman. London, Oxford University Press, 1967.
272p.

895. United Nations. Yearbook. New York, Columbia
University Press in cooperat'ɔn with the United
Nations, 1946/47-   v. 1-   (annual)

Record of activities of the United Nations. Good
coverage of all U. N. happenings for the year.
An indispensible source for information on the role
of the U. N. in international diplomacy.

896. _____. International Law Commission. Yearbook.
New York, 1957-   v. 1-   (United Nations document A/CN. 4)

Is issued in two volumes of which v. 1 contains
summary records of the session and v. 2, documents relating to the subject discussion, including reports of the General Assembly. Each
volume has a separate index.

897. The Yearbook of world polity. New York, Praeger,
1957-   v. 1-   (irregular)

A collection of essays on subjects of international
law and organizations. Many of the essays deal
with areas and problems of diplomacy. Also
includes some extensive bibliographies compiled
by scholars in the field. Title varies and some
volumes have distinctive titles.

VII

Diplomatic Documents and Organization

This chapter has been designed to provide illustrative examples of key diplomatic documents which will supplement the material contained in the main body of this work. Such illustrations will help enrich the user's understanding of the functions and organization of diplomatic relations between nations.

Where possible the documents included here have been selected to emphasize the significance, scope, and limitations of diplomatic activity. Admittedly, they do not satisfy all of these criteria. Some, while not inherently significant, none-the-less are presented to illustrate an important function or procedure.

The format of this chapter is arranged in such a way that some documents are directly reproduced to give as accurate a representation of the original as possible. Actual facsimilies, in some cases, are reproduced. The machinery and structure for the conduct of international affairs, particularly the structure of foreign offices, diplomatic missions, international conferences, etc. is presented in chart form. Other documents are presented in a pattern to portray their use in diplomatic relations. [19]

Diplomatics

Diplomatics is the science and/or art of deciphering and studying the old official and historical documents, determining their authenticity, age, etc. The relationship as well as importance of diplomatics to the study of diplomacy is obvious. Official documents have played a major role in the development and conduct of diplomatic relations throughout history. Below are cited a few works in this area.

212

898.   Giry, Arthur.   Manuel de diplomatique; diplômes
        et chartes, chronologie technique, éléments
        critiques, et parties constitutués de la teneur
        des chartes, les chancelleries, les actes privés.
        Nouv. ed.   Paris, F. Alcan, 1925.   944p.

        Contains bibliographies including an appendix to
        book 1, chapter 1, (p. 37-50), footnotes, and
        "Index bibliographique" (p. 893-907)

899.   Mabillon, Jean.   De re diplomatica libri vi ...
        Neapili, ex typographia Vincentii Orsini, 1789.
        2v. in 1.

        A handbook on paleography and diplomatics along
        with an essay on the history of writing.

900.   Tessier, Georges.   Diplomatique royale française.
        Paris, A. et J. Picard, 1962.   340p.   (Includes
        bibliography)

        A detailed study of diplomatics and the French
        diplomatic archives.

Organization for the Conduct of Diplomacy

Diplomatic relations between modern nation-states
requires an extremely complex network of governmental
machinery on national and international levels. Vast
agencies ranging from manifold international bodies such as
the United Nations are used in the conduct of common bilateral negotiations.

Governments of states throughtout the world employ
a variety of agencies to manage their foreign and diplomatic
relations. The main agency for the United States, of course,
is the Department of State. Although going through some
modification at times, the State Department has developed
an emerging structural pattern. Often other governments
call the central agency which conducts its foreign relations
the Foreign Office or Ministry of Foreign Affairs, which
varies in the structure and organization with the particular
circumstances and traditions of the state concerned.

In foreign capitals a government is represented by
embassies and legations of varying sizes, composition and
functions. Those of a less complex structure are located
in capitals where a small amount of diplomatic business
is transacted; those of a more complicated structure are
found in the important capitals of the world. To handle
commercial and other essentially non-political activities,
consular offices are maintained in the principal ports and
industrial centers of foreign countries. Their organizational structure is much less complex than that of diplomatic missions. [20]

1. Executive Organization for Foreign Relations (Simplified)[21]

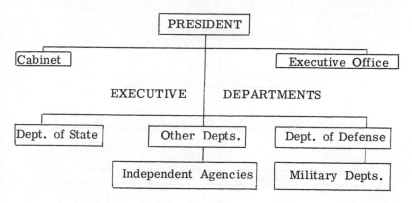

2. Department of State Structure Chart (Simplified)[22]

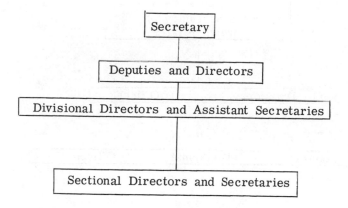

3.   British Foreign Office Structure Chart (Simplified)[23]

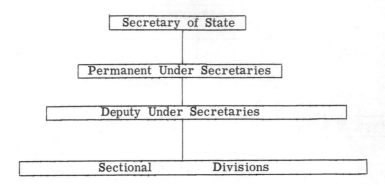

4.   German Foreign Office Structure Chart (Simplified)[24]

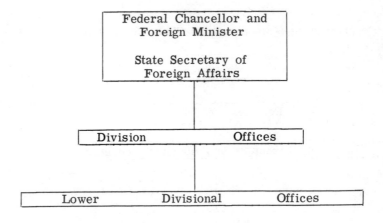

5. DIPLOMATIC MISSION: STRUCTURE CHART OF 25 TYPICAL UNITED STATES MISSION

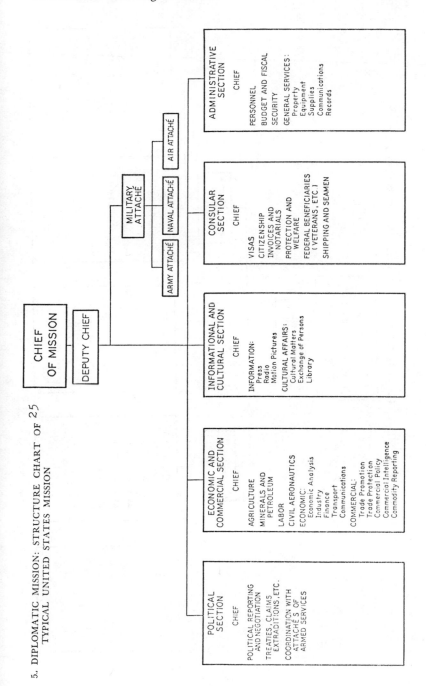

CHIEF OF MISSION

DEPUTY CHIEF

MILITARY ATTACHÉ
ARMY ATTACHÉ   NAVAL ATTACHÉ   AIR ATTACHÉ

POLITICAL SECTION

CHIEF

POLITICAL REPORTING AND NEGOTIATION
TREATIES, CLAIMS EXTRADITIONS, ETC.
COORDINATION WITH ATTACHÉ'S OF ARMED SERVICES

ECONOMIC AND COMMERCIAL SECTION

CHIEF

AGRICULTURE
MINERALS AND PETROLEUM
LABOR
CIVIL AERONAUTICS
ECONOMIC:
  Economic Analysis
  Industry
  Finance
  Transport
  Communications
COMMERCIAL:
  Trade Promotion
  Trade Protection
  Commercial Policy
  Commercial Intelligence
  Commodity Reporting

INFORMATIONAL AND CULTURAL SECTION

CHIEF

INFORMATION:
  Press
  Radio
  Motion Pictures
CULTURAL AFFAIRS:
  Cultural Matters
  Exchange of Persons
  Library

CONSULAR SECTION

CHIEF

VISAS
CITIZENSHIP
INVOICES AND NOTARIALS
PROTECTION AND WELFARE
FEDERAL BENEFICIARIES (VETERANS, ETC.)
SHIPPING AND SEAMEN

ADMINISTRATIVE SECTION

CHIEF

PERSONNEL
BUDGET AND FISCAL
SECURITY
GENERAL SERVICES:
  Property
  Equipment
  Supplies
  Communications
  Records

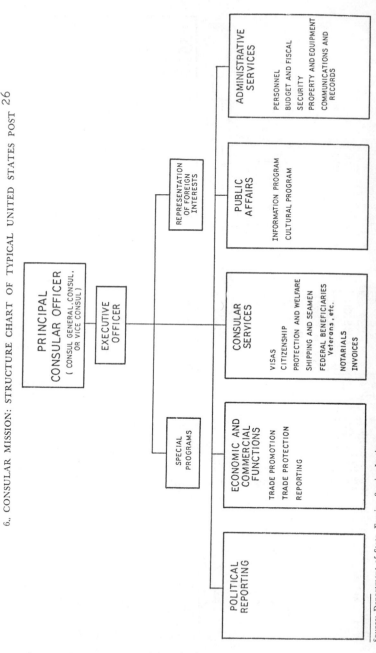

6. CONSULAR MISSION: STRUCTURE CHART OF TYPICAL UNITED STATES POST 26

PRINCIPAL
CONSULAR OFFICER
(CONSUL GENERAL, CONSUL,
OR VICE CONSUL)

EXECUTIVE
OFFICER

SPECIAL
PROGRAMS

REPRESENTATION
OF FOREIGN
INTERESTS

POLITICAL
REPORTING

ECONOMIC AND
COMMERCIAL
FUNCTIONS

TRADE PROMOTION
TRADE PROTECTION
REPORTING

CONSULAR
SERVICES

VISAS
CITIZENSHIP
PROTECTION AND WELFARE
SHIPPING AND SEAMEN
FEDERAL BENEFICIARIES
Veterans, etc.
NOTARIALS
INVOICES

PUBLIC
AFFAIRS

INFORMATION PROGRAM
CULTURAL PROGRAM

ADMINISTRATIVE
SERVICES

PERSONNEL
BUDGET AND FISCAL
SECURITY
PROPERTY AND EQUIPMENT
COMMUNICATIONS AND
RECORDS

Source: Department of State, Foreign Service Institute.

7. Diplomatic Mission: Structure Chart of the United States
   Mission to the United Nations (Simplified)[27]

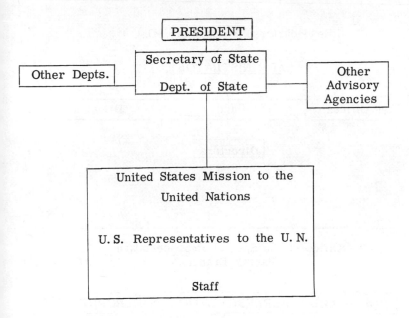

8. Economic Cooperation Administration Structure Chart
   (Simplified)[28]

Headquarters, Washington, D. C.

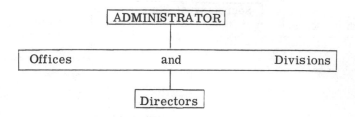

Office of the Special Representative
Paris, France

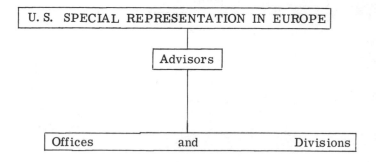

9. AGENCY FOR INTERNATIONAL DEVELOPMENT STRUCTURE CHART [29]

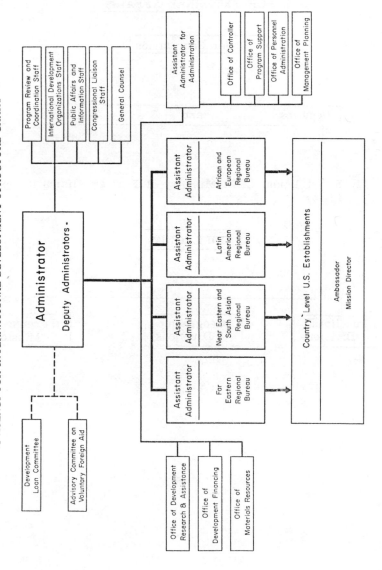

10. Canada: Department of External Affairs (Simplified)[30]

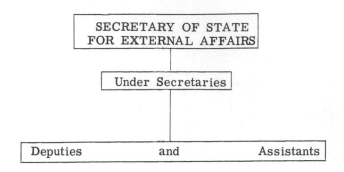

11. Soviet Union: USSR Ministry of Foreign Affairs (Simplified)[31]

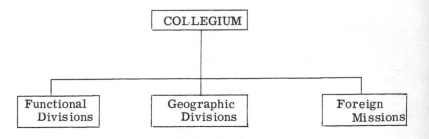

Diplomatic and Consular Credentials and Immunities

Diplomatic and consular affairs have always been handled by agents who have been officially accredited for this purpose. Throughout history states have exercised their inherent right to diplomatic representation. Principles covering these rights have been codified in some detail by the Vienna Convention of 1961. The Congress of Vienna (1815) and Aix-la-Chapelle (1818) established the rules which affect the official and social position of a diplomat in a foreign capital.

Prior to any appointment of an individual to a diplomatic post, agrément must be reached regarding his acceptability to the receiving government. Normally the appointee is persona grata, but occasionally he proves to be persona non grata in which case he must be replaced. If acceptable, the sending government verifies his appointment by issuing a diplomatic commission.

The diplomat is further furnished with a number of additional credentials by his home government. Among the more important of these is a "letter of credence" which identifies him as the official emissary of the sending government. The envoy presents this letter to the head of the receiving government at a formal reception. Upon this occasion, the newly-appointed diplomat customarily makes a few circumspect remarks, to which the head of the receiving government makes an equally discreet reply. When a diplomatic agent is appointed for the specific purpose of negotiating and signing an agreement, he is supplied with what is known as "full power."

Diplomatic vacancies are usually created by the resignation of a diplomat. In many cases an envoy will be recalled by his home government for appointment to some other post. This recall is formally verified in a letter addressed to the government to which the diplomat has been accredited. It is presented in accordance with a prescribed procedure. In case the diplomat is declared persona non grata during his incumbency, the receiving government may request his recall. In extreme cases, should the sending government refuse to comply with a request for recall, the receiving government may dismiss the diplomat.

Consular credentials are somewhat less complex. Upon appointment the consular official, like the diplomat, is commissioned by his home government. Concomitantly,

the foreign government, to whose territory he is assigned,
supplies him with an "exequatur," which authorizes him
to perform his duties within the jurisdiction of that foreign
state.

Privileges and immunities granted to diplomats are
not enjoyed by the ordinary alien.   In the past these special
arrangements were based largely upon general principles
of customary international law and often were implemented
by the municipal (national) law of a state.   In recent times,
however, they have been incorporated into a multilateral
convention.   Consular privileges and immunities, on the
other hand, have usually been founded on conventional international law and are prescribed in detail in consular conventions. [32]

PRINCIPLES OF DIPLOMATIC REPRESENTATION:
VIENNA CONVENTION OF 1961[33]

Article 4.

1.   The sending state must make certain that the agrément of the receiving state has been given for the person
it proposes to accredit as head of the mission to that
state.

2.   The receiving state is not obligated to give reasons
to the sending state for a refusal of agrément.

Article 6.

Two or more states may accredit the same person as
head of mission to another state, unless objection is offered
by the receiving state.

Article 9.

1.   The receiving state may at any time and without
having to explain its decision, notify the sending state that
the head of the mission or any member of the diplomatic

staff of the mission is <u>persona</u> <u>non</u> <u>grata</u> or that any other member of the staff of the mission is not acceptable.   In any such case, the sending state shall, as appropriate, either recall the person concerned or terminate his func- tions with the mission.   A person may be declared <u>non</u> <u>grata</u> or not acceptable before arriving in the territory of the receiving state.

2. If the sending state refuses or fails within a reason- able period to carry out its obligations under paragraph 1 of this article, the receiving state may refuse to recognize the person concerned as a member of the mission.

Article 11.

1. In the absence of specific agreement as to the size of the mission, the receiving state may require that the size of a mission be kept within limits considered by it to be reasonable and normal, having regard to circum- stances and conditions in the receiving state and to the needs of the particular mission.

2. The receiving state may equally, within similar bounds and on a non-discriminatory basis, refuse to accept officials of a particular category.

Article 14.

1. Heads of mission are divided into three classes, namely:
    (a) that of ambassadors or nuncios accredited to Heads of State, and other heads of mission of equivalent rank;
    (b) that of envoys, ministers and internuncios accred- ited to Heads of State;
    (c) that of <u>chargé d'affaires</u> accredited to Ministers for Foreign Affairs.

2. Except as concerns precedence and etiquette, there shall be no differentiation between heads of mission by rea- son of their class.

Article 15.

The class to which the heads of their missions are to be

assigned shall be agreed between states.

Article 18.

The procedure to be observed in each state for the reception of heads of mission shall be uniform in respect of each class.

Article 21.

1. The receiving state shall either facilitate the acquisition on its territory, in accordance with its laws, by the sending state of premises necessary for its mission or assist the latter in obtaining accommodation in some other way.

2. It shall also, where necessary, assist missions in obtaining suitable accommodation for their members.

Article 43.

The function of a diplomatic agent comes to an end inter alia;

    (a) on notification by the sending state to the receiving state that the function of the diplomatic agent has come to an end.

    (b) on notification by the receiving state to the sending state that, in accordance with paragraph 2 of Article 9, it refuses to recognize the diplomatic agent as a member of the mission.

Article 46.

A sending state may, with the prior consent of a receiving state, and at the request of a third state not represented in the receiving state, undertake the temporary protection of interests of the third state and of its nationals.

2. RULES OF DIPLOMATIC PRECEDENCE[34]

... The Department has adopted the following rules,
based upon those laid down at the Congress of Vienna and
the Congress of Aix-la-Chapelle, on the precedence and
relative rank of diplomatic representatives of the various
nations:
(a) Order of Precedence. The order of precedence is:
   (1) Ambassadors extraordinary and plenipotentiary.
   (2) Envoys extraordinary and ministers plenipotentiary.
   (3) Ministers resident.
   (4) Chargés d'affaires ad hoc.
   (5) Chargés d'affaires ad interim.

(b) Precedence among representatives of the same rank.
   Diplomatic representatives take precedence in their
   respective classes according to the date of the official notification of their arrival.

3. AGRÉMENT: UNITED STATES PROCEDURE[35]

Upon the appointment of an ambassador or minister by
the President, inquiry is made through the Department of
State of the head of the government to which he is to be
accredited whether the appointment is agreeable to the
government. Upon the receipt of a reply in the affirmative,
the name of the ambassador or minister is sent by the
President to the Senate for confirmation of his appointment
in conformity with the provisions of Paragraph 2, Section
2, Article II of the Constitution of the United States.

4. AGRÉMENT: PERSONA NON GRATA[36]

...Our objections to Mr. Keiley's appointment as minister of the United States to the Imperial Court (of Austria-
Hungary) are founded upon want of political tact evinced on
his part on a former occasion, in consequence of which a
friendly power (Italy) declined to receive him; and upon the
certainty that his domestic relations preclude that reception
of him by Vienna society which we judge desirable for the
representative of the United States, with which power we
wish to continue the friendly relations existing between the
two governments.

5. LETTER OF CREDENCE OF AN AMBASSADOR[37]

(Name of President)
President of the United States of America

(address to head
of foreign country)

Great and Good Friend:
        I have made choice of (name of appointee)
as a distinguished citizen of the United States to reside
near the Government of Your Excellency in the quality of
Ambassador Extraordinary and Plenipotentiary of the United
States of America.   He is well informed of the relative
interests of the two countries and of the sincere desire
of this Government to cultivate to the fullest extent the
friendship which has long subsisted between them.   My
knowledge of his high character and ability gives me entire
confidence that he will constantly endeavor to advance the
interests and prosperity of both Governments and so render
himself acceptable to Your Excellency.

        I therefore request Your Excellency to receive him
favorably and to give full credence to what he shall say on
the part of the United States and to the assurances which I
have charged him to convey to you of the best wishes of this
Government for the prosperity of (name of foreign country).

May God have Your Excellency in His wise Keeping

Your Good Friend,

By the President: (Signature of President)

(Signature of Secretary
    of State)

Secretary of State

Washington, (Date).

6. DIPLOMATIC CREDENTIALS: PRESENTATION OF LETTER OF CREDENCE--PROCEDURE IN UNITED STATES[38]

The newly-arrived Ambassador having called upon the Secretary of State and left a copy of his Letters of Credence with the Secretary, as well as a copy of the Letters of Recall of his predecessor and a copy of the remarks he will make upon the occasion of presenting his Letters of Credence to the President, an appointment for his reception by the President is made by the Chief of Protocol of the Department of State through the Executive Office. The appointed Ambassador is in due time notified of the day and hour upon which the President will receive him, and, at that time, he is called for at the Embassy by the Chief of Protocol accompanied by either the senior Military or Naval White House Aide (in full-dress uniform) in the President's automobile. The Department of State provides such other cars as may be necessary to accommodate the staff .... the Ambassador, in full uniform or formal day dress, awaits them with all the members of his staff (also in full uniform or formal day dress)...

Upon the arrival of the party at the White House four White House Aides are awaiting the Ambassador in the entrance hall, and will precede the party into the Green Room.

When the President is ready and standing in the center of the Blue Room, with the Military and Naval Aides to his

right and left, a junior White House Aide announces to the
Chief of Protocol that the President will be pleased to receive the Ambassador.   The Ambassador, with the Chief
of Protocol walking at his left, then enters the Blue Room
by way of the corridor preceded by four White House Aides
who take position uncovered in the Blue Room on either
side of the entrance, the senior to the right of the President.   The Chief of Protocol at the same time presents
him to the President, using his full title.

The Ambassador then advances to where the President
stands and shakes hands with him.   He then presents his
Letters of Credence and a copy of the remarks which he
has prepared.   In return he is handed a copy of the President's remarks in reply.   It should be noted that the remarks are not read.   An informal conversation follows,
after which the Ambassador asks permission to present
his staff to the President. . . .

Formal leave is then taken by the Ambassador. . . .

7. DIPLOMATIC CREDENTIALS: PRESENTATION OF LETTER OF CREDENCE--PROCEDURE FOR AMERICAN DIPLOMAT ABROAD[39]

. . . Upon the arrival at the seat of mission, the newly
appointed diplomatic representative shall request, through
the actual incumbent of the mission, an informal conference
with the Minister for Foreign Affairs, or such other officer
of the government to which he is accredited as may be
found authorized to act in the premises, in order to arrange
for his official reception.   He shall at the same time, in
his own name, address a formal note to the Minister for
Foreign Affairs, communicating the fact of his appointment
and requesting the designation of a time and place for presenting his letter of credence and the letter of recall of
his predecessor.

When the representative is accredited by the President
to the Chief of State, he shall, on requesting audience for
the purpose of presenting the original sealed letter of
credence in person, communicate to the Minister for

Foreign Affairs the open office copy thereof accompanying
his original instructions.

If the diplomatic representative be of the rank of chargé
d'affaires, bearing a letter of credence addressed to the
Minister for Foreign Affairs, he shall, on addressing to
the Minister the formal note, convey to him the office copy
of his letter of credence and shall await the Minister's
pleasure for presentation of the original.

... On the occasion of presenting letters of credence it
is usual at most capitals for the incoming diplomatic representative to make a brief address.   A representative of
the United States delivering such address shall write and
speak it in English.   A copy of the address should be furnished the Minister for Foreign Affairs in advance.   Copies
of the address and of the reply must be sent to the Department.

... The newly appointed diplomatic representative should
be accompanied by all Foreign Service officers assigned to
the mission in a diplomatic capacity and by all attachés
of the mission when presenting his letter of credence.

8. DIPLOMATIC CREDENTIALS: FULL POWER TO NEGOTIATE[40]

PRESIDENT OF THE UNITED STATES OF AMERICA

To all to whom these presents shall come, Greeting:

KNOW YE, That reposing special trust and confidence in the integrity, prudence, and ability of_____

Delegates of the United States of America to the_____ International Conference of American States which is to con- vene at_____on or about_____, I have in- vested them jointly and severally with full and all manner of power and authority for and in the name of the United States of America to meet and confer with any person or persons duly authorized by the respective Governments of the States represented at the said Conference, being invested with like power and authority, and with the said person or persons to negotiate, conclude, and sign any treaty, con- vention, or other act which may be agreed on at the said Conference.

IN TESTIMONY WHEREOF, I have caused the Seal of the United States of America to be hereunto affixed.

DONE at the city of Washington this_____day of_____ in the year of our Lord_____ _____and of the Independence of the United States of America the_____.

By the President:

Secretary of State

9. DIPLOMATIC CREDENTIALS:
FULL POWER TO SIGN SURRENDER INSTRUMENT[41]

HIROHITO,

By the Grace of Heaven, Emperor of Japan, seated on the Throne occupied by the same Dynasty changeless through ages eternal,

To all to whom these Presents shall come, Greeting!

We do hereby authorise Mamoru Shigemitsu, Zyosanmi, First Class of the Imperial Order of the Rising Sun to attach his signature by command and in behalf of Ourselves and Our Government unto the Instrument of Surrender which is required by the Supreme Commander for the Allied Powers to be signed.

In witness whereof, We have hereunto set Our signature and caused the Great Seal of the Empire to be affixed.

Given at Our Palace in Tōkyō, this first day of the ninth month of the twentieth year of Syowa, being the two

---

thousand six hundred and fifth year from the Accession of the Emperor Zinmu.

Signed: HIROHITO

Seal of

the

Empire   Countersigned: Naruhiko-ō
                                        Prime Minister

(Translation of Foreign Minister Shigemitsu's Credentials)

10. RESIGNATION OF DIPLOMAT:
LETTER TO THE PRESIDENT[42]

Dear Mr. President:

When my service as Personal Representative of the President to the Pope was undertaken at Christmas time in 1939, it was regarded by President Franklin D. Roosevelt and by myself as a temporary mission, to be terminated when circumstances permitted. At the end of hostilities, you asked me to continue this service and I was happy to do so, again on a temporary basis. To my great regret, personal considerations of a compelling nature make in necessary for me now to ask to be released from this service. Accordingly, I hereby tender my resignation as Personal Representative of the President of the United States of America to Pope Pius XII.

The mission arose because of the war and of the vital interests of the United States in the reestablishment, when hostilities ended, of world peace on a surer foundation....

I visited Rome for President Roosevelt seven times in the years 1940-1945. The activities of my mission in this period were indicated in Wartime Correspondence Between President Roosevelt and Pope Pius XII, which was published in 1947 with your approval and that of His Holiness.

. . . .

The continuance of the mission beyond the close of hostilities is a part of the history of the struggle for an enduring peaceful world order that the free nations have unflaggingly made in the presence of adverse and discouraging circumstances....

Six visits followed, the first in the spring of 1946, the last in November and December, 1949. These visits were concerned primarily with the continuing problems of attaining a peaceful and advancing world in accordance with Christian principles, and with the new problems of sustaining the hopes of the enslaved victims of communist tyranny....

It is a matter of particular regret to me that I find it necessary to withdraw from official service in this field at

a time when the great objectives sought by you and your
predecessor are as yet not fully attained. . . .

In returning to private life, I wish to express my pro-
found appreciation of the opportunity given me over the last
ten years to serve, under the wise leadership of two Presidents of the United States, in behalf of the cause of peace
and humanity for which the free world fought the war and
which it upholds today. . . .

So far as my abilities and my remaining years permit,
I shall endeavor, as a private citizen, to devote myself
to the taks of helping to strengthen cooperation and unity
among all the moral forces working for a better world.

With high esteem and affectional regard, believe me

Faithfully yours,

MYRON C. TAYLOR

11. LETTER OF RECALL OF DIPLOMAT[43]

(Name of President)
PRESIDENT OF THE UNITED STATES OF AMERICA

To His Majesty
  (Name of Monarch)
    of Great Britain, Ireland and the British Dominions
    beyond the Seas, King, etc. , etc. , etc.

Great and Good Friend:

Mr. _____, who has for some time been
the Ambassador Extraordinary and Plenipotentiary of the
United States of America to _____, having been
transferred to another post, and being unable to present
his letter of recall in person, I have entrusted to his
successor the duty of placing it in the hands of Your Majesty.

I am pleased to believe that Mr. _____, during his mission, devoted all his efforts to strengthening the good understanding and the friendly relations existing between the Governments of the United States of America and _____, and I entertain the hope that while fulfilling satisfactorily the trust imposed upon him he succeeded in gaining Your Majesty's esteem and good will.

                                    Your Good Friend,
                                    (Signature)

By the President:

            Secretary of State.
Washington, (Date)

12. LETTER OF RECALL: PROCEDURE IN UNITED STATES[44]

All plenipotentiary representatives--both Ambassadors and Ministers--present their Letters of Credence to the President at a formal audience at the White House, but it is the exception rather than the rule for a retiring Ambassador or Minister to present in person his Letter of Recall, such being usually presented by his successor at the time of the presentation of his Letter of Credence.

It has been the practice of the President, during this Administration at least, to receive Ambassadors, upon the relinquishment of their plenipotentiary capacity, in equally formal audience at the White House, whether they present at that time their Letters of Recall or merely take formal leave of the President. Irrespective of the practice followed in previous Administrations, it is my impression and recollection that at least one Minister who presented in person his Letter of Recall was received by the President at the Executive Office, and that an Assistant Secretary of State was present during the interview: all Ministers desiring to take final leave of the President without presentation of Letter of Recall have also been received at the Executive Office.

In view of the fact that the presentation of a Letter of
Recall by a departing plenipotentiary representative may be
considered as a ceremonial almost equal in importance
with the presentation of a Letter of Credence, I therefore
suggest, for the consideration of the President, that the
following procedure be adopted, which, it is hoped, will
occasion the President no additional inconvenience, and
which will more nearly accord with the general practice of
nations upon such ceremonial occasions:

1. That, as heretofore, presentation of all Letters of
Credence take place at formal audience at the White House.
2. That presentation, in person, by Ambassadors Extraordinary and Plenipotentiary, and by Envoys Extraordinary
and Ministers Plenipotentiary of their Letters of Recall,
take place at formal audience at the White House.
3. That Ambassadors, when taking formal and final
leave of the President, without presentation of Letters of
Recall, be received in formal audience at the White House.
4. That Envoys Extraordinary and Ministers Plenipotentiary when taking final and formal leave of the President,
without presentation of their Letters of Recall, be received
at the Executive Office, and that an appropriate officer of
the Executive Office and be present during the interview.
5. That the formalities to be observed at such ceremonies as shall take place at the White House shall be identical
with those observed upon the occasion of the presentation
of Letters of Credence by such officers-- with the exception
that in no case shall the retiring Chief of Mission be
accompanied by any member of his staff.

13. REQUEST FOR RECALL OF DIPLOMAT: PERSONA NON GRATA[45]

Mr. Constantin Dumba, the Austro-Hungarian Ambassador
at Washington, has admitted that he proposed to his Government plans to instigate strikes in American manufacturing
plants engaged in the production of munitions of war. The
information reached the Government through a copy of a
letter of the Ambassador to his Government. The bearer
was an American citizen named Archibald, who was traveling under an American passport. The Ambassador has admitted that he employed Archibald to bear official despatches

from him to his Government.

By reason of the admitted purpose and intent of Mr.
Dumba to conspire to cripple legitimate industries of the
people of the United States and to interrupt their legitimate
trade, and by reason of the flagrant violation of diplomatic
propriety in employing an American citizen protected by
an American passport as a secret bearer of official despatches through the lines of the enemy of Austria-Hungary,
the President directs me to inform your excellency that Mr.
Dumba is no longer acceptable to the Government of the
United States as the Ambassador of His Imperial Majesty
at Washington.

Believing that the Imperial and Royal Government will
realize that the Government of the United States has no
alternative but to request the recall of Mr. Dumba on
account of his improper conduct, the Government of the
United States expresses its deep regret that this course
has become necessary and assures the Imperial and Royal
Government that it sincerely desires to continue the cordial
and friendly relations which exist between the United States
and Austria-Hungary.

14. DISMISSAL OF DIPLOMAT: <u>PERSONA NON GRATA</u>[46]

My Lord: The President of the United States has instructed me to inform you that for good and sufficient causes,
which are known to yourself, and have been duly brought to
the knowledge of your government, he has with great regret
become convinced that it would be incompatible with the
best interests and detrimental to the good relations of both
Governments that you should any longer hold your present
official position in the United States, and that accordingly
the Government of Her Britannic Majesty will without delay
be informed of this determination, in order that another
channel may be established for the transmission of such
communications as may be found desirable by two Governments in the transaction of their business.

Whenever it is your pleasure to depart from the United
States, I am instructed to furnish you with the usual facili-

ties, and with that view I now beg leave to inclose a passport in the customary form.

15. COMMISSION OF APPOINTMENT AS FOREIGN SERVICE OFFICER[47]

THE PRESIDENT OF THE UNITED STATES OF AMERICA

To _____ Greeting:

Reposing special trust and confidence in your Integrity, Prudence and Ability, I do appoint you a Foreign Service Officer _____ of the United States of America and do authorize and empower you to do and perform all such matters and things as to the said office do appertain and to hold and exercise the said office during the pleasure of the President of the United States and until the end of the next Session of the Senate of the United States and no longer.

In testimony whereof, I have caused the Seal of the United States to be hereunto affixed.

Done at the City of Washington this _____ day of _____ in the year of our Lord one thousand nine hundred and _____ and of the Independence of the United States of America the one hundred and _____

By the President:

_____
Secretary of State

(Great Seal of the
United States)

16. COMMISSION OF APPOINTMENT AS DIPLOMATIC OFFICER[48]

THE PRESIDENT OF THE UNITED STATES OF AMERICA

To _____
a Foreign Service Officer of the United States of America, Greeting:

Reposing special trust and confidence in your Integrity, Prudence and Ability, I do appoint you a Secretary in the Diplomatic Service of the United States of America, and do authorize and empower you to have and to hold the said office and to exercise and enjoy all the rights, privileges and immunities thereunto during the pleasure of the President of the United States and until the end of the next session of the Senate of the United States and no longer.

In testimony whereof, I have caused the Seal of the United States to be hereunto affixed.

Done at the City of Washington this _____ day of _____
in the year of our Lord one thousand nine hundred and _____
and of the Independence of the United
States the one hundred and _____

By the President

Secretary of State

(Great Seal of the
United States)

17. COMMISSION OF APPOINTMENT AS CONSULAR OFFICER[49]

The PRESIDENT OF THE UNITED STATES OF AMERICA

To _____

a Foreign Service Officer of the United States of America, Greeting:

Reposing special trust and confidence in your Integrity, Prudence and Ability, I do appoint you a _____ Consul _____ of the United States of America, and do authorize and empower you to have and to hold the said office and to exercise and enjoy all the rights, privileges and immunities thereunto during the pleasure of the President of the United States and until the end of the next session of the Senate of the United States and no longer.

In testimony whereof, I have caused the Seal of the United States to be hereunto affixed.

Done at the City of Washington this _____ day of _____ in the year of our Lord one thousand nine hundred and _____ and of the Independence of the United States the one hundred and _____

By the President:

Secretary of State

(Great Seal of
the United States)

18. DIPLOMATIC PRIVILEGES AND IMMUNITIES: VIENNA CONVENTION OF 1961[50]

Article 22.

1. The premises of the (diplomatic) mission shall be inviolable. The agents of the receiving state may not enter them, except with the consent of the head of the mission.

2. The receiving state is under a special duty to take all appropriate steps to protect the premises of the mission against any intrusion or damage and to prevent any disturbance of the peace of the mission or impairment of its dignity.

3. The premises of the mission, their furnishings and other property thereon and the means of transport of the mission shall be immune from search, requisition, attachment or execution.

Article 23.

1. The sending state and the head of the mission shall be exempt from all national, regional or municipal dues and taxes in respect of the premises of the mission, whether owned or leased, other than such as represent payment for specific services rendered.

Article 24.

The archives and documents of the mission shall be inviolable at any time and wherever they may be.

Article 27.

1. The receiving state shall permit and protect free communication on the part of the mission for all official purposes. . . .

2. The official correspondence of the mission shall be inviolable. Official correspondence means all correspondence relating to the mission and its functions.

Article 29.

The person of a diplomatic agent shall be inviolable. He shall not be liable to any form of arrest or detention. The receiving state shall treat him with due respect and shall take all appropriate steps to prevent any attack on his person, freedom or dignity.

Article 30.

1. The private residence of a diplomatic agent shall enjoy the same inviolability and protection as the premises of the mission.

2. His papers, correspondence and, except as provided (herein), his property, shall likewise enjoy inviolability.

Article 31.

1. A diplomatic agent shall enjoy immunity from the criminal jurisdiction of the receiving state. He shall also enjoy immunity from its civil and administrative jurisdiction, except (three exemptions are specified)...

2. A diplomatic agent is not obliged to give evidence as a witness.

Article 34.

A diplomatic agent shall be exempt from all dues and taxes, personal or real, national, regional or municipal, except: (Exceptions are specified)...

Article 36.

1. The receiving state shall, in accordance with such laws and regulations as it may adopt, permit entry of and grant exemption from all customs duties, taxes, and related charges other than charges for storage, cartage and similar services, on:

(a) articles for the official use of the mission;

(b) articles for the personal use of a diplomatic agent
or members of his family forming part of his house-
hold, including articles intended for his establishment.

2. The personal baggage of a diplomatic agent shall be
exempt from inspection...

Article 41.

1. Without prejudice to their privileges and immunities,
it is the duty of all persons enjoying such privileges and
immunities to respect the laws and regulations of the receiving state. They also have a duty not to interfere in the
internal affairs of that state.

. . . .

3. The premises of the mission must not be used in
any manner incompatible with the functions of the mission
as laid down in the present Convention...

19. Consular Privileges and Immunities: Consular Convention[51]

PART III. LEGAL RIGHTS AND IMMUNITIES

Article 7.

(1) The sending state may acquire ... land, buildings,
parts of buildings, and appurtenances located in the territory and required by the sending state for the purpose of
a consular office, or of a residence for a consular officer
or employee, ...

Article 8.

(1) There may be placed, on the outer enclosure and
outer wall of the building in which a consulate is installed,
the coat-of-arms or national device of the sending state

with an appropriate inscription designating the consulate in
the official language of the sending state. . . .

(2) The flag of the sending state and its consular flag
may be flown at the consulate. . . .

(4) A consular office shall not be entered by the police
or other authorities of the territory, provided such office
is devoted exclusively to consular business, except with the
consent of the consular officer . . . The consent of the consular officer shall be presumed in the event of fire or other
disaster or in the event that the authorities of the territory
have probable cause to believe that a crime of violence has
been or is being or is about to be committed in the consular
office. . . .

(5) Neither a consular office, nor the flag of the sending state, shall be used to afford asylum to fugitives from
justice. . .

Article 10.

(1) The archives and all other official documents and
papers kept in a consulate shall at all times be inviolable
and the authorities of the territory may not under any pretext examine or detain any of them . . .

(2) A consular officer may communicate with his government, or with the diplomatic mission under whose superin-
tendence he is, by post, telegraph, telephone and wireless,
. . . In addition, he may send and receive official correspondence by sealed consular pouches, bags, and other con-
tainers and may use secret language. . . .

(3) The official consular correspondence referred to in
the preceding paragraph shall be inviolable and the authorities of the territory shall not examine or detain it. . . .

(4) A consular officer or employee shall be entitled to
refuse a request from the courts or authorities of the
territory to produce any documents from his archives or
other official papers or to give evidence relating to matters
within the scope of his official duties.   Such a request
shall, however, be complied with in the interests of justice
if, in the judgment of the consular officer or employee, it
is possible to do so without prejudicing the interests of the
sending state. . .

Article 11.

(1) (a) A consular officer or employee shall not be liable, in proceedings in the courts of the receiving state, in respect of acts performed in his official capacity, falling within the functions of a consular officer under this Convention, unless the sending state requests or assents to the proceedings through its diplomatic representative.

. . . .

(2) It is understood that the provisions of paragraph (1) (a) of this Article do not preclude a consular officer or employee from being held liable in a civil action arising out of a contract concluded by him in which he did not expressly contract as agent for his government and in which the other party looked to him personally for performance, ...

(3) A consular officer or employee may be required to give testimony in either a civil or a criminal case, except as provided in paragraph (4) of Article 10. The authorities and court requiring his testimony shall take all reasonable steps to avoid interference with the performance of his official duties. The court requiring the testimony of a consular officer shall, wherever possible or permissible, arrange for the taking of such testimony, orally or in writing, at his residence or office.

(Followed by listing of financial privileges.)

Documents Relating to International Conferences

Over the past century and a half international relations
have tended to become more and more multilateral in nature.
As a consequence, bilateral direct negotiation has been supplemented by conference diplomacy.   Following are a number of illustrative documents in relation to diplomacy by
conference.   This aspect of diplomacy is discussed in more
detail in Chapter III.

1. INVITATION TO ATTEND INTERNATIONAL CONFERENCE:
SELECT ILLUSTRATIONS[52]

A.

The Secretary of State presents his compliments to
their Excellencies and Messieurs the Chiefs of Mission whose
Governments are indicated on the attached list and has the
honor to call attention to the invitation which this Government has extended to their respective Governments to be
represented at an International Wheat Conference which will
be convened at Washington, D. C. , on January 25, 1949.

The Chiefs of the respective United States Missions
have been requested to communicate this invitation to the
Governments to which they are accredited.

This Conference is being convened to negotiate a new
international wheat agreement.

.   .   .   .

(List of 60 missions not included)

B.

The Economic and Social Council, taking note of the
declaration proposed jointly by the delegations of Brazil
and China at San Francisco, which was unanimously approved,
regarding an International Health Conference, and recogniz-
ing the urgent need for international action in the field of

public health,

1. decides to call an international conference to consider the scope of, and the appropriate machinery for, international action in the field of public health and proposals for the establishment of a single international health organization of the United Nations;

2. urges the Members of the United Nations to send as representatives to this conference experts in public health;

3. established a Technical Preparatory Committee to prepare a draft annotated agenda and proposals for the consideration of the Conference, ...

. . . .

6. instructs the Secretary-General to call the Conference not later than 20 June 1946, and, in consultation with the President of the Council, to select the place of meeting.

C.

The Government of the United States of America, on behalf of itself and of the Governments of the United Kingdom of Great Britain and Northern Ireland, the Union of Soviet Socialist Republics, and the Republic of China invites the Government of (name of Government invited was inserted here) to send representatives to a conference of the United Nations to be held on April 25, 1945, at San Francisco in the United States of America to prepare a charter for a general international organization for the maintenance of international peace and security.

The above-named Governments suggest that the conference consider as affording a basis for such a charter the proposals for the establishment of a general international organization, which were made public last October as a result of the Dumbarton Oaks Conference, ...

Further information as to arrangements will be transmitted subsequently.

In the event that the Government of (name of Government invited was inserted here) desires in advance of the Conference to present views or comments concerning the proposals, the Government of the United States of America will be pleased to transmit such views and comments to the other participating Government.

D.

WHEREAS:

On the supposition that the war may continue for a more or less extended period, and the state of emergency which now exists may, a year hence, have become accentuated or that there may exist an abnormal post-war situation which may require consideration,

The Meeting of the Foreign Ministers of the American Republics

RESOLVES:

To suggest to the respective governments the desirability of having their Ministers of Foreign Affairs meet in the City of Habana, capital of the Republic of Cuba, on October 1, 1940, without prejudice to an earlier meeting if this should be found necessary.

(Approved October 3, 1939.)

2. CONFERENCE STRUCTURE:
SAN FRANCISCO CONFERENCE, 1945 (Simplified)[53]

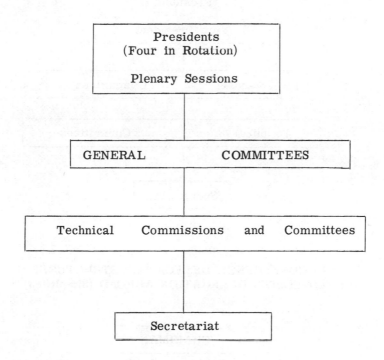

3. CONFERENCE DELEGATION STRUCTURE: UNITED STATES AS HOST STATE (Simplified)[54]

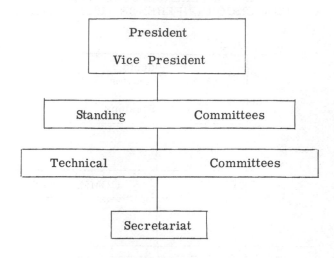

4. CONFERENCE DELEGATION STRUCTURE: UNITED STATES DELEGATION ABROAD (Simplified)[55]

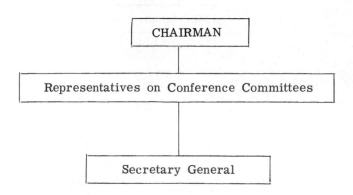

5. CONFERENCE CHAIRMANSHIP:
SELECT ILLUSTRATIONS[56]

A.

Section 1.   Temporary President

Art. 1.   The President of the Republic of Uruguay shall
designate the temporary president who shall preside at the
opening session and shall continue to preside until the Conference elects a permanent president.

Section II.   Permanent President

Art. 2.   The permanent president of the Conference
shall be elected by an absolute majority of the states represented at the Conference.

Section III.   Vice Presidents

Art. 4.   In the first session there shall be settled by
lot the numerical order of the delegations for the purpose
of establishing the order of precedence of their location.   In
this order the presidents of the delegations shall be called
to occupy the chair in the absence of the president as provided by these regulations.

B.

There shall be four Presidents (representing the U. S. ,
U. K. , U. S. S. R. , and China) who will preside in rotation
at the plenary sessions.   These four may meet from time
to time, with Mr. Stettinius presiding over the meetings and
Mr. Stettinius to be Chairman of the Executive and Steering
Committees, the three others delegating full powers to Mr.
Stettinius for conducting the business of the Conference.

C.

Adolf A. Berle, Jr. , Chairman of the Delegation of the
United States of America, was elected Permanent President
of the Conference at the Second Plenary Session, held on
November 2, 1944.

Max Hymans, Chairman of the Delegation of France, and Kia-ngau Chang, Chairman of the Delegation of China, were elected Vice Presidents of the Conference.

D.

The post of President of the Conference was originally occupied by His Excellency Laureano Gómez, the Minister of Foreign Affairs of Colombia, and subsequently by His Excellency Eduardo Zuleta Angel, who succeeded him in the aforesaid Ministry.

6. CONFERENCE SECRETARY GENERAL: SELECT ILLUSTRATIONS[57]

A.

The Secretary General of the Conference shall be appointed by the President of the Republic of Brazil.

B.

In accordance with the Regulations, the Government of Colombia appointed His Excellency Camilo de Brigard Silva as Secretary General of the Conference.

C.

Warren Kelchner, Chief of the Division of International Conferences, Department of State of the United States, was designated, with the approval of the President of the United States, as Secretary General of the Conference; Frank Coe, Assistant Administrator, Foreign Economic Administration of the United States, as Technical Secretary General; and Philip C. Jessup, Professor of International Law at Columbia University, New York, New York, as Assistant Secretary General.

7. CONFERENCE AGENDA: SELECT ILLUSTRATIONS[58]

A.

Mr. Stettinius: Fellow Delegates, Ladies and Gentlemen, the Second Plenary Session of the United Nations Conference on International Organization is hereby convened.

The first part of our session this afternoon will be devoted to the business of organizing the Conference....

Mr. Belt (Rapporteur for delegations): Agenda of the Conference:
The meeting recommends that the Conference approve as its agenda the Dumbarton Oaks Proposals as supplemented at the Crimea Conference and by the Chinese proposals agreed to be all the sponsoring governments, and the comments thereon submitted by the participating countries.

Mr. Stettinius: Has any delegate any comment on this recommendation? If there is no comment, the recommendation stands approved.

B.

1. Complementary measures to intensify the cooperation in the war effort to complete victory.

2. Consideration of problems of international organization for the maintenance of peace and collective security.
   a) World organization;
   b) The further development of the inter-American system and its coordination with the world organization.

3. Consideration of the economic and social problems of the Americas.
   a) Economic cooperation during the war and in the transition period.
   b) Consideration of methods to develop such cooperation for the improvement of economic and social conditions of the peoples of the America, with a view to raising their standard of living.

C.

1. Opening Proceedings
2. Adoption of Rules of Procedure
3. Appointment of Credentials Committee
4. Report of Credentials Committee
5. Adoption of Provisional Agenda
6. Election of President
7. Election of Vice-Presidents
8. Presentation of the Report of the Technical Preparatory Committee by the Chairman (who will be accompanied by the Vice-Chairman and Rapporteur)
9. Statements by Delegates on the general attitudes of
   their Governments on the Report of the Technical
   Preparatory Committee.
10. Establishment of Committees
11. Final Consideration of Reports of Committees
12. Resolutions
13. Consideration of Draft Final Act and Protocols
14. Special Report of Legal Committee on Draft of Final
    Act and Protocols
15. Adoption of Final Act and Protocols
16. Signing of Final Act and Protocols

8. CONFERENCE PROCEDURE: FLOW CHART [59]

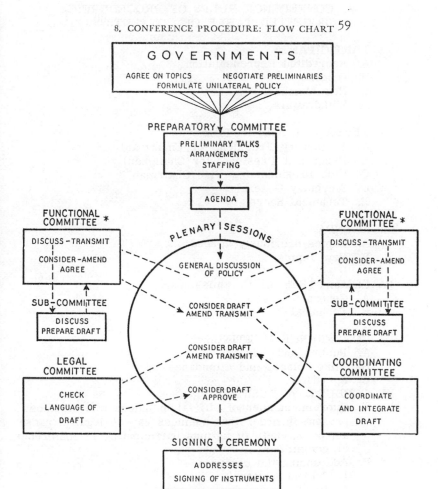

* There may be two or more functional committees, depending on conference organization.

9. CONFERENCE RULES OF PROCEDURE: SUGGESTED TABLE OF CONTENTS[60]

I. PARTICIPANTS
   A. Accredited Representation
   B. Others
   C. New Members
   D. Withdrawals

II. PERSONNEL AND DUTIES
   A. Temporary President (or Chairman)
   B. Permanent President (or Chairman)
   C. Vice President (or Vice Chairman)
   D. Secretary General
   E. Technical Secretary

III. AGENDA
   A. Topics previously agreed
   B. New Topics

IV. COMMITTEES (or Commissions)
   A. General
   B. Technical

V. CONFERENCE MEETINGS
   A. Public, and private
   B. Time, place, and attendance
   C. Agenda

VI. CONDUCT OF BUSINESS
   A. Quorum: number of official members who must be present in order that business can be legally transacted; majority of nations participating in conference, or committee
   B. Addressing the conference
      1. Subject matter
      2. Right
      3. Precedence
      4. Length of time
   C. Points of Order
   D. Submission, and handling of proposals, etc.
   E. Precedence, and handling of motions, resolution, etc.
   F. Invitations to non-members to attend conference to furnish information to conferees
   G. Measures to expedite conference work

VII. VOTING
   A. By Delegation
   B. Absentee Ballot
   C. On agenda subjects
   D. Proposals, Reports, and Projects

VIII. LANGUAGES
   A. Official
   B. Working
   C. Others

IX. RECORDS OF THE CONFERENCE
   A. Meetings
   B. Final Decision

X. ADOPTION, AND AMENDMENT OF RULES AND
   REGULATIONS
   A. Adoption
   B. Amendment

10. CONFERENCE RULES OF PROCEDURE: EXCERPTS[61]

3.
Opening Session

The first plenary session shall be opened by a representative of the country organizing the conference.

4.
Selection of the Chairman and the Vice-Chairman

The Chairman and the Vice-Chairman shall be selected at the first plenary session.

5.
General Secretariat

The first plenary session shall constitute a General Secretariat of the Conference consisting of employees of the Bureau of the Union and, if necessary, of employees of the administrations which are parties to the Convention.

7.
Appointment of Committees

The plenary session may establish committees to carry on the work of the Conference and submit questions to them for study. These committees may appoint subcommittees or sub-subcommittees.

10.
Minutes of Plenary Session

1. The minutes of plenary sessions shall be drafted by the General Secretariat.

2. As a general rule, the minutes shall include only proposals and conclusions, with the principal reasons relative thereto, in concise form.

14.
Order of Seating

In plenary sessions the delegations shall be seated according to the alphabetical order in the French language of the names of the countries represented.

15.
Order of Discussion

1. Persons desiring to speak may take the floor only after having obtained recognition from the Chairman. As a general rule, they shall begin by announcing the name of their country.

2. Any person having the floor must express himself slowly and distinctly, separating his words well and making frequent pauses, so as to make it possible for all his colleagues to understand his meaning clearly

19.
Voting in Plenary Sessions

1. For a valid vote to be taken at Plenary Sessions, at least onehalf of the delegations accredited to the Conference

and having the right to vote must be present or represented at the session during which the vote is cast.

2. In Plenary Sessions, no proposal or amendment shall be adopted unless it is supported by a majority of the delegations present and voting.   In determining the number of votes required for a majority, abstentions shall not be taken into account.   In case of a tie the measure shall be considered rejected.

3. Exceptions to the above rule shall be made with respect to proposals to admit, suspend, or exclude a country (in connection with the list of countries in Article 18 entitled to participate and vote in the Conference) and proposals to move the seat of the Union.   In such cases, a 2/3 majority of the positive and negative votes cast shall be required.

4. If the number of abstentions exceeds 50% of the delegations present and voting, the measure shall be reconsidered at a subsequent meeting.

23.
Drafting Committee

1. After the texts have been drafted as nearly as possible in final form by the committees, they shall be submitted to a drafting committee charged with perfecting the form thereof without modifying the meaning.

2. The complete text, after having been properly edited, shall be submitted to the Plenary Assembly for consideration on a first reading.

24.
Final Approval

The vote of the conference shall be final only after a second reading of the complete set of texts, followed by their approval.

26.
Signature

The documents resulting from the deliberations of the

conference shall be submitted for signature to the delegates provided with the necessary powers, following the alphabetical order in the French language of the names of the countries.

11. CONFERENCE VOTING FORMULAE: SELECT ILLUSTRATIONS[62]

A.

1. Each Delegation shall have one vote in each body of the Conference on which it is represented.

2. Any question of procedure put to the vote shall be decided by a majority of the votes of the Delegations present and voting.   All other questions put to the vote shall be decided by two-thirds of the votes of the Delegations present and voting.

3. If there is a substantial degree of uncertainty prior to a vote on any given question as to whether that question is or is not one of procedure, the Presiding Officer of the body concerned shall submit the question to the Executive Committee, which shall decide.

4. The Conference shall normally vote by a show of hands except that any Delegation in any body of the Conference may request a roll call, which shall then be taken by countries in English alphabetical order.....

B.

(a) Plenary Conference.
   The decisions of the Conference on questions of procedure shall be taken by a simple majority.

   The decisions concerning all other questions shall be taken by two-thirds majority of the votes cast.

   The recommendations of the Plenary Conference shall be of two kinds:

1) Recommendations adopted by a <u>two-thirds majority</u> of members of the Conference.
2) Recommendations which have secured more than half, but less than two-thirds of the votes of members of the Conference.

Both kinds of recommendation shall be submitted for the consideration of the Council of Foreign Ministers.

C.

Article 29

In the deliberations in the plenary sessions as well as in the committees, the delegation of each Republic represented at the Conference shall have but one vote, and the votes shall be taken separately by countries and shall be recorded in the minutes.

Votes as a general rule shall be taken orally, unless any delegate should request that they be taken in writing. In this case each delegation shall deposit in an urn a ballot containing the name of the nation which it represents and the sense in which the vote is cast. The Secretary shall read aloud these ballots and count the votes.

Article 30

The Conference shall not proceed to vote on any report, project, or proposal relating to any of the subjects included in the program except when at least two thirds of the nations attending the Conference are represented by one or more delegates. In the voting account shall be taken of the votes sent in writing as provided for in articles 24 and 34, the absent delegations being considered present, only for the purposes of the vote, when they have submitted their vote in the manner indicated.

Article 34

Except in cases expressly indicated in these regulations, proposals, reports and projects under consideration by the Conference shall be considered approved when they have obtained the affirmative vote of an absolute majority of the delegations represented by one or more of their members

at the meeting where the vote is taken.   The delegation which
may have sent its vote to the Secretary shall be considered
as present at the meeting.

12. CONFERENCE COMMITTEE ACTION:
VERBATIM MINUTES[63]

President (Mr. Para Pérez, Venezuela, of Commission
IV, on Judicial Organization) (Speaking in French; English
version as delivered by interpreter follows): If there are no
remarks, Article 68 is also approved.

We now come to the Statute of the International Court
of Justice.   As you know, this Statute is composed of 70
different articles in five different chapters.   The text of
the Statute has been circulated in both languages and if no-
body requests that it should be read, we shall not read it,
and I shall open discussion of the whole of the Statute.

Mr. Aglion (France):   I ask for the floor.

President: I call on the delegate of France.

Mr. Aglion (speaking in French; English version as delivered by interpreter follows):   Only on a point of form Mr.
President.   I should like to point out that the French text of
the Statute, as circulated, does not include all the latest
amendments which were made on the French text, and I
understand that such a text, fully corrected, is now in existence, and it is that fully corrected text which we should
now be understood to approve.

President (speaking in French; English version as delivered by interpreter follows):   You have heard the remark
made by the Honorable Delegate of France.   I understand
that his remark should be applied-- should be understood to
apply-- to all the texts in the five languages.

No further remark?   I shall now submit the Statute of
the Court to your approval.   I take it that the text is unanimously approved.

Now that the Statute of the Court has been adopted by
the Commission, I should like to add a few words to say
how I view this decision of our Commission as both symbol-
ical and encouraging. The Statute of the Court has now
become the first text which received the full approval of a
plenary commission and will receive, undoubtedly, the full
approval of the Conference itself.

13. CONFERENCE PLENARY ACTION:
VERBATIM MINUTES[64]

Lord Halifax: ... Now, Ladies and Gentlemen of the
Conference, we come to the final action of this, the penul-
timate plenary session.   The rapporteurs of the four commissions and of the Steering Committee have reported on the
work of those bodies in the formulation of the provisions of
the Charter of the United Nations, including the Statute of
the International Court and the Agreement on Interim Arrangements, providing for the establishment of the Preparatory
Commission.   These texts have, I think been distributed to
delegates and it is now my duty, my honor, and my privilege
in the Chair, to call for a vote on the approval of the Charter of the United Nations, including the Statute of the International Court, and also of the Agreement on Interim Arrangements.   I feel, Ladies and Gentlemen, that in view of
the world importance of this vote that we are collectively
about to give, it would be appropriate to depart from the
usual method of signifying our feeling by holding up one hand.
If you are in agreement with me, I will ask the leaders of
delegations to rise in their places in order to record their
vote on an issue that I think is likely to be as important
as any of us in our lifetime are ever likely to vote upon.

If I have your pleasure, may I invite the leaders of
delegations who are in favor of the approval of the Charter
and the Statute and the Agreement on Interim Arrangements
to rise in their places and be good enough to remain standing while they are counted.
            (Vote taken.)
Thank you. Are there any against?

The Charter and the other documents are unanimously

approved.   (At this point the delegates and the entire audience rose and cheered.)

I think, Ladies and Gentlemen, we may all feel that
we have taken part, as we may hope, in one of the great
moments of history.

14. CONFERENCE FINAL ACT:
SELECT ILLUSTRATIONS[65]

A.

The Ninth International Conference of American States,
composed of the Delegations of (names of 21 states attending follow here) met at the City of Bogotá, Capital of the
Republic of Colombia, in accordance with· Resolution CVIII
of the Lima Conference, on March 30, 1948, the date fixed
by the Governing Board of the Pan American Union in
agreement with the Government of Colombia.

The following were the accredited Delegations, listed
in the order of precedence established at the preliminary
session:
(Delegation membership and Conference officers follow here.)

The Program and Regulations of the Conference were
approved by the Governing Board of the Pan American
Union at its meetings of July 23, 1947, and March 6, 1946,
respectively.
(Conference Committee structure follows here.)

As a result of its deliberations, in addition to the
Charter of the Organization of American States, the Amer-
ican Treaty on Pacific Settlement--the "Pact of Bogotá,"
the Economic Agreement of Bogotá the Inter-American Con-
vention on the Granting of Political Rights to Women, and
the Inter-American Convention on the Granting of Civil
Rights to Women, the Conference approved the following
Resolutions, Declarations, Recommendations, Agreements,
Votes and Motions:
(Texts follow here.)

IN WITNESS WHEREOF the respective Delegates Plenipotentiary sign and affix their seals to the present Final
Act, in the Spanish language, at Bogotá on May the second,
one thousand nine hundred forty-eight, which shall be deposited in the archives of the Pan American Union, where
it shall be sent by the Secretary General of the Conference,
in order that certified copies may be sent to the Governments of the American Republics.

(Signatures follow here.)

B.

The Economic and Social Council of the United Nations,
by a resolution dated February 18, 1946, resolved to call
an International Conference on Trade and Employment for
the purpose of promoting the expansion of the production,
exchange and consumption of goods.

The Conference, which met at Havana on November 21,
1947, and ended on March 24, 1948, drew up the Havana
Charter for an International Trade Organization to be submitted to the Governments represented. The text of the
Charter in the English and French languages is annexed
hereto and is hereby authenticated. The authentic text of
the Charter in the Chinese, Russian and Spanish languages
will be established by the Interim Commission of the International Trade Organization, in accordance with the procedure approved by the Conference.

There are also annexed to this Final Act a resolution
of the Conference establishing an Interim Commission of
the International Trade Organization and the other resolutions of the Conference.

This Final Act and the Documents annexed shall be
deposited with the Secretary-General of the United Nations,
who will send certified copies to each of the Governments
represented at the Conference.

IN WITNESS WHEREOF, the duly authorized representatives of their Governments have subscribed their names
below.

DONE at Havana, this twenty-fourth day of March,
one thousand nine hundred and forty-eight, in a single copy
in the Chinese, English, French, Russian and Spanish

languages.

(Here follow names of delegates.)

Documents Relating to Treaties

Negotiations leading to treaties are highly important within the scope of diplomatic activity. At times this process is detailed and complex. The documents given below portray some of the many facets of this process which is discussed more fully in Chapter III.

1. TREATY PRINCIPLES: INTER-AMERICAN CONVENTION[66]

Article 1. Treaties will be concluded by the competent authorities of the States or by their representatives, according to their respective internal law.

Article 2. The written form is an essential condition of treaties.

. . . .

Article 4. Treaties shall be published immediately after exchange of ratifications. The failure to discharge this international duty shall affect neither the force of treaties nor the fulfillment of obligations stipulated therein.

Article 5. Treaties are obligatory only after ratification by the contracting states, even though this condition is not stipulated in the full powers of the negotiators or does not appear in the treaty itself.

Article 6. Ratification must be unconditional and must embrace the entire treaty. It must be made in writing pursuant to the legislation of the state.

. . . .

Article 8. Treaties shall become effective from the date of exchange or deposit of ratification, unless some other date has been agreed upon through an express provision.

. . . .

Article 10. No state can relieve itself of the obligations of a treaty or modify its stipulations except by the agreement, secured through peaceful means, of the other contracting parties.

. . . .

Article 12. Whenever a treaty becomes impossible of execution through the fault of the party entering into the obligation, or through circumstances which at the moment of concluding it were under control of this party and unknown to the other party, the former shall be responsible for damages resulting from its non-execution.

. . . .

Article 14. Treaties cease to be effective:
a) When the stipulated obligation has been fulfilled;
b) When the length of time for which it was made has expired;
c) When the resolutory condition has been fulfilled;
d) By agreement between the parties;
e) By renunciation of the party exclusively entitled to a benefit thereunder;
f) By total or partial denunciation, if agreed upon;
g) When it becomes incapable of execution.

. . . .

Article 17. Treaties whose denunciation may have been agreed upon and those establishing rules or international law, can be denounced only in the manner provided thereby.

In the absence of such a stipulation, a treaty may be denounced by any contracting state, which state shall notify the others of this decision, provided it has complied with all obligations convenanted therein.

In this event the treaty shall become ineffective, as far as the denouncing state is concerned, one year after the last notification, and will continue in force for any other signatory states, if any.

2. UNITED STATES TREATY PROCEDURE[67]

Part 111--NEGOTIATION OF TREATIES

111.1 General provisions regarding the negotiation of treaties. Bilateral treaties to which the United States is one of the parties may be negotiated and concluded either at Washington or at the capital of the foreign country. When circumstance or convenience makes it desirable to negotiate and conclude a treaty at the capital of the other contracting party, the American diplomatic agent will be furnished with a full power from the President authorizing him to negotiate, conclude, and sign the treaty. If the proposal originates with the United States, there will also be furnished to the diplomatic agent a tentative draft of the proposed treaty for submission by him to the other government for its consideration. The diplomatic agent shall submit to the Department any modification of the draft or counter-proposal made by the other government and shall await instructions from the Department. If the original proposal emanates from a foreign government, the diplomatic agent shall forward the proposal to the Department and await its instructions. In no case shall a diplomatic agent sign a treaty until finally advised by the Department to do so after an accord has been reached. The treaty should then be signed in two originals, one for each government.

111.2 The principle of the "alternat." In the preparation of a treaty for signature, after an accord has been reached, the principle of the alternat should be observed, that is to say:

(a) When English and a language other than English are both used, the texts in the two languages should be placed either in parallel vertical columns on the same page, half the width of the page, or on opposite pages of the document, the entire width of the page. The former style is preferred, as it lends itself more conveniently to the binding and sealing of the treaty. If the two languages are placed in parallel columns on the same page, the English text should occupy the left-hand column of each page and the foreign text the right-hand column, in the original to be retained by the United States; in the original to be retained by the foreign government, the foreign text should occupy the left-hand column and the English text the right-hand column. If the two languages are placed on opposite pages of the document, the English text should occupy the left-hand page and the foreign text the right-hand page, in the United States' original, and conversely in the foreign government's original.

In certain oriental countries where by its nature the written language is not adapted to contracted space, the expedient may be resorted to of making and signing two separate originals in each language, but in no other case is this desirable or advisable.

(b) In the original to be retained by the United States, the United States and the plenipotentiary of the United States should be named first in both the English and the foreign texts wherever the names of the countries of the plenipotentiaries occur, and the signature of the plenipotentiary of the United States should appear above the signature of the foreign plenipotentiary. Conversely, in both texts throughout the original to be retained by the foreign government, that government and its plenipotentiary should be named first and the signature of the foreign plenipotentiary should appear above the signature of the plenipotentiary of the United States.

111.3 Conformity of texts. Before signing the treaty, the diplomatic agent of the United States shall see that the texts in the two languages of both originals of the prepared treaty are in exact conformity with the texts of the two languages in the drafts agreed upon, and that the foreign text is essentially in accord with the English text. The punctuation of the two texts should be brought into substantial conformity.

3. TREATY FORM: INTER-AMERICAN
PROTOCOLARY PRINCIPLES[68]

Article 42. The protocolary articles that shall be used in the treaties and conventions signed at the Conference (Lima, 1938) are appended to these regulations. The Conference may, if it deems it advisable, modify the wording of these protocolary articles.

Annex

Protocolary Articles

The preamble to treaties and conventions signed at the Conference shall be as follows:

The Governments represented at the Eighth International Conference of American States:
Wishing to conclude a treaty (convention) on . . . . ,
have appointed the following plenipotentiaries:
(Here shall follow the names of the plenipotentiaries.)
Who, after having deposited their full powers, found to be in good and due form, have agreed as follows:

ARTICLE I, ETC;

The concluding articles of treaties and conventions shall be as follows:

ARTICLE --

The present treaty (convention) shall be ratified by the high contracting parties in conformity with their respective constitutional procedures. The original instrument shall be deposited in the Ministry of Foreign Affairs of the Republic of Peru, which shall transmit authentic certified copies to the governments for the aforementioned purpose of ratification. The instruments of ratification shall be deposited in the archives of the Pan American Union in Washington, which shall notify the signatory governments of said deposit. Such notification shall be considered as an exchange of ratifications.

ARTICLE --

The present treaty (convention) will come into effect between the high contracting parties in the order in which they deposit their respective ratifications.

ARTICLE --

The present treaty (convention) shall remain in effect indefinitely, but may be denounced by means of one year's notice given to the Pan American Union, which shall transmit it to the other signatory governments. After the expiration of this period the treaty (convention) shall cease in its effects as regards the party which denounces it, but shall remain in effect for the remaining high contracting parties.

ARTICLE --

The present treaty (convention) shall be open to the adherence and accession of American states which may not have signed. The corresponding instruments shall be deposited in the archives of the Pan American Union, which shall communicate them to the other high contracting parties.

In witness whereof, the above-mentioned plenipotentiaries sign the present treaty (convention), and hereunto affix their respective seals, at the city of Lima, Capital of the Republic of Peru, on the ...... day of the month of ....

4. TREATY FORM: UNITED STATES INSTRUCTIONS[69]

The convention should be signed in two originals--one to be transmitted by you to the Department, and the other to be retained by the Argentine Government. The English and Spanish texts should be prepared in parallel columns on the same page. Separate copies in English and in Spanish are not advisable. In the signed original to be transmitted by you to the Department, the English text should occupy the left hand column, the United States should be named first throughout both texts in all places where the principle of the alternat is to be observed, and your signature should appear above that of the Argentine Plenipotentiary. Conversely, throughout the two texts of the signed original to be retained by the Argentine Government, the Spanish text should occupy the left hand column, Argentina

should be named first, and your signature should be subscribed below that of the Argenine Plenipotentiary.

5. TREATY APPROVAL: UNITED STATES RATIFICATION PROCEDURE[70]

111. 5 <u>Ratification of treaties</u>. After the signature of
a treaty, the original intended for the Government of the
United States shall be forwarded by the diplomatic agent to
the Secretary of State to be laid before the President and,
if approved, to be transmitted by him to the Senate to receive the advice and consent of the Senate to ratification.

Since all treaties signed on the part of the United States
are subject to ratification by and with the advice and consent of the Senate, and foreseen, it is preferred by this
Government that it be provided in the treaties signed on its
part that the exchange of ratifications shall be effected "as
soon as possible" rather than within a specified period.

111. 6 <u>Exchange of ratification</u>. Exchange of ratifications is effected by the plenipotentiary of the United States
handing to the plenipotentiary of the foreign government a
copy of the United States' original of the treaty ratified by
the President and the plenipotentiary of the foreign government handing to the plenipotentiary of the United States a
copy of the foreign government's original of the treaty ratified by the head of the foreign government.   A protocol
attesting the exchange of ratifications should be signed by
the two plenipotentiaries at the time the exchange is made.
The protocol should be signed in duplicate originals, one
for each government, in which the principle of the <u>alternat</u>
is observed the same as in the treaty.

Before making the exchange of ratifications the diplomatic agent of the United States shall satisfy himself that
the texts in the two languages as incorporated in the instrument of ratification of the foreign government are, with the
exception of the observance of the alternat, in exact conformity with the two texts as contained in the President's
instrument of ratification.

111. 7 <u>Date of Exchange to be cabled</u>. As most treaties
stipulate for their going into effect on the day of the exchange
of ratifications, the date of exchange and the date of the instrument of ratification of the foreign government shall be
cabled to the Department of State at once in order that the
treaty may be proclaimed by the President.   The instrument of ratification of the foreign government and one original of the signed protocol of exchange shall be forwarded
to the Department by the first following mail.

6. TREATY APPROVAL: SENATE RESOLUTION[71]

A.

<u>Resolved (two-thirds of the Senators present concurring
therein</u>), That the Senate advise and consent to the ratification of Executive A, Seventieth Congress, second session,
a multilateral treaty for renunciation of war, signed in Paris
August 27, 1928.   (Roll call vote-yeas 85, nay 1.)

B.

<u>Resolved (two-thirds of the Senators present concurring
therein</u>), That the Senate advise and consent to the ratification of Executive L, Eighty-first Congress, first session,
the North Atlantic Treaty, signed at Washington on April
4, 1949.   (Roll call vote--yeas 82, nays 13, not voting 1.)

7.   TREATY APPROVAL: CONGRESSIONAL ACT[72]

Resolved by the Senate and House of Representatives of
the United States of America in Congress assembled, That
the President is hereby authorized to approve, on behalf
of the United States, the trusteeship agreement between the
United States of America and the Security Council of the
United Nations for the former Japanese mandated islands (to

be known as the Territory of the Pacific Islands) which was approved by the Security Council at the seat of the United Nations, Lake Success, Nassau County, New York, on April 2, 1947.

Approved July 18, 1947.

8. TREATY APPROVAL: RESERVATIONS-- SELECT ILLUSTRATIONS[73]

A.

Nothing contained in this convention shall be so construed as to require the United States of America to depart from its traditional policy of not intruding upon, interfering with, or entangling itself in the political questions of policy or internal administration of any foreign State; nor shall anything contained in the said convention be construed to imply a relinguishment by the United States of its traditional attitude toward purely American questions.

B.

The United States understands that under the statement in the preamble or under the terms of this treaty there is no commitment to armed force, no alliance, no obligation to join in any defense.

C.

1. The ratification of this international sanitary convention (1926) is not to be construed to mean that the United States of America recognizes a régime or entity acting as government of a signatory or adhering power when that regime or entity is not recognized by the United States as the government of that power.

2. The participation of the United States of America in this international sanitary convention does not involve any contractual obligation on the part of the United States to a signatory or adhering power represented by a regime or

which the United States does not recognize as representing the government of that power until it is represented by a government recognized by the United States.

9. TREATY RATIFICATION: INSTRUMENT OF RATIFICATION[74]

CALVIN COOLIDGE, President of the United States of America

To all to whom these presents shall come, greeting:

. . . .

AND WHEREAS, the Senate of the United States, by their resolution of January 15, 1929, (two-thirds of the Senators present concurring therein) did advise and consent to the ratification of the said Treaty;

NOW THEREFORE, be it known that I, Calvin Coolidge, President of the United States of America, having seen and considered the said Treaty, do hereby, in pursuance of the aforesaid advice and consent of the Senate, ratify and confirm the same and every article and clause thereof.

IN TESTIMONY WHEREOF, I have caused the seal of the United States to be hereunto affixed.

DONE at the city of Washington this seventeenth day of January in the year of our Lord one thousand nine hundred and twenty-nine, and of the Independence of the United States of America the one hundred and fifty-third.

CALVIN COOLIDGE

By the President:

FRANK B KELLOGG
Secretary of State.

GASTON DOUMERGUE, President of the French Republic.

To all those who shall see these present letters, greeting:

The General Pact for Renunciation of War having been signed in Paris, August 27, 1928, which pact reads as follows:

(Here follows the text of the Treaty.)

We, having seen and examined the said pact, have approved and do approve it by virtue of the provisions of the law passed by the Senate and Chamber of Deputies; declare that it is accepted, ratified, and confirmed and promise that it shall be inviolably observed.

In faith whereof, we have given these presents sealed with the seal of the Republic.

At Paris, April 6, 1929.

GASTON DOUMERGUE
By the President of the
Republic:

(SEAL)   Minister for Foreign
Affairs
B (RIAND)

10. TREATY RATIFICATION: PROTOCOL OF RATIFICATION[75]

WHEREAS, paragraph 3 of Article 110 of the Charter of the United Nations, signed at San Francisco on June 26, 1945, provides as follows:

"3. The present Charter shall come into force upon the deposit of ratifications by the Republic of China, France, the Union of Soviet Socialist Republics, the United Kingdom of Great Britain and Northern Ireland, and the United States of America, and by a majority of the other signatory states. A protocol of the ratifications deposited shall thereupon be drawn up by the Government of the United States of America which shall communicate copies thereof to all the signatory states. ";

. . . .

AND WHEREAS, the requirements of paragraph 3 of Article 110 with respect to the coming into force of the Charter have been fulfilled by the deposit of the aforementioned instruments of ratification;

NOW THEREFORE, I, James F. Byrnes, Secretary of State of the United States of America, sign this Protocol in the English language, the original of which shall be deposited in the archives of the Government of the United States of America and copies thereof communicated to all the states signatory of the Charter of the United Nations.

DONE at Washington this twenty-fourth day of October, one thousand nine hundred forty five.

JAMES F. BYRNES
Secretary of State
of the United States of America

11. TREATY RATIFICATION: ACCESSION AND ADHERENCE[76]

1. Any member of the United Nations, not a signatory to the present Treaty, which is at war with Italy, and Albania, may accede to the Treaty and upon accession shall be deemed to be an Associated Power for the purposes of the Treaty.

2. Instruments of accession shall be deposited with the Government of the French Republic and shall take effect upon deposit.

B.

The Federal President of the Republic of Austria hereby declared his adherence in the name of the Republic of Austria, to the antiwar pact, signed on August 27, 1928, at Paris, by the plenipotentiaries of the German Reich, the United States of America, Belgium, the French Republic, the British Empire, Italy, Japan, Poland, and the Czechoslovak Republic, this pact having first been constitutionally ratified by the National Council, and the tenor thereof being as follows:

(Here follows the text of the treaty.)

and the promised conscientious observance of the pact on behalf of the said Republic.

In witness whereof the present instrument of adherence has been signed by the Federal President and countersigned by the Federal Chancellor, and the state seal of the Republic of Austria has been affixed thereto.

Done at Vienna, November 28, 1928.

The Federal President:
HAINISCH

The Federal Chancellor:
SEIPEL

12. PRESIDENTIAL TREATY PROCLAMATION[77]

. . . .

AND WHEREAS the Senate of the United States of America by their Resolution of July 28 (legislative day of July 9), 1945, two-thirds of the Senators present concurring therein, did advise and consent to the ratification of the said Charter, with annexed Statute;

AND WHEREAS the said Charter, with annexed Statute, was duly ratified by the President of the United States of America on August 8, 1945, in pursuance of the aforesaid advice and consent of the Senate;

AND WHEREAS it is provided by paragraph 3 of Article 110 of the said Charter that the Charter shall come into force upon the deposit of ratifications by the Republic of China, France, the Union of Soviet Socialist Republics, the United Kingdom of Great Britain and Northern Ireland, and the United States of America, and by a majority of the other signatory states, and that a protocol of the ratifications deposited shall thereupon be drawn up by the Government of the United States of America;

AND WHEREAS the Secretary of State of the United States of America signed on October 24, 1945 a protocol of deposit of ratifications of the Charter of the United Nations stating that the requirements of the said paragraph 3 of Article 110 with respect to the coming into force of the said Charter have been fulfilled by the deposit of instruments of ratification of the said Charter by the following states:
(Here follow names of states, with date of ratification.)

NOW, THEREFORE, be it known that I, Harry S. Truman, President of the United States of America, do hereby proclaim and make public the said Charter of the United Nations, with the Statute of the International Court of Justice annexed thereto, to the end that the same and every article and clause thereof may be observed and fulfilled with good faith, on and from the twenty-fourth day of October, one thousand nine hundred forty-five, by the United States of America and by the citizens of the United States of America and all other persons subject to the jurisdiction thereof.

IN TESTIMONY WHEREOF, I have hereunto set my hand and caused the Seal of the United States of America to be affixed.

DONE at the city of Washington this thirty-first day of October in the year of our Lord one thousand nine hundred forty-five and of the Independence of the United States of America the one hundred seventieth.

                                        HARRY S TRUMAN
By the President:

JAMES F. BYRNES,
    Secretary of State

13. TREATY REGISTRATION AND PUBLICATION: UNITED NATIONS RULES[78]

. . . .

1. Every treaty or international agreement whatever its form and descriptive name entered into by one or more Members of the United Nations after 24 October 1945, the date of the coming into force of the Charter, shall as soon as possible be registered with the Secretariat in accordance with these regulations.

. . . .

4. The Secretariat shall record the treaties and international agreements so registered in a Register established for that purpose.

. . . .

Article 5.

A party or specialized agency, registering a treaty or international agreement under Article 1 or 4 of these regulations, shall certify that the text is a true and complete copy thereof and includes all reservations made by parties thereto.

The certified copy shall reproduce the text in all languages in which the treaty or agreement was concluded and shall be accompanied by two additional copies and by a statement setting forth, in respect of each party:
(a) the date on which the treaty or agreement has come into force;
(b) the method whereby it has come into force (for example: by signature, by ratification or acceptance, by accession, et cetera).

Article 6.

The date of receipt by the Secretariat of the United Nations of the treaty or international agreement registered shall be deemed to be the date of registration, provided that the date of registration of a treaty or agreement

registered <u>ex officio</u> by the United Nations shall be the date
on which the treaty or agreement first came into force between two or more of the parties thereto.

Article 7.

A certificate of registration signed by the Secretary-
General or his representative shall be issued to the registering party or agency and also to all signatories and parties
to the treaty or international agreement registered.

Article 8.

1. The Register shall be kept in the five official languages of the United Nations.   The Register shall comprise,
in respect of each treaty or international agreement, a record of:
  (a) the serial number given in the order of registration;
  (b) the title given to the instrument by the parties;
  (c) the names of the parties between whom it was con-
      cluded;
  (d) the dates of signature, ratification or acceptance,
      exchange of ratifications, accession, and entry into
      force;
  (e) the duration;
  (f) the language or languages in which it was drawn up;
  (g) the name of the party or specialized agency which
      registers the instrument and the date of such regis-
      tration;
  (h) particulars of publication in the treaty series of the
      United Nations.

. . . .

Article 12.

1. The Secretariat shall publish as soon as possible in
a single series every treaty or international agreement
which is registered, or filed and recorded, in the original
language or languages, followed by a translation in English
and in French.   The certified statements referred to in
Article 2 of these regulations shall be published in the same
manner . . .

14. TREATY REGISTRATION AND PUBLICATION: SELECT ILLUSTRATIONS[79]

A.

1. Every treaty and every international agreement entered into by any Member of the United Nations after the present Charter comes into force shall as soon as possible be registered with the Secretariat and published by it.

2. No party to any such treaty or international agreement which has not been registered in accordance with the provisions of paragraph 1 of this Article may invoke that treaty or agreement before any organ of the United Nations.

B.

The Eighth International Conference
of American States

RESOLVES:

1. To recommend to the American Governments, which have not yet done so, that they comply as soon as possible with the resolution of the Inter-American Conference for the Maintenance of Peace on the organization of National Committees of Intellectual Cooperation.

2. To recommend to the National Committees of Intellectual Cooperation that they publicize in their respective countries in every possible way the treaties, conventions, resolutions and recommendations which have been adopted, or which may in the future be adopted, by the International Conferences of American States.

(Approved December 24, 1938.)

C.

This Agreement shall be registered with the United Nations.

D.

The present Charter shall be registered with the Secretariat of the United Nations through the Pan American Union.

E.

The present Treaty shall be registered with the Secretariat of the United Nations through the Pan American Union, when two-thirds of the Signatory States have deposited their ratifications.

15. TREATY SUSPENSION DURING WAR[80]

Whereas the conditions envisaged by the Convention have been, for the time being, almost wholly destroyed, and the partial and imperfect enforcement of the Convention can operate only to prejudice the victims of aggression, whom it is the avowed purpose of the United States of America to aid; and

Whereas it is an implicit condition to the binding effect of the Convention that those conditions envisaged by it should continue without such material change as has in fact occurred; and

Whereas under approved principles of international law it has become, by reason of such changed conditions, the right of the United States of America to declare the Convention suspended and inoperative:

NOW, THEREFORE, I, FRANKLIN D. ROOSEVELT, President of the United States of America, exercising in behalf of the United States of America an unquestioned right and privilege under approved principles of international law, do proclaim and declare the aforesaid International Load Lines Convention suspended and inoperative in the ports and waters of the United States of America, and in so far as the United States of America is concerned, for the duration of the present emergency.

16. TREATY TERMINATION: SUPERSESSION-- SELECT ILLUSTRATIONS[81]

A.

The Government of the United States of America considers that the Final Protocol concluded at Peking on September 7, 1901, between the Chinese Government and other governments, including the Government of the United States of America, should be terminated and agrees that the rights accorded to the Government of the United States of America under that Protocol and under agreements supplementary thereto shall cease.

B.

It comes into force immediately on the exchange of the instruments of ratification and shall thereupon replace the Agreement between the Government of the Union of Soviet Socialist Republics and His Majesty's Government in the United Kingdom, signed at Moscow on the 12th July, 1941.

C.

The provisions of Article IV of the Treaty of Commerce and Navigation, signed at London on July 3, 1815, and the provisions of Article III of the Convention relating to the Tenure and Disposition of Real and Personal Property, signed at Washington on March 2, 1899, are hereby superseded in respect of the territories to which this Convention applies.

17. TREATY TERMINATION: SELECT EXPIRATION CLAUSES[82]

A.

Part I of the present Treaty shall remain in force until the reestablishment of peace between the High Contracting Parties and Germany and the Powers associated with her in acts of aggression in Europe.

Part II of the present Treaty shall remain in force for a period of twenty years. Thereafter, unless twelve months' notice has been given by either Party to terminate the Treaty at the end of the said period of twenty years, it shall continue in force until twelve months after either High Contracting Party shall have given notice to the other in writing of his intention to terminate it.

B.

This agreement shall take effect as from this day's date. It shall continue in force until a date to be agreed upon by the two governments.

C.

The present treaty is concluded for a period of ten years, with the proviso that, in so far as one of the High Contracting Parties does not denounce it one year prior to the expiration of this period, the validity of this treaty shall automatically be extended for another five years.

D.

The present Agreement shall enter into force upon its acceptance by the two governments and shall remain in force for a period of ninety-nine years subject to extension thereafter as agreed by the two Governments.

E.

After the Treaty has been in force for twenty years, any Party may cease to be a party one year after its notice of denunciation has been given to the Government of the United States of America, which will inform the Governments of the other Parties of the deposit of each notice of denunciation.

18. TREATY TERMINATION: INSTRUMENT OF DENUNCIATION[83]

A.

...I am directed to add that my Government considers the decision utterly untenable and a clear violation of the American-Hellenic treaty of extradition signed at Athens May 6th, 1931.

Inasmuch as the Greek authorities have now seen fit on two occasions to deny the just requests of the United States made under the provisions of the above mentioned treaty, it is apparent that this treaty, although similar in terms to treaties which the United States has found effective in extraditing fugitives from other countries, cannot be relied upon to effect the extradition of fugitives who have fled to Greece. My Government therefore considers that from the American point of view the treaty is entirely useless. Accordingly I am instructed to give formal notice herewith of my Government's denunciation of the treaty with a view to its termination at the earliest date possible under its pertinent provisions.

B.

Whereas the treaties concluded between the United States and France have been repeatedly violated on the part of the French Government; and the just claims of the United States for reparation of the injuries so committed have been refused, and their attempts to negotiate an amicable adjustment of all complaints between the two nations have been repelled with indignity; and whereas, under authority of the French Government, there is yet pursued against the United States a system of predatory violence, infracting the said treaties and hostile to the rights of a free and independent nation:

Be it enacted by the Senate and House of Representatives of the United States of America in Congress assembled, that the United States are of right freed and exonerated from the stipulations of the treaties and of the consular convention, heretofore concluded between the United States and France, and that the same shall not henceforth be regarded as legally obligatory on the Government or citizens of the United States.

19. TREATY TERMINATION: NOTE TERMINATING EXECUTIVE AGREEMENT[84]

... Inasmuch as the abstention on the United States from such an exercise of its right of statutory control over immigration was the condition upon which was predicated the undertaking of the Japanese Government contained in the Gentlemen's Agreement of 1907-08 with respect to the regulation of the emigration of laborers to the United States, I feel constrained to advise you that this Government cannot but acquiesce in the view that the Government of Japan is to be considered released, as from the date upon which Section 13 (c) of the Immigration Act comes into force, from further obligation by virtue of that understanding.

20. TREATY TERMINATION:
DIPLOMATIC NOTE OF TERMINATION[85]

When the German Government proposed an interpretative and supplementary agreement regarding article 23 of the treaty of 1799 between the United States and Prussia, Secretary Lansing refused to enter into such negotiations and said of the existing treaty:

I feel constrained in view of the circumstances to add that this Government is seriously considering whether or not the treaty of 1828 and the revived articles of the treaties of 1785 and 1799 have not been in effect abrogated by the German Government's flagrant violations of their provisions, for it would be manifestly unjust and inequitable to require one party to an agreement to observe its stipulations and to permit the other party to disregard them. It would appear that the mutuality of the undertaking has been destroyed by the conduct of the German authorities.

21. TREATY TERMINATION: DENIAL OF
VALIDITY OF UNILATERAL TERMINATION[86]

...the Government of the United States does not acquiesce in the endeavor of the Imperial Government to set aside the Capitulations, and does not recognize that the Ottoman Government has a right so to do, or that its action to this end, being unilateral, can have any effect upon the rights and privileges enjoyed by American citizens under the Capitulatory Conventions.

...the Department of State cannot agree with the position taken by the Imperial Government in this matter; but, on the contrary the Department holds that a convention by which one country gives the right to exercise certain rights of sovereignty within its territory to another country is absolute in its nature, and the grantor, having parted with the rights unconditionally, cannot resume their exercise except by a reconveyance or a formal consent on the part of the grantee who is entitled to exercise them.

. . . .

The chief reason for obtaining the right of extraterritoriality is to insure protection for the life, liberty and
interests of the nationals of one State while within the territory of the State granting the right. ... Following the
practice in similar cases with other countries in which the
United States exercised extraterritorial rights under treaty,
this Government will, upon the establishment of judicial
and administrative reforms in Turkey, consider whether
they are of such a character as to warrant the surrender
of the extraterritorial rights of such American citizens in
the Ottoman Empire.

In conclusion, the American Embassy is further instructed to notify the Imperial Ottoman Government that the
United States will hold it responsible for any injury which
may be occasioned to the United States or to its citizens,
through any interference on the part of the Ottoman authorities with the extraterritorial rights possessed by the United
States and its citizens in the Ottoman Empire.

Notes

1. Charles O. Lerche, Jr. and Abdul A. Said, Concepts of International Politics (Englewood Cliffs, N. J.: Prentice-Hall, 1963), pp. 73-75.

2. Lennox A. Mills and Charles H. McLaughlin, World Politics in Transition (New York: Holt, 1956), p. 189.

3. Ibid.

4. Ibid., p. 190.

5. Lerche, op. cit., pp. 25-28.

6. John F. Simmons, "The Story Behind Protocol," in I. Monte Radlovic, Etiquette & Protocol (New York: Harcourt, Brace, 1956), pp. ix-xii.

7. Mills & McLaughlin, op. cit., p. 203.

8. Elmer Plischke, International Relations, Basic Documents 2d ed. (Princeton, N. J.: Van Nostrand, 1962), pp. 38-39.

9. Ibid., pp. 24-25.

10. Mills & McLaughlin, op. cit., pp. 260-268.

11. Ibid.

12. Ibid.

13. Ernest Satow, A Guide to Diplomatic Practice, 3d ed. (New York: Longmans, Green, 1932), pp. 161-211.

14. Ibid.

15. Clyde Eagleton, International Government, 3d ed. (New York: Ronald Press Co., 1957), pp. 126-129.

16. Harold Nicolson, _Diplomacy_, 2d ed. (New York: Oxford University Press, 1958), pp. 219-226.

17. _Ibid._

18. For a detailed study on the language of diplomacy see Alexander Ostrower, _Language, Law, and Diplomacy; A Study of Linguistic Diversity in Official International Relations and International Law_ (Philadelphia: University of Pennsylvania Press, 1965), 2v.

19. Plischke, _International Relations,_ p. iv.

20. _Ibid._ , p. 1.

21. _Ibid._ , p. 2.

22. _United States Government Organization Manual_, 1969-70.

23. Plischke, _International Relations,_ p. 4.

24. U. S. Office of the High Commissioner for Germany, _7th Quarterly Report on Germany, April 1-June 30, 1951_, p. 22. See also Plischke, _International Relations,_ p. 5.

25. Plischke, _International Relations,_ p. 6. Source: Based upon charts of Department of State, Foreign Service Institute.

26. _Ibid._ , p. 7. Source: Department of State, Foreign Service Institute.

27. _Ibid._ , p. 8.

28. U. S. Economic Cooperation Administration, _European Recovery Program: A Report on Recovery Progress and United States Aid_ (Washington: 1949), pp. 128, 133. See also Plischke, _International Relations,_ p. 9. Whereas these charts are now obsolete, they represent the ECA structure at its peak.

29. Plischke, _International Relations,_ p. 10.

30. Canada. Dept. of External Affairs. _Reference Papers,_ no. 69 (Revised, January 1969), p. 16.

31. U. S. Congress. Senate. National Policy Machinery in the Soviet Union (Washington: G. P. O. , 1960), p. 43.

32. Plischke, International Relations, pp. 11-12.

33. U. N. Document A/CONF. 20/13, April 16, 1961. See also Plischke, International Relations, p. 13.

34. Foreign Service Regulations of the United States, II-5, n. 4, Jan. 1941; in Green H. Hackworth, Digest of International Law, vol. IV (1942), pp. 632-633. Note: In the course of time, the rank of Minister Resident fell into disuse. Also see the preceding Document, Art. 14, for contemporary version. See also Plischke, International Relations, p. 14.

35. Communication from Chief of Division of Foreign Service Administration, Department of State, Jan. 25, 1934; in Green H. Hackworth, Digest of International Law, vol. IV (1942), p. 446. See also Plischke, International Relations, p. 14.

36. Note of Austro-Hungarian Government to Secretary of State Bayard, June 11, 1885; in John Bassett Moore, A Digest of International Law (1906), vol. IV, p. 482. See also Plischke, International Relations, p. 14.

37. Source: Department of State.

38. Chief of Division of Protocol. Department of State, to the Belgian Ambassador, May 2, 1938; in Green H. Hackworth, Digest of International Law, vol. IV (1942), pp. 443-444. See also Plischke, International Relations, p. 16.

39. Foreign Service Regulations of the United States, II-4 and nn. 1 and 2, Jan. 1941; in Green H. Hackworth, Digest of International Law, vol. IV (1942), pp. 442-443. See also Plischke, International Relations, p. 16.

40. Plischke, International Relations, p. 17.

41. Ibid.

42. White House Press Release, Jan. 18, 1950. See also Plischke, International Relations, p. 18.

43.   Source: Department of State.   See also Plischke, International Relations, p. 18.

44.   Prepared by Under Secretary of State and approved by the President, 1927: In Green H. Hackworth, Digest of International Law, vol. IV (1942), pp. 444-445.   See also Plischke, International Relations, p. 19.

45.   Secretary of State to Austro-Hungarian Government, Sept. 8, 1915; in U. S. Dept. of State, Foreign Relations of the United States, 1915, Supplement (1928), pp. 933-934. A copy of this note was delivered to the Ambassador in New York by Special Messenger, Sept. 9.   See also Plischke, International Relations, p. 20.

46.   Secretary of State Bayard to Lord Sackville-West, British Minister, Oct. 30, 1888; in John Bassett Moore, A Digest of International Law (1906), vol. IV, p. 537.

47.   Source: Department of State.

48.   Source: Department of State.

49.   Source: Department of State.

50.   U. N. Document A/CONF. 20/13, April 16, 1961. See also Plischke, International Relations, p. 22.

51.   United States-United Kingdom Consular Convention: in Department of State, Press Release No. 91, Feb. 16, 1949.   See also Plischke, International Relations, p. 23.

52.   (A) Dec. 15, 1948, Dept. of State; (B) Resolution of the Economic and Social Council of the United Nations, Feb. 15, 1946, quoted in Final Act, International Health Conference, New York, 1946, in Dept. of State, International Health Conference (no date), pp. 35-36; (C) Quoted in "Protocol of the Proceedings of the Crimea Conference," in Department of State, Press Release No. 239, Mar. 24, 1947; (D) Resolution 12 of Panama Meeting of American Foreign Ministers, 1939, Appendix 18 in Dept. of State, Report of the Delegates of the United States of America to the Meeting of the Foreign-Ministers of the American Republics, Panama, 1939 (1940), p. 62.   See also Plischke, International Relations, p. 40.

53.   Plischke, International Relations, p. 41.

54.   U.S. Dept. of State, Participation of the United States Government in International Conferences, July 1, 1946-June 20, 1947, Dept. of State Pub., 3031 (1948), p. xix. See also Plischke, International Relations, p. 41.

55.   Ibid., p. xx. See also Plischke, International Relations, p. 41.

56.   (a) Rules of Procedure, Montevideo Conference, 1933, in U. S. Dept. of State, Report of the Delegates of the United States of America to the Seventh International Conference of American States (1934), pp. 69-70; (B) U. S. Dept. of State, The United Nations Conference on International Organization (1946), p. 20; (C) Final Act of International Civil Aviation Conference, Chicago, 1944, in U. S. Dept. of State, International Civil Aviation Conference (1945), p. 31; (D) Final Act of Bogotá Conference, 1948, in U. S. Dept. of State, Ninth International Conference of American States (1948), p. 229. The first two illustrations are from rules of procedure prescribing the method of selection, the last two are from final acts explaining who served as chairmen. See also Plischke, International Relations, p. 43.

57.   (A) Rules of Procedure, Art. 9, Rio de Janeiro Conference, 1947, in U. S. Dept. of State, Inter-American Conference for the Maintenance of Continental Peace and Security (1948), p. 158; (B) Final Act, Bogotá Conference, 1948, in U. S. Dept. of State, Ninth International Conference of American States (1948), p. 229; (C) Final Act, United Nations Monetary Conference, Bretton Woods, 1944, in U. S. Dept. of State, United Nations Monetary and Financial Conference (1944), p. 18. The first illustration is from rules of procedure prescribing the method of selection; the other two illustrations are from Final acts explaining who served as secretary general. See also Plischke, International Relations, p. 43.

58.   (A) U. S. Dept. of State, The United Nations Conference on International Organization, San Francisco, California, 1945-Selected Documents (1946), pp. 264-266; (B) U. S. Dept. of State, Report of the Delegation of the United States of America to the Inter-American Conference on Problems of Peace and War, Mexico City, 1945 (1946), p. 51; (C) Summarized from draft agenda, International Health Conference, 1946, in U. S. Dept. of State, International Health Conference (no date), pp. 124-126. First document illustrates conference approval

of agenda, second document depicts substantive issues on
agenda, and the third shows conference steps according to
agenda items. See also Plischke, International Relations, p.
44.

59.   Elmer Plischke, The Conduct of American Diplomacy,
3d ed. , (New York: Van Nostrand, 1967), p. 623.

60.   U. S. Dept. of State, Conference Procedure Series,
Checklist on Rules and Regulations of an International Conference (no date), pp. 4-6. See also Plischke, International Relations, p. 46.

61.   Regulations, International Telecommunication Conference, Atlantic City, N. J. , 1947; in U. S. Dept. of State, International Telecommunication Conferences (1948), pp. 165-171.
See also Plischke, International Relations, pp. 46-47.

62.   (A) United Nations Information Organization, Docu-
ments of the United Nations Conferences on International Organ-
ization, San Francisco, 1945, vol. II (1945), p. 4652; (B) U. S.
Dept. of State, Record of Paris Peace Conference Commission
on Procedure (typewritten, 1946); (C) Regulations of Bogotá
Conference, 1948, in U. S. Dept. of State, Ninth International
Conference of American States (1948) pp. 298-300. See also
Plischke, International Relations, p. 48.

63.   U. S. Dept. of State, The United Nations Conference
on International Organization, San Francisco, California, 1945-
Selected Documents (1946), pp. 893-894. See also Plischke,
International Relations, p. 49.

64.   U. S. Dept. of State, The United Nations Conference
on International Organization (1946), p. 919. See also above,
Document 7A and Plischke, International Relations, p. 49.

65.   (A) Bogotá Conference, 1948; in U. S. Dept. of State,
Ninth International Conference of American States (1948), pp.
272-276; (B) Havana Trade Conference, 1948; in U. S. Dept. of
State, Havana Charter for an International Trade Organization
(1948), p. 19. See also Plischke, International Relations, p. 50.

66.   Inter-American Covention on Treaties, Havana, 1928;
in U. S. Dept. of State, Report of the Delegates of the United
States of America to the Sixth International Conference of American States (1928), pp. 197-201. See also Plischke, International Relations, p. 25.

67. Executive Order 8016, Dec. 1, 1938, U. S. Code of Federal Regulations, Cumulative Supplement, Title 22, Part III, pp. 5436-5437. See also Plischke, International Relations, p. 26.

68. "Regulations of the Conference," Lima, 1938, Appendix 3; in U. S. Dept. of State, Report of the Delegation of the United States of America to the Eighth International Conference of American States, Lima, 1938 (1941), pp. 58-59. See also Plischke, International Relations, p. 27.

69. Secretary of State Lansing to Ambassador to Argentina, Dec. 23, 1917; in Green H. Hackworth, Digest of International Law, vol. V (1943), p. 36. See also Plischke, International Relations, p. 28.

70. Executive Order 8016, Dec. 1, 1938, U. S. Code of Federal Regulations, Cumulative Supplement, Title 22, Part III, p. 5437. See also Plischke, International Relations, p. 28.

71. (A) Jan. 15, 1929, Congressional Record, vol. 70, p. 1731; (B) July 21, 1949, ibid. , vol. 95, p. 10114. See also Plischke, International Relations, p. 29.

72. Public Law 204, 80th Cong. , 1st Sess. In United States Constitutional practice. This arrangement with the United Nations is an "executive agreement" rather than a formal "Treaty." See also Plischke, International Relations, p. 29.

73. (A) Hague Convention on Pacific Settlement, 1909, in William M. Malloy, Treaties, Conventions, International Acts, Protocols and Agreements Between the United States of America and Other Powers, 1776-1909, vol. II (1910), p. 2247: (B) Four Power Pact, 1921, in C. F. Redmond, ibid. , 1910-1923, vol. III (1923), p. 3096; C. Sanitary Convention, 1926, in Edward J. Trentworth, ibid. , 1923-1937, vol. IV (1938), p. 5018. Also see Document 16. See also Plischke, International Relations, p. 29.

74. U. S. Dept. of State, Treaty for the Renunciation of War (1933), pp. 104 and 91 respectively. See also Plischke, International Relations, p. 30.

75. U. S. Dept. of State, Bulletin, vol. XIII, Oct. 28,

1945, pp. 679-680. See also Plischke, International Relations, p. 31.

76. (A) Italian Peace Treaty, Art. 88 (Paris, 1947), in United States, Treaties and Other International Acts, series no. 1638 (1947), p. 169; (B) U. S. Dept. of State, Treaty for the Renunciation of War (1933), p. 125. See also Plischke, International Relations, p. 31.

77. U. S. Congress. Senate. A Decade of American Foreign Policy: Basic Documents, 1941-1949, Senate Document 123, 81st Cong., 1st sess. (1950), pp. 154-155. See also Plischke, International Relations, p. 31.

78. General Assembly Resolution, Dec. 14, 1946; in United Nations, Yearbook of the United Nations, 1946-47 (1947), pp. 252-254. See also Plischke, International Relations, p. 33.

79. (A) Charter of the United Nations, art. 102: (B) Resolution XCVII in U. S. Dept. of State, Report of the Delegation of the United States of America to the Eighth International Conference of American States, Lima, 1938 (1941), p. 179; (C) U. S. Agreement on Aid to Greece, Art. 12, in A Decade of American Foreign Policy, Basic Documents, 1941-1949 (1950), p. 1264; (D) Charter of the Organization of American States, Art. 110; (E) Inter-American Treaty of Reciprocal Assistance, Art. 24, in North Atlantic Treaty, Senate Doc. No. 48, 81st Cong., 1st Sess. (1949) p. 23. Also consult League of Nations Covenant, Appendix A, Art. 18. See also Plischke, International Relations, p. 34.

80. Presidential proclamation, Aug. 9, 1941; in Green H. Hackworth, Digest of International Law, vol. V (1943), pp. 355-356. See also Plischke, International Relations, p. 34.

81. (A) U. S. -Chinese Treaty for Relinquishment of Extraterritoriality, Art. II, 1943, in U. S. Dept. of State, United States Relations with China (1949), p. 514; (B) British-Soviet Alliance, Art. VIII, 1942, in North Atlantic Treaty, Senate Doc. No. 48, 81st Cong., 1st Sess. (1949), p. 106; (C) U. S. -U. K. Consular Convention, art. 29, 1949, in Senate Executive A, 81st Cong., 2d Sess. (1950). See also Plischke, International Relations, p. 35.

82.   (A) British-Soviet Alliance, Art. VIII, 1942, in North Atlantic Treaty, Senate Doc. No. 48 81st Cong. 1st Sess. (1949), p. 106; (B) U. S. Agreement to Aid to Turkey, Art. VII, 1947, in A Decade of American Foreign Policy: Basic Documents, 1941-1949 (1950), p. 1267; (C) Soviet-German Non-Aggression Treaty, Art. VI, 1939, in U. S. Dept. of State, Nazi-Soviet Relations, 1939-1941 (1948), p. 77; (D) U. S. -Philippine Agreement, Art. XXIX, 1947, in A Decade of American Foreign Policy: Basic Document 1941-1949 (1950), p. 880; (E) North Atlantic Treaty, Art. 13, in U. S. Dept. of State, The Signing of the North Atlantic Treaty (1940).   See also Plischke, International Relations, p. 35.

83.   (A) U. S. Minister to Greek Minister of Foreign Affairs, Nov. 5, 1933; in Foreign Relations of the United States, 1933, vol. II (1949), p. 566; (B) Enactment of 1798 annulling Treaties of 1778, in John Bassett Moore, A Digest of International Law (1906), vol. V, p. 356.   See also Plischke, International Relations, p. 36.

84.   Secretary of State Hughes to Japanese Ambassador June 16, 1924; in Green H. Hackworth, Digest of International Law, vol. V (1943), p. 344.   See also Plischke, International Relations, p. 36.

85.   Secretary of State Lansing, March 20, 1917; in Green H. Hackworth, Digest of International Law, vol. V (1943), pp. 343-344.   See also Plischke, International Relations, p. 37.

86.   Dept. of State to Turkish Government, Sept. 10, 1914, and Feb. 19, 1916; in Green H. Hackworth, Digest of International Law, vol. II (1941), pp. 527-528.   See also Plischke, International Relations, p. 37.

Akzin, B. , Propaganda by diplomats, 72.
Albèri, E. , Relazioni degli ambasciatori veneti al Senato, 136.
Albertini, L. E. , Derecho diplomático en sus aplacaciones especiales á las repúblicas sud-americanas, 501.
Albrecht-Carrié, R. , Diplomatic history of Europe since the Congress of Vienna, 137.
Allen, F. E. , Treaty as an instrument of legislation, 240.
Allué Salvador, M. , Condición juridica de los cónsules, 255.
Almanac of current world leaders, 788.
Almanach de Gotha, 867.
Almanach diplomatique & Consulaire, 394.
Almanach du corps diplomatiques, Congo (Leopoldville) Ministère des affaires étrangères, 385.
Alphabetical list of the foreign embassies and legations in London, Gr. Brit. Foreign Office, 814.
Alting von Geusau, F. A. M. , European organizations and foreign relations of states, 138.
Ambasciate elegazioni in Italia, Italy. Ministero degli affari esteri, 817.
Ambasciatore, G. Bragaccia, 590.
Ambassades anglaises pendant la guerre de cent ans, L. Mirot, 601.
Ambassador, J. Hotman, 598.
Ambassador and his functions, A. Wicqueford, 614.
Ambassador Dodd's diary, 1933-1938, W. E. Dodd, 93.
Ambassador Extraordinary Clare Boothe Luce, A. Hatch, 104.
Ambassadors and secret agents, A. Cobban, 87.
Ambassadors ordinary and extraordinary, E. W. Spaulding, 125.
Ambassador's report, C. Bowles, 77.
American agencies interested in international affairs, Council on foreign relations, 799.
American ambassador, W. H. Heinrichs, 107; U. S. Dept. of State, 613.
American Assembly, Representation of the United States abroad, 522.
American consular bulletin, 840.
American consular jurisdiction in the Orient, F. E. Hinckley, 548.
American diplomacy, E. Plischke, 749.
American diplomacy and emergent patterns, K. W. Thompson, 572.
American diplomacy and the furtherance of commerce, E. Schuyler, 560.
American diplomat in China, P. S. Reinsch, 120.

American diplomatic and consular practice, G. H. Stuart, 570.
American diplomatic code, J. Elliot, 537.
American foreign relations, E. Plischke, 750.
American foreign service, J. R. Childs, 532.
American Foreign Service Association. Committee on Career Principles, Toward a modern diplomacy, 523.
American journal of international law, 841.
American political science review, 842.
American Secretaries of State and their diplomacy, S. F. Bemis, 75.
American Secretary of State, an interpretation, A. DeConde, 534.
America's ambassadors to England, B. Willson, 581.
America's ambassadors to France, B. Willson, 582.
Amiama Tió, F. A., Functiones consulares, 389.
Anatomy of the Foreign Service, J. E. Harr, 542.
Anatomy of the State Department, S. Simpson, 564.
Annuaire de l'Institut de droit international, Institute of International Law, 882.
Annuaire des ministères, 789.
Annuaire diplomatique, 868.
Annuaire diplomatique et consulaire, Belgium. Ministère des affaires étrangères, 360.
Annuaire diplomatique et consulaire de la Rèpublique Française, 790.
Annuaire français de droit international, 869.
Antokoletz, D., Manual diplomatico y consular, 350; Tratado teórico y práctico de derecho diplomático y consular, 256.
Anuario hispano-luso-americano de derecho internacional, 870.
Anuario juridico interamericano, 871.
Anuario uruguayo de derecho internacional, 872.
Archives diplomatiques pour l'histoire du temps et des états, 139.
Archives diplomatiques; recueil mensuel de diplomatie, d'histoire et droit international, 843.
Arduino, M., Consoli, consolati e diritto consolare, 257; Diplomazia ed agenti diplomatici, 258.
Argentine republic, Ministerio de relaciones exteriores y culto, Cuerpo consular extranjero, 351.
Arms control & disarmament, 707.
Arnold, R., Treaty-making procedure, 241.
Arntz, E. R. N., Précis méthodique des Règlements consulaires de Belgique, 359.

305

Art and practice of diplomacy, C. K. Webster, 64.
Art of diplomacy, T. A. Bailey, 524.
Art of the possible; government and foreign policy in Canada,
J. Eayrs, 370.
Ashton-Gwatkin, F. T. A., British Foreign Service, 450.
Asile diplomatique d'après la pratique des États latino-amér-
icains, F. Villagran Kramer, 345.
Asmundo, M., Diplomazia europea, 140.
Asociación Francisco de Vitoria, Anuario, 873.
Asociación Guatemalteca de Derecho Internacional, Revista,
874.
Aspaturian, V. V., Union Republics in Soviet diplomacy, 504.
Aspetti della diplomazia contemporanea, P. Quaroni, 52.
Asylum in legations and consulates and in vessels, J. B.
Moore, 313.
At the Court of St. James's, 451.
Atribuciones i perrogativas de los cónsules, A. Hernández-
Bretón, 626.
Attachés militaires, attachés navals et attachés de l'air,
A. P. Beauvais, 259.
Audisio, G., Idea storica erazionale della diplomazia eccles-
iastica, 1; Idée historique et rationnelle de la diplomatie
ecclésiastique, 141.
Aufricht, H., Guide to League of Nations publications, 832.
Aussenpolitik und Diplomatie, F. W. Pritwitz und Gaffron,
51.
Australia, Dept. of External Affairs, Diplomatic list, 791.
Australian yearbook of international law, 875.
Austria. Bundesministerium für Auswärtige Angelegenheiten,
Bundeministerium für Auswärtige Angelegenheiten, 1959-
1962, 355.
Austria. Bundeskanzleramt, Auswärtige Angelegenheiten,
Verzeichnis der ausländischen Konsularämter, 356.
Auswärtige dienst Deutschen Reiches (diplomatie und konsul-
arwesen), H. Kraus, 436.
Auswärtige Dienst Frankrechs, L. Dischler, 403.
Auvergne, E. B. F., Envoys extraordinary, 73.
Azbuka diplomatii, A. Kovolev, 508.
Azud, J., Diplomaticke imunity a výsady, 652.

Background on world politics, See International Studies Quart-
erly, 717.
Bailey, T. A., Art of diplomacy, 524.
Baillou, J., Affaires étrangères, 395.
Barceló, S., Manual diplomático y consular hispano-amer-
icano, 502.

Barghoorn, F. C. , Soviet cultural offensive, 505.
Barnes, W. , Foreign Service of the United States, 525.
Barraza, R. , Vademécum diplomático, 2.
Barron, B. , Inside the State Department, 526.
Barthélemy, J. , Démocratie et politique étrangère, 142.
Bastid, S. B. , Fonctionnaires internationaux, 653.
Bates, L. T. , Unauthorized diplomatic intercourse by American citizens with foreign powers as a criminal offense under the laws of the United States, 527.
Battaglini, G. , Protezione diplomatica delle società, 684.
Beard, C. A. , Cross currents in Europe today, 143.
Beaulac, W. L. , Career ambassador, 74; Career diplomat, 528.
Beauvais, A. P. , Attachés militaires, attachés navals et attachés de l'air, 259.
Bedjaoui, M. , Fonction publique internationale et influences nationales, 654.
Before the war, C. P. Gooch, 163.
Beginnings of diplomacy, R. J. Numelin, 41.
Beichman, A. , Other State Department, 529.
Beiträge zur reform und kodifikation des völkerrechtlichen immunitats-rechts, K. Strupp, ed. , 338.
Beladiez, E. , Diplomacia y diplomáticos, 3.
Belgium. Ministère des affaires étrangères, Annuaire diplomatique et consulaire, 360.
Beloff, M. , New dimensions in foreign policy, 452.
Bemis, S. F. , American Secretaries or State and their diplomacy, 75; Diplomacy of the American revolution, 530; Guide to the diplomatic history of the United States, 1775-1921, 833.
Benedetti, V. , Studies in diplomacy, 144.
Berding, A. H. T. , Making of foreign policy, 531.
Berkes, R. N. , Diplomacy of India, 476.
Berlin embassy, W. R. Russell, 122.
Bernal de O'Reilly, A. , Practica consular de España, 511.
Bernard, M. , Four lectures on subject connected with diplomacy, 4.
Bertoni, K. , Praktyka dyplomatiyczna i kinsularna, 260.
Bertschy, R. , Schutzmacht im Völkerrecht, 685.
Beruf des diplomaten, S. Clemens, 85.
Best, G. L. , Diplomacy in the United Nations, 209.
Bettanini, A. M. , Lo stile diplomatico, 261.
Beytrage zu dem neuesten europaischen gesandtschafftsrecht, J. J. Moser, 602.
Bibliographic register, U. S. Dept. of State, 824.
Bibliographie du droit des gens et des relations internationales, K. Strupp, 753.

Bragaccia, G. , Ambasciatore, 590.

Bratt, E. , Diplomater och konsuler, 266.

Brauer, A. , Deutschen justizgestze in ihrer anwendung auf die amtliche thätigkeit der konsuln und diplomatischen agenten und die kinsulargerichtsbarkeit, 427.

Braun, W. , Démarche, ultimatun, sommation, 7.

Brazil. Departamento diplomatico e consular. Divisãro consular, Lista do corpo consular estrangerio, 792.

Breviate of British diplomatic Blue Books, R. Vogel, 761.

Briggs, E. O. , Farewell to Foggy Bottom, 79.

Brinckmeier, E. , Glossarium diplomaticum zur erläuterung schwieriger, einer diplomatischen, historischen, sachlicher, 766.

British consuls abroad, R. Fynn, 461.

British consuls in the confederacy, M. L. Bonham, 455.

British consuls manual, E. W. A. Tuson, 471.

British diplomatic representatives, 1689-1789, D. B. Horn, 464.

British diplomatic representatives, 1789-1852, S. T. Bindoff, 453.

British diplomatic service, 1689-1789, D. B. Horn, 465.

British Foreign Service, F. T. A. Ashton-Gwatkin, 450.

British imperial calendar and civil service list, 793.

British year book of international law, 876.

Brock, C. , Literature of political science, 834.

Broglie, A. , Histoire et diplomatie, 146.

Brooks, P. C. , Diplomacy and the border lands, 147.

Brown, J. C. , Administration of United States foreign affairs, 732.

Brunner, S. , Humor in der diplomatie und regierungskunde des 18. jahrhunderts, 148.

Buchanan, M. , Diplomacy and foreign courts, 149.

Buchanan, W. T. , Red carpet at the White House, 131.

Buch, P. W. , Control of foreign relations in modern nations, 267.

Bullard, A. , Diplomacy of the great war, 150.

Bulletin...annual cumulation, Public affairs information service, 727.

Bulmerincq, A. , Consularrecht, 618.

Bundesministerium für Auswärtige Angelegenheiten, 1959-1962, Austria, Bundesministerium für Auswärtige Angelegenheiten, 355.

Burchfield, L. , Student's guide to materials in political science, 835.

Bursotti, G. , Guide des agents consulaires, 268.

Burton, J. W. , Systems, states, diplomacy and rules, 211.

Busk, D. L. , Craft of diplomacy, 456.
Bustos, L. , E. , Lejislacion diplomática i consular de Chile, 372.
Byrnes, J. F. , Speaking frankly, 80.

Cadieux, M. , Canadian diplomat, 368.
Cagiati, A. , Diplomazia dalle origini al xvii secdo, 8.
Cahier, P. , Droit diplomatique contemporain, 269.
Caleb, R. , Konsulargerichtsbarkeit in Bulgarien auf grund der capitulationen mit Türkei, 367.
Calendar of Soviet documents on foreign policy, 1917-1941, J. T. Degras, 734.
California. University, Berkeley. Bureau of International Relations, International relations digest of periodical literature, 709.
Callières, F. , On the manner of negotiating with princes, 9.
Calvo, C. , Dictionnaire manuel de diplomatie et de droit international public et privé, 767.
Calvo, J. A. , Prontuario consular colombiano, 382.
Cambon, J. M. , Diplomatist, 81.
Cambon, P. , Correspondence, 1870-1924, 82.
Campbell, G. , Of true experience, 83.
Canada. Dept. of External Affairs, Canadian representatives abroad and representatives of other countries in Canada, 369, 794.
Canadian yearbook of international law, 877.
Candioti, A. M. , Historia de la institución consular en la antigüedad y en la e dad media, 619.
Caraffa, C. M. , Embaxador politico-christiano, 591.
Cardozo, M. H. , Diplomats in international cooperation, 84.
Career ambassador, W. L. Beaulac, 74.
Career diplomat, W. L. Beaulac, 528.
Carlino, P. , Genesi e fondamento delle immunitá diplomatiche, 592.
Carnegie Endowment for International Peace. Library, Select bibliographies, 723.
Carnegie Institute in Diplomacy, University College, Dar es-Salaam, 1965, Report and general information, 10.
Carneiro de Mencoça Franco, M. , Consular regulations of the empire of Brazil, 364.
Cartilla consular, A. Ramirez Peña, 499.
Castro y Casaleiz, A. , Guía practica del diplomático Español, 512.
Catalog of international law and relations, Harvard University. Law School. Library, 742.
Centeno, F. , Digesto de relaciones exteriores, 1810-1913, 352.

Century of diplomatic blue books, H. W. V. Temperley, ed. , 754.

Ceylon, Ministry of External Affairs, Diplomatic, consular and other representation in Ceylon and Ceylon representation abroad, 795.

Chaco dispute, W. R. Garner, 235.

Chambrun, C. , Esprit de la diplomatie, 11.

Chao, C. , Chinese diplomatic practice and treaty relations, 1842-1943, 377.

Chazelle, J. , Diplomatie, 12.

Chevrey-Rameau, P. , Répertoire diplomatique et consulaire, 399; Supplement pour les années 1886-1887, 400.

Child, R. W. , Diplomat looks at Europe, 151.

Childs, J. R. , American foreign service, 532.

Chile. Laws, statutes, etc. , Servicio diplomatico i consular, 373.

Chile through embassy windows, 1939-1953, C. G. Bowers, 76.

China's entrance into the family of nations, C. Hsü, 378.

Chinese diplomatic practice and treaty relations, 1842-1943, C. Chao, 377.

Chinese foreign affairs--organization and control, P. C. Liu, 379.

Chinese representation in the United States, E. Swisher, 381.

Classification, immunities and privileges of diplomatic agents, F. Deak, 656.

Classification of diplomatic agents, D. J. Hill, 585.

Clemens, S. , Der beruf des diplomaten, 85.

Clercq, A. J. H. , Guide pratique des consultats, 401.

Cleugh, E. A. , Without let or hindrance, 86.

Clippers and consuls, E. Griffin, 541.

Co je diplomacie, J. Pokstefl, 49.

Cobban, A. , Ambassadors and secret agents, 87.

Code diplomatique de l'Europe, G. Garden, 286.

Code diplomatique et consulaire, 796.

Code-memorial international & maritame des consulats, G. Rosa Rullo, 643.

Cold war diplomacy, C. E. Wilson, 681.

Collection of the diplomatic and consular laws and regulations of various countries, A. H. Feller, 282.

Columbia. Ministerio de relaciones exteriores, Lista consular, 797.

Comercio y servicio exterior mexicanos, A. López Romer, 487.

Committee on Foreign Affairs Personnel, Personnel for the new diplomacy, 533.

Course in European diplomacy, D. J. Hill, 167.
Craft of diplomacy, D. L. Busk, 456.
Craft sinister; a diplomatico-political history of the great
    war and its causes, G. A. Schreiner, 200.
Craig, G. A., Diplomats: 1919-1939, 88; From Bismarck to
    Adenauer: aspects of German statecraft, 428; War,
    politics and diplomacy, 152.
Crandall, S. B., Treaties, their making and enforcement,
    244.
Cresson, W. P., Diplomatic portraits, 89.
Cross currents in Europe today, C. A. Beard, 143.
Crosswell, C. M., Protection of international personnel
    abroad, 655.
Cuba. Servicio de Protocolo, Lista del cuerpo diplomático
    extranjero, 387.
Cuerpo consular extranjero, Argentia republic. Ministerio
    de relaciones exteriores y culto, 351.
Cuerpo diplomático de Venezuela, Ministerio de Relaciones
    Exteriores, 830.
Culbertson, W. S., International economic policies, 214.
Cultural attaché, H. L., Nostrand, 321.
Culture and communication, R. T. Oliver, 43.
Current abstracts of the Soviet Press, 710.
Current digest of the Soviet press, 711.
Current thought on peace and war, 712.
Cussy, F., Dictionnaire, ou, Manuel-lexique du diplomate et
    du consul, 768; Règlements consulaires principaux états
    maritimes de l'Europe et de l'Amérique, 274.
Cuttino, G. P., English diplomatic administration, 1259-
    1339, 153.
Czartoryski, A. J., Essai sur la diplomatie, 14.
Czechoslovak Republic. Ministerstuo zahranicnich veci,
    Diplomatická korespondence, 699.
Czechoslovak yearbook of international law, 878.

Damiron, P., De l'incompétence des tribunaux français dans
    les litiges concernant les agents diplomatiques, 402.
Daniels, J., Shirt-sleeve diplomat, 90.
Daring diplomacy; the case of the first American ultimatum,
    A. Klay, 694.
Davies, J. E., Mission to Moscow, 91.
De foro legatorum liber singularis, C. van Bijnkershoek,
    589.
De la juridiction des consuls de France à l'étranger et des
    devoirs et obligations qu'ont à remplir ces foncionnaires,
    ainsi que les armateuis, négocians, navigateus, Lagét
    de Podio, 410.

Dictionnaire diplomatique, Academie Diplomatique Internationale, 764.
Dictionnaire manuel de diplomatie et de droit international public et privé, C. Calvo, 767.
Dictionnaire, ou, Manuel-lexique du diplomate et du consul, F. Cussy, 768.
Dietrich, V., De l'inviolabilité et de l'exemption de juridiction des agents diplomatiques et consolaires en pays de chrétienté, 276.
Digest of international law, G. H. Hackworth, 714; J. B. Moore, 718; M. M. Whiteman, 721.
Digest of the international law of the United States, F. Wharton, ed., 720.
Digesto de relaciones exteriores, 1810-1913, F. Centeno, 352.
Dimensions of diplomacy, E. A. J. Johnson, 30.
Dinstein, Y., Consular immunity from judicial process, 657.
Diplomacia, R. Rodriquez Araya, 353.
Diplomacia universitaria americana, J. L. Suárez, 503.
Diplomacia y diplomáticos, E. Beladiez, 3.
Diplomacia y literatura, P. Ugarteche, 207.
Diplomáciai és nemzetközi jogi lexika, G. Hajdu, 773.
Diplomáciai kapcsolatok joga, F. Ustor, 343
Diplomacy, H. G. Nicolson, 40; J. R. R. Rennell, 55.
Diplomacy and dogmatism, D. Jensen, 170.
Diplomacy and foreign courts, M. Buchanan, 149.
Diplomacy and peace, R. B. Mowat, 184.
Diplomacy and the border lands, P. C. Brooks, 147.
Diplomacy and the communist challenge, Council on Foreign Relations, 213.
Diplomacy and the study of international relations, D. P. Heatley, 27.
Diplomacy as a career, H. R. Wilson, 128.
Diplomacy by conference, M. P. A. H. Hankey, 237.
Diplomacy in a changing world, S. D. Kertesz, 31; R. Regála, 54.
Diplomacy in a democracy, H. M. Wriston, 583.
Diplomacy in evolution, D. L. B. Hamlin, 236.
Diplomacy in fetters, V. Wellesley, 65.
Diplomacy in the Near and Middle East, J. C. Hurewitz, 169.
Diplomacy in the nuclear age, L. B. Pearson, 225.
Diplomacy in the United Nations, G. L. Best, 209.
Diplomacy in transition, 15.
Diplomacy of appeasement, A. H. Furnia, 160.
Diplomacy of economic development, E. R. Black, 210.
Diplomacy of imperialism, 1890-1902, W. L. Langer, 173.

318

Diplomatic prelude, 1938-1939, L. B. Namier, 190.
Diplomatic press directory of Ghana, 800.
Diplomatic press directory of Jamaica, 801.
Diplomatic press directory of the Federation of Nigeria, 802.
Diplomatic press directory of the Republic of Cyprus, 803.
Diplomatic press directory of the State of Singapore, 804.
Diplomatic press Hong Kong trade directory, 805.
Diplomatic press trade directory of Malta, 806.
Diplomatic press trade directory of the Empire of Ethiopia, 807.
Diplomatic press trade directory of Trinidad and Tobago, 808.
Diplomatic privileges and immunities, C. E. Wilson, 682.
Diplomatic protection of Americans in Mexico, F. S. Dunn, 688.
Diplomatic protection of citizens abroad, E. M. Borchard, 686.
Diplomatic protest in foreign policy, J. C. McKenna, 304.
Diplomatic quarter in Peking, its juristic nature, M. I. Pergament, 380.
Diplomatic service list, 809.
Diplomatic staffs of Commonwealth and foreign missions in Accra, Ghana. High Commissioner for the United Kingdom, 449.
Diplomatic terms, M. al-Hamawi, 774.
Diplomatic year book, 879.
Diplomatically speaking, L. C. Griscom, 101.
Diplomaticheskii slovar'. V trek tomakh, Glavnaia redaktsiia A. A. Gromyko i dr. 770.
Diplomatická korespondence, Czechoslovak Republic, Ministerstuo, 699.
Diplomatické imunity a vysady, J. Azud, 652.
Diplomatie, J. Chazelle, 12; Economie, 17; L. Essen, 157; H. L. Krekeler, 33; A. Mendelssohn Bartholdy 438; O. G. Wesendonk, 66.
Diplomatie au temps de Machiavel, M. A. R. Maulde La Clavière, 178.
Diplomatie contemporaine, F. Moussa, 748.
Diplomatie du droit, L. V. A. Bourgeois, 6.
Diplomatie française, C. Laroche, 412.
Diplomatie française au temps de Louis xiv (1661-1715) institutions, moeurs et coutumes, C. G. Picavet, 196.
Diplomatie im Sprachgebrauch, F. Stieve, 337.
Diplomatie, les consulats et le commerce français, Z. Marcas, 415.

Diplomatie und diplomaten, W. Zechlin, 68.
Diplomatie unserer zeit, International Seminar for Diplomats, Klessheim, 1959?, 29.
Diplomatie, Wesen, Rolle und Wandlung, H. von Dirksen, 16.
Diplomatique royale française, G. Tessier, 900.
Diplomatische Asyl in deutschen Vertretungen Lateinamerikas, W. Ungerer, 340.
Diplomatische Dienst, R. Sallet, 423.
Diplomatische verhandlungen, G. B. Mably, 37.
Diplomatischen privilegien, M. S. Kebedgy, 664.
Diplomatischen Vertretug gen unter besonder Berücksichtigung der schweizerischen, A. Redard, 520.
Diplomatist, 848; J. M. Cambon, 81.
Diplomatists: 1919-1939, G. A. Craig, 88.
Diplomat's annual, 810.
Diplomat's directory, 811.
Diplomat's handbook of international law practice, B. Sen, 334.
Diplomats in international cooperation, M. H. Cardoza, 84.
Diplomat's wife, R. F. Boyce, 78.
Diplomazia dalle origini al xvii secdo, A. Cagiati, 8.
Diplomazia ed agenti diplomatici, M. Arduino, 258.
Diplomazia europea, M. Asmundo, 140.
Directorio consular de México, Mexico. Direccion general de comercio exterior y del servicio consular, 488.
Directory of Commonwealth commissioners and the consular corps, Kenya Colony and Protectorate, 819.
Direito consular internacional, A. Martins, 497.
Diritto diplomatic e giurisdizione internazionale maritima, P. Esperson, 280.
Diritto diplomatico consolare, parte generale, V. Corsini, 271.
Dirksen, H. , Diplomatie, Wesen, Rolle und Wandlung, 16.
Dischler, L. , Auswärtige Dienst Frankrechs, 403.
Discours sur l'art de négocier, A. Pecquet, 46.
Dissertation inauguralis, juris gentium, De legatis rebusque, ab his agendis, A. C. Snouckaert van Schauburg, 611.
Dissertation juridica inauguralis, J. Kannes, 295.
Documents politiques, diplomatiques et financiers, 849.
Dodd, W. E. , Ambassador Dodd's diary, 1933-1938, 93.
Doehring, K. , Pflicht des Staates zur Gewährung diplomatischen Schutzes, 687.
Dollot, R. , Du secret diplomatique, 404.
Donnadier, J. , Consuls de France, 405.
Douma, J. , Bibliography on the International court including the Permanent Court, 1918-1964, 735.

153.
Entwicklung der diplomatischen Rang stufen; E. H. Markel, 308.
Entwicklung der ständigen diplomatie vom fünfzehnten jahrhundert bis zu den beschlüssen von 1815 und 1818, O. Krauske, 32.
Envoy unextraordinary, D. C. Dunham, 94.
Envoys extraordinary, E. B. F. Auvergne, 73.
Erice y O'Shea, J. S., Derecho diplomático, 278; Noras de diplomacia y de derecho diplomático, 279.
Eroğlu, H., Représentation internationale en vue de protéger les intéréts des belligérants, 690.
Ersuchen um rechtshilfe im internationalen verkehr, für die preussischen gerichte bearbeitet von landgerichtssekretär, W. Peil, 443.
Escher, A., Schutz der staatsangerhörigen im ausland durch fremde gesandtschaften und konsulate, 691.
Escott, T. H. S., Story of British diplomacy, 156.
Esperson, P., Diritto diplomatico e giurisdizione internazionale maritima, 280.
Esprit de la diplomatie, C. Chambrun, 11.
Essai sur la diplomatie, A. J. Cazrtoryski, 14.
Essai sur la diplomatie nouvelle, A. A. Forgac, 20.
Essen, J. L. F., Immunities in international law, 736; Ontwikkeling en codifictie van de diplomatieke voorechten, 281.
Essen, L., Diplomatie, 157.
Estudios realizados para formular un proyecto de ley organicando el servicio diplomático y consular de la república de Cuba, J. M. Cortina, 386.
Etats et souverains, L. J. D. Féraud-Giraud, 283.
Etiquette & protocol, I. M. Radlovic, 133.
Etudes diplomatiques, H. Bonneval, 5.
Etudes sur la juridiction consulaire en pays chrétiens et en pays non chrétiens, et sur l'extradition, W. B. Lawrence, 630.
Eubank, K., Summit conferences, 1919-1960, 234.
Europäische gesandschaftrecht, A. Miruss, 181.
Europäisches gesandschaftsrecht, F. X. Moshamm, 39.
Europäisches Wörterbuch, H. Grosse, 772.
European organizations and foreign relations of states, F. A. M. Alting von Geusau, 138.
Evolution de la diplomatie, C. S. Blaga, 145.
Evolution des méthodes diplomatiques, P. Granet, 218.
Evolution of diplomatic method, H. G. Nicolson, 224.
Evolution of personnel systems for U. S. foreign affairs, A. G. Jones, 550.

Flassan, G. , Histoire générale et raisonnée de la diplomatie française, 406.
Florio, F. , Nozioni di diplomazia e diritto diplomatico, 19.
Flynn, A. H. , World understanding, 737.
Fonction publique internationale et influences nationales, M. Bedjaoui, 654.
Fonctionnaires internationaux, S. Bastid, 653.
Fonctions diplomatiques en temps de paix, H. C. R. Lisboa, 302.
Foreign affairs; an American quarterly review, 850.
Foreign affairs bibliography, 738.
Foreign consul, J. I. Puente, 638.
Foreign consular offices in the United States, U. S. Dept. of State, 826.
Foreign office, W. S. Strang, 468; J. A. C. Tilley, 470.
Foreign office list and diplomatic and consular yearbook, 812.
Foreign office organization, H. K. Norton, 320.
Foreign policy and diplomacy, B. Pradhan, 50.
Foreign relations of the United States, U. S. Dept. of State, 574.
Foreign secretaries of the xix century to 1834, P. M. Thornton, 127.
Foreign service journal, 851.
Foreign service list, U. S. Dept. of State, 827.
Foreign service of the United States, W. Barnes, 525; T. H. Lay, 552.
Forgac, A. A. , Essai sur le diplomatie nouvelle, 20.
Forgac, A. T. New diplomacy and the United Nations, 284.
Formación del diplomático peruano, P. Ugarteche, 495.
Formen und Stile der Diplomatie, P. Gerbore, 25.
Formulaire des consulats, F. Borel, 264.
Formularios consulares, F. Iturriage y Codes, 514.
Formulation and administration of United States foreign policy, H. F. Haviland, 546.
Foster, J. W. , Practice of diplomacy as illustrated in the foreign relations of the United States, 538.
Foundations of American foreign policy, A. B. Hart, 545.
Four lectures on subjects connected with diplomacy, M. Bernard, 4.
Fraga Iribarne, M. , Guerra y diplomácia en el sistema actual de las relaciones internacionales, 21.
Français dans les relations diplomatiques, H. Roumiguière, 705.
Français, langue diplomatique moderne, J. B. Scott, 706.
France vue de l'étranger, A. Mousset, 418.

328

Huddleston, S. , Popular diplomacy and law, 220.
Hudson, M. O. , International legislation, 248.
Hugessen, H. M. K. , Diplomat in peace in war, 109.
Hull, C. , Memoirs of Cordell Hull, 110.
Humanismo y politica exterior, J. J. Santa Pinter, 57.
Humor in der diplomatie und regierungskunde des 18 jahr-
    hunderts, S. Brunner, 148.
Huntington-Wilson, F. M. , Memoirs of an ex-diplomat, 111.
Hunziker, A. , Konsularische eheschliessung ihre grundlagen
    und ihre stellung im schweizersichen recht, 627.
Hurewitz, J. C. , Diplomacy in the Near and Middle East,
    169.
Huyn, H. , Tragedy of errors, 112.
Hyamson, A. M. , Dictionary of international affairs, 776.

I saw Poland betrayed, A. B. Lane, 115.
Iceland.   Utanrickisraouneytio, Diplomatic list, 815.
Idea storica erazionale della diplomazia ecclesiastica, G.
    Audisio, 1.
Iklé, F. C. , How nations negotiate, 292.
Ilchman, W. F. , Professional diplomacy in the United
    States, 1779-1939, 549.
Im wandel der aussenpolitik, U. Hassell, 103.
Immunità giurisdizionale degli organi stranieri, M. Miele,
    668.
Immunität der nicht-diplomaten, S. Kauffmann, 663.
Immunité civile de juridiction des agents diplomatiques, C.
    Ozanam, 603.
Immunité judiciaire civile des agents diplomatiques étrangers,
    U. Sinner, 677.
Immunités consulaires dans les pays de chrétienté, A. Bodin,
    616.
Immunités diplomatiques des représentants des états membres
    et des agents de la Société des nations, J. Secretan, 676.
Immunities and privileges of international officials, W. M.
    Hill, 660.
Incident diplomatique, K. G. Katakazi, 662.
Index to legal periodicals, 724.
India (Republic) Central Hindi Directorate, List of technical
    terms in Hindi, 777.
Indian yearbook of international affairs, 881.
Inmunidades consulares, J. Pareja Paz Soldan, 672.
Inside the State Department, B. Barron, 526.
Institucion consular, J. L. Fuenzalida Lamas, 374.
Institucion diplomática, J. Peralta Peralta, 47.
Institute of International Law, Annuaire de l'Institut de droit

330

international, 882.

Institutes du droit consulaire, J. Toubeau, 425.

Institution consulaire en Belgique depuis 1830, J. Mees, 363.

Institution des consulats, G. Salles, 331.

Institutions spécialisées, problèmes juridiques et diplomatiques de l'administration internationale, C. Labeyrie-Ménahem, 297.

Instruments of America's foreign policy, B. Westerfield, 580.

International administrative jurisdiction, J. K. King, 665.

International affairs, 852; Metron, inc., New York, Universal Reference System, 746.

International bibliography of political science, 725.

International communication and the new diplomacy, 221.

International economic policies, W. S. Culbertson, 214.

International immunities, C. W. Jenks, 661.

International law and custom of ancient Greece and Rome, C. Phillipson, 195.

International law as a substitute for diplomacy, M. D. A. Redlich, 53.

International law relating to diplomatic practice, B. Sen, 335.

International law reports: 1919-1922, 715.

International legislation, M. O. Hudson, 248.

International political science abstracts, 716.

International politics, 726.

International relations, U. S. Information Agency, 759.

International relations digest of periodical literature, California. University, Berkeley. Bureau of International Relations, 709.

International seminar for Diplomats, Klessheim, 1959?, 29.

International studies, 853.

International studies quarterly, 717.

International yearbook and statesman's who's who, 816.

Internationale Politik, 883.

Internationale Terminologie, G. Hanesch, 775.

Introducteurs des ambassadeurs, 1585-1900, A. Boppe, 396.

Irizarry y Puente, J., Traité sur les fonctions internationales des consuls, 293.

Istituzione dei consolati ed il diritto internazionale europeo nella sua applicabilità in Oriente, F. P. Contuzzi, 620.

Italy. Ministero degli affari esteri, Ambasciate elegazioni in Italia, 817.

Iturriage y Codes, F., Formularios consulares, 514.

Jahrbuch des völkerrechts, 884.

Jahrbuch für internationales Recht, 885.

Jameson, J. F., Provisional list of printed lists of ambas-

sadors and other diplomatic representatives, 743.
Janner, A. , Puissance protectrice en droit international
d'après les expériences faites par la Suisse pendant la
seconde guerre mondiale, 693.
Japanese annual of international law, 886.
Jenks, C. W. , International immunities, 661.
Jensen, D. , Diplomacy and dogmatism, 170.
Jessup, P. C. , Parliamentary diplomacy, 222.
Jewish yearbook of international law, 887.
Joekes, A. M. , Schets van de bevoegdheden der hederland-
sche consuls, 489.
Johnson, E. A. J. , Dimensions of diplomacy, 30.
Jones, A. G. , evolution of personnel systems for U. S.
Foreign affairs, 550.
Jones, C. L. , Consular service of the United States, 551.
Jones, J. M. , Full powers and ratification, 249.
Jordan. Ministry of Foreign Affairs, Diplomatic list, 818.
Journal of conflict resolution, 854.
Journal of international affairs, 855.
Joy, C. T. , How Communists negotiate, 294.
Juridical basis of diplomatic immunity, M. Ogdon, 670.
Jurisdiktionsverhältinisse der frendländischen konsuln in
Deutschland, R. Zimmer, 651.
Jus gentium, 888.
Jusserand, J. A. A. J. , School for ambassadors, 599.

Kameke, C. , Palais Beauharnais, 431.
Kannes, J. , Dissertatio juridica inauguralis, 295.
Katakazi, K. G. , Incident diplomatique, 662.
Kauffmann, S. , Immunität der nicht-diplomaten, 663.
Kaufmann, J. , Conference diplomacy, 238.
Kebedgy, M. S. , Diplomatschen privilegien, 664.
Kelly, D. V. , Ruling few, 113.
Kennan, G. F. , Memoirs, 1925-1950, 114.
Kennedy, A. L. , Old diplomacy and new, 1876-1922, 171.
Kenya Colony and Protectorate, Directory of Commonwealth
commissioners and the consular corps, 819.
Kertesz, S. D. , Diplomacy in a changing world, 31; Quest
for peace through diplomacy, 172.
Ketchkitch, D. , Mariages diplomatiques ou consulaires et
leurs effets internationaux, 628.
Key officers of foreign service posts, U. S. Dept. of State,
828.
King, J. K. , International administrative jurisdiction, 665.

List of books, pamphlets, U. S. Dept. of State. Library, 758.

List of books received at the library of the Department of State, U. S. Dept. of State. Library, 757.

List of local notabilities, Council of Europe. Secretariat, 798.

List of technical terms in Hindi: diplomacy, India (Republic) Central Hindi Directorate, 777.

Lista consular, Colombia. Ministerio de relaciones exteriores, 797.

Lista del cuerpo diplotmático extranjero, Cuba. Servicio de Protocolo, 387.

Lista de corpo consular estrangerio, Brazil, Departamento diplomatico e consular. Divisão consular, 792.

Liste de MM. les membres du corps diplomatique à Damas, Syria Ministère des affaires étrangères, 823.

Liste des diplomatischen Korps in Bonn, Germany (Federal Republic, 1949-   ) Auswärtiges Amt. , 813.

Literature of political science, C. Brock, 834.

Liu, C. , Practical diplomatic correspondence, 701.

Liu, P. C. , Chinese foreign affairs--organization and control, 379.

Llaverias, F. Manual de derecho consular dominicano, 390.

Lodge, R. , Studies in eighteenth century diplomacy, 1740-1748, 175.

Lombard, H. C. C. , Washington waltz; diplomatic people and policies, 116.

López Romero, A. , Comercio y servicio exterior mexicanos, 487.

Ludwig, E. , Consular treaty rights and comments on the "most favored nation" clause, 633.

Maag, J. , Konsularische und diplomatische schutz des Auslandschweizers, 695.

Mabillon, J. , De re diplomatica libri vi, 899.

Mably, G. B. , Diplomatische verhandlungen, 37; Principes des négotiations, 303.

McCamy, J. L. , Conduct of the new diplomacy, 553.

Mackay, B. L. , Moderne diplomatie, 176.

McKay, V. , African diplomacy, 348.

McKenna, J. C. , Diplomatic protest in foreign policy, 304.

Madiedo, M. M. , Tratado de derecho de jentes, internacional, diplómatico i. consular, 305.

Magnone, F. , Manuel des officiers consulaires sardes et étrangers, 500.

Majistraturen des völkerrechtlichen verkehrs (gesandtschafts-

und konsularrecht) und die exterritorialität, B. Hübler, 291.

Making of foreign policy, A. H. T. Berding, 531.

Making of United States foreign policy, B. M. Sapin, 558.

Makowski, J. , O. konsulach i konsulatach, 306.

Malfatti di Monte Tretto, J. , Hanbuch desösterreichisch-ungarischen konsularwesens, nebst einem anhange, 357.

Maluquer y Salvador, M. , Derecho consular español, 516; Apéndice. Años 1900-1901, 516A; Apéndice. Años 1902-1907, 516B.

Manning, C. A. W. , Nature of international society, 38.

Mansoor, M. , ed. , Legal and documentary Arabic reader, 778.

Mantovani, M. , Agenti diplomatici di cittadinanza italiana presso il sommo pontefice ne Trattato lateranense, 667.

Manual de derecho consular, G. E. N. Silva, 366.

Manual de derecho consular, R. Torre y Reiné, 388.

Manual de derecho consular dominicano, F. Llaverias, 390.

Manual de derecho diplomático, J. Peréz de Cuéllar, 494.

Manual diplomatico y consular, D. Antokoletz, 350.

Manual diplomatico y consular colombiano, J. M. Perez-Sarmiento, 384.

Manual diplomático y consular hispano-americano, S. Barcelo, 502.

Manual for United States consuls, J. S. Henshaw, 547.

Manual para diplomáticos y consules, R. Vera, 376.

Manuale di diritto consolare, F. Ferrara, 479; G. Zampaglione, 483.

Manuale teorico pratico del servizio consolare, ad uso degli uffici consolari avvocati, notai e studi legali en geuere, G. Bionell, 477.

Manuel à l'usage des consuls des pays-bas, J. Wertheim, 490.

Manuel de diplomatique, G. Airy, 898.

Manuel de droit consulaire, J. Pillaut, 421.

Manuel des agents consulaires, français étrangers, L. J. A. Moreüil, 417.

Manuel des consuls, A. Miltitz, 312.

Manuel des officiers consulaires sardes et étrangers, F. Magnone, 500.

Manuel diplomatique, K. Martens, 745.

Manuel diplomatique et consulaire, R. Monnet, 416.

Manuel pratique de consulat, F. A. Mensch, 439.

Manuel pratique de protocole, J. C. Serres, 134.

Manuel pratique des consulats, A. L. Verdier, 426.

Manuel théorique et pratique des agents diplomatiques et con-

337

338

Orbis, 857.
Organization of American States style manual, Pan American Union, 781.
Orientations and behavioral styles of Foreign Service officers, R. Walther, 577.
Origin of the capitulations and of the consular institution, G. B. Ravndal, 328.
Origines de la diplomate, R. J. Numelin, 42.
Origins of American diplomacy, M. Savelle, 559.
Ormesson, W. , Enfances diplomatiques, 323.
Ostrower, A. , Language, law, and diplomacy, 703.
Other State Department: The United States Mission to the United Nations, A. Beichman, 529.
Our foreign affairs, P. S. Mowrer, 189.
Our foreign service, F. Van Dyne, 575.
Outline lectures on the history, organization, jurisdiction and practice of the ministerial and consular courts of the United States and Japan, G. H. Scidmore, 561.
Overseas representation and services for Federal domestic agencies, R. E. Elder, 536.
Ozanam, C. , Immunité civile de juridiction des agents diplomatiques, 603.

Pacassi, J. B. , Einleitung in die sammtlichen gesandschaftsrechte, 604.
Pagès, F. J. H. , De l'inferiorité sociale des affrancis à Rome et des moyens de la relever, 636.
Palais Beauharnais, C. Kameke, 431.
Palau, Lisimaco, Guía para los cónsules colombianos, 383.
Palomar, J. I. , Diccionario diplomatico consular, 780.
Pan American Union, Organization of American States style manual, 781.
Panama (Republic) Ministerio de relaciones exteriores, Guía consular, 491; Guía diplomática, 492.
Panikkar, K. M. , Principles and practice of diplomacy, 44.
Panorama de la literatura diplomatica, P. Ugarteche, 756.
Pantzer, R. F. H. , Neuere fortbildungen im system der völkerrechtlichen exemtionen, 671.
Pareja Paz Soldán, J. , Inmunidades consulares, 672.
Parfait ambassadeur, J. A. V. Z. F. Roca, 608.
Paris embassy, B. Willson, 473.
Parliamentary diplomacy, P. C. Jessup, 222.
Paschal, C. , Legatus, 605.
Pastuhov, V. D. , Guide to the practice of international conferences, 239.
Patau, P. , De la situation comparée des agents diplomatiques et consulaires, 324.

343

Prontuario de derecho consular chileno, J. Guerra Araya, 375.

Prontuario diplomatico y consular y resumen de los derechos y deberes de los estrangeres en los paises donde risden, J. J. G. Cortina, 272.

Propaganda by diplomats, B. Akzin, 72.

Protection des nationaux à l'étranger, E. Pittard, 696.

Protection diplomatique et consulaire dans les échelles du Levant et de Barbaric, F. Rey, 641.

Protection of foreign interests, W. M. Franklin, 692.

Protection of international personnel abroad, C. M. Crosswell, 655.

Protection of nationals, F. S. Dunn, 689.

Protezione diplomatica delle societá, C. Battaglini, 684.

Provisional list of printed lists of ambassadors and other diplomatic representatives, J. F. Jameson, 743.

Public affairs information service, Bulletin, 727.

Publicity and diplomacy, O. J. Hale, 219.

Puente, J. I. , Foreign consul, 638; Traité sur les fonctions internationales des consuls, 639.

Puig Vilazar, C. , Derecho consular ecuatoriano, 392.

Puissance protectrice en droit international d'après les expériences faites par la Suisse pendant la seconde guerre mondiale, A. Janner, 693.

Punishment of ambassadors who transgress the laws of countries where they reside, R. Zouche, 615.

Quaroni, P. , Aspetti della diplomazia contemporanea, 52.

Queller, D. E. , Office of ambassador in the Middle Ages, 606.

Quest for peace through diplomacy, S. D. Kertesz, 172.

Raccolta di norme per l'applicazione della tariffa consolare, A. Fano, 478.

Radlovic, I. M. , Etiquette & protocol, 133.

Ramirez Peña, A. , Cartilla consular, 499.

Rappaport, A. , ed. , Sources in American diplomacy, 557.

Rapports des consuls avec la marine marchande, E. Roman, 642.

Rappresentanza del diritto internazionale, A. P. Sereni, 336.

Ravaut-Bignon, R. , Du droit de police des consuls dans les pays horschrétienté, 640.

Ravndal, G. B. , Origin of the capitulations and of the consular institution, 328.

Rayneli, E. T. , Derecho diplomático moderno, 329.

Recent revelations of European diplomacy, G. P. Gooch, 164.
Rechliche stellung der deutschen konsuln in Bulgarien einst und jetzt, P. Tromborn, 446.
Recollections of the old Foreign Office, E. Hertslet, 463.
Red carpet at the White House, W. T. Buchanan, 131.
Redard, A. , Diplomatischen Vertretuggen unter besonder Berücksichtigung des schweizerischen, 520.
Redlich, M. D. A. , International law as a substitute for diplomacy, 53.
Ragala, R. , Diplomacy in a changing world, 54; Trends in modern diplomatic practice, 228; World peace through diplomacy and law, 229.
Régime des privilèges et immunités des missions diplomatiques étrangères et des organisations internationales en Suisse, G. Perrenoud, 325.
Register of the Department of State, U. S. Dept. of State, 829.
Règlements consulaires des principaux états maritimes de l'Europe et de l'Amérique, F. de C. , baron de Cussy, 274.
Reiff, H. , Diplomatic and consular privileges, immunities, and practice, 673.
Reinsch, P. S. , American diplomat in China, 120; Secret diplomacy, 230.
Relazioni degli ambasciatori veneti al Senato, E. Alberi, 136.
Renaissance diplomacy, G. Mattingly, 177.
Rendel, G. , Sword and the olive, 466.
Rennell, J. R. R. , Diplomacy, 55.
Répertoire diplomatique, annales du droit des gens et de la politique extérieure, G. Garden, 247.
Répertoire diplomatique et consulaire, P. Chevrey-Rameau, 399; Supplement, 400.
Repertorium der diplomatischen Vertreter aller Länder seit dem Westfälischen Frieden (1648), 822.
Report and general information, Carnegie Institute in Diplomacy, University College, Dares-Salaam, 1965, 10.
Représentation internationale en vue de protéger les intérêts des belligérants, H. Eroğlu, 690.
Representation of the United States abroad, American Assembly, 522.
Research resources, J. B. Mason, 837.
Resources and needs of American diplomacy, S. Simpson, 565.
Reuter, P. , ed. , Traités et documents diplomatiques, 704.
Revista de derecho internacional y ciencias diplomáticas, 858.

senção de direitos advaneiros em geral e para automóveis, em favor los diplomatas e consules, 675.

347

Secretan, J. , Immunités diplomatiques des représentants des états membres et des agents de la Société des nations, 676.
Secretary of State and the Ambassador, U. S. Congress. Senate. Committee on Government Operations, 573.
Seelos, G. , Moderne diplomatie, 232.
Sekiguchi, N. K. , First Japanese ambassadors to America, 484.
Select bibliographies, Carnegie Endowment for International Peace. Library, 723.
Sen, B. , Diplomat's handbook of international law practice, 334; International law relating to diplomatic practice, 335.
Senga, T. , Gestaltung und kritik der heutigen konsulargerichtsbarkeit in Japan, 485.
Sereni, A. P. , Rappresentanza del diritto internazionale, 336.
Serial bibliographies in the humanities and social sciences, R. A. Gray, 740.
Serres, J. C. , Manuel pratique de protocole, 134.
Service diplomatique des États arabes, F. Moussa, 521.
Servicio diplomático i consular, Chile. Laws, statutes, etc. , 373.
Seward, G. F. , United States consulates in China, 562.
Shackled diplomacy, M. J. Demiashkevich, 155.
Shaw, G. H. , State Department and its foreign service in wartime, 563.
al-Shawi, K. A. , Role of the corporate entity in international law, 697.
Shirt-sleeve diplomat, J. Daniels, 90.
Silva, G. E. N. , Manual de derecho consular, 366.
Simpson, S. , Anatomy of the State Department, 564; Resources and needs of American diplomacy, 565.
Sinner, U. , Immunité judiciaire civile des agents diplomatiques étrangers, 677.
Sistema della diplomazia, S. Nava, 319.
Skilling H. G. , Canadian representation abroad, 371.
Snouckaert van Schauburg, A. C. , Dissertation inauguralis, 611.
Snow, F. , Treaties and topics in American diplomacy, 566.
So-called right of asylum in legations, A. P. Morse, 314.
Social sciences and humanities index, 729.
Sources in American diplomacy, A. Rappaport, 557.
South African diplomats abroad, E. Rosenthal, 349.
Sovetskii ezhegodnik mezhdunarodnogo prava, Soviet yearbook of international law, 891.

Soviet cultural offensive, F. C. Barghoorn, 505.
Soviet yearbook of international law, Sovetskii exhegodnik mezhdunarodnogo prava, 891.
Spanish guide to diplomatic procedure in the last quarter of the seventeenth century, Embajada española; an anonymous contemporary, 513.
Spaulding, E. W. , Ambassadors ordinary and extraordinary, 125.
Speaking frankly, J. F. Byrnes, 80.
Sperduti, G. , Competenza dei consoli nelle controversie marittime, 644.
Stakes of diplomacy, W. Lippmann, 36.
State Department and its foreign service in wartime, G. H. Shaw, 563.
State Department and the Foreign Service, Z. S. Steiner, 568.
Statesman's yearbook, 892.
Statut des schweizerischen diplomatischen personals, K. Greisler, 518.
Steiner, Z. S. , Present problems of the Foreign Service, 567; State Department and the Foreign Service, 568.
Stewart, I. , Consular privileges and immunities, 645.
Stieve, F. , Diplomatie im Sprachgebrauch, 337.
Stile diplomatico, A. M. Bettanini, 261.
Sto je diplomacija, B. Krizman, 35.
Stock, L. F. , Consular relations between the United States and the Papal states, 569.
Story of British diplomacy, T. H. S. Escott, 156.
Stowell, E. C. , Consul, 646; Consular cases and opinions, 647.
Straelen, H. , New diplomacy in the Far East, 205.
Strang, W. S. , Diplomatic career, 467; Foreign Office, 468.
Strupp, K. , Beiträge zur reform und kodifikation des völkerrechtlichen immunitätsrechts, 338; Bibliographie du droit des gens et des relations internationales, 753; Wörterbuch des Völkerrechts, 783.
Stuart, G. H. , American diplomatic and consular practice, 570.
Stuart, J. , L. , Fifty years in China, 126.
Student's guide to materials in political science, L. Burchfield, 835.
Studies in diplomacy, V. Benedetti, 144.
Studies in diplomacy and statecraft, G. P. Gooch, 165.
Studies in diplomatic history and historiography in honor of G. P. Gooch, A. O. Sarkissian, 199.

search in foreign affairs, 760.
U. S. Superintendent of Documents, Monthly catalog of
United States government publications, 730.
United States treaties and other international agreements,
U. S. Treaties, etc. , 252.
U. S. Treaties, etc. , Treaties, conventions, international
acts, protocols, and agreements between the United
States of America and other powers, 253; United States
treaties and other international agreements, 252.
Ustor, E. , Diplomáciai kapcsolatok joga, 343.

Vademêcum diplomâtico, R. Barraza, 2.
Vagts, A. , Defense and diplomacy, 344.
Valija den un diplomático peruano, P. Ugarteche, 496.
Van Dyne, F. , Our foreign service, 575.
Vasco, M. A. , Diccionairo de derecho internacional, 785.
Vatican diplomacy, R. A. Graham, 166.
Venezuela. Ministerio de Relaciones Exteriores, Cuerpo
diplomático de Venezuela, 830.
Ventures in diplomacy, W. Phillips, 119.
Vera, R. , Manual para diplomáticos y consules, 376.
Verdier, A. L. , Manuel pratique des consulats, 426.
Verge, J. , Consuls dans les pays d'Occident, 649.
Vero diplomatico, P. Gerbore, 287.
Verzeichnis der ausländischen konsularämter, Austria.
Bundeskanzleramt Auswärtige Angelegenheiten, 356.
Vidal y Saura, G. , Tratado de derecho diplomático, con-
tribución al estudio sobre los principlos y usos de la
diplomaccia moderne, 62.
Vienna convention on diplomatic relations, United Nations
Conference on Diplomatic Intercourse and Immunities,
Vienna, 1961. Delegation from the United States, 680.
Villagran Kramer, F. , Asile diplomatique d'après la
pratique des États latino-américains, 345.
Villard, H. S. , Affairs of State, 576.
Villaseñor, V. M. , Nacionalidad de las soiedades y la pro-
tección diplomatica de los intereses extranjeros en
Mexico, 698.
Voci del servizio diplomatico-consolare italino e straniero,
L. Testa, 482.
Vogel, R. , Breviate of British diplomatic Blue Books, 1919-
1939, 761.
Völkerrechtliche sonderstellung der diplomatischen agenten,
R. Schwerdtfeger, 123.
Völkerrechtliche sonderstellung des gesanden, C. Hothorn,
597.

353

Wakelin, J. , Roots of diplomacy, 63.
Walther, R. , Orientations and behavioral styles of Foreign Service officers, 577.
War and diplomacy in the French republic, F. L. Schuman, 202.
War and diplomacy in the Japanese empire, T. Takeuchi, 486.
War, politics and diplomacy, G. A. Craig, 152.
Warden, D. B. , On the origin, nature, progress and influence of consular establishments, 346.
Wartime mission in Spain, 1942-1945, C. J. H. Hayes, 105.
Washington waltz; diplomatic people and policies, H. C. C. Lombard, 116.
Waters, M. , Ad hoc diplomat, 578.
Webster, C. K. , Art and practice of diplomacy, 64.
Wege und Irrwege der Diplomatie, W. von Blücher, 263.
Weintal, E. , Facing the brink, 579.
Weiser, W. , Deutsche konsulargerichtsbarkeit in zivilsachen, 447.
Weiske, C. A. , Considerations historiques et diplomatiques sur les ambassades des Romains comparées aux modernes 208.
Wellesley, V. , Diplomacy in fetters, 65.
Welt der Diplomatie, W. Zechlin, 69.
Wertheim, J. , Manuel à l'usage des consuls des pays-bas, 490.
Wesendonk, O. G. , Diplomatie, 66.
Westerfield, B. , Instruments of America's foreign policy, 580.
Westphal, H. , Konsulargestzgebung im deutschen und ausländischen Recht, 650.
Whang, P. K. , Matter of elevating diplomatic rank, 586.
Wharton, F. , Digest of the international law of the United States, 720.
What is diplomacy, C. W. Hayward, 26.
Whiteman, M. M. , Digest of international law, 721.
Wicqueford, A. , Ambassador and his functions, 614.
Wildik, P. A. , Bibliotheca consular, 498, 762.
Wildner, H. , Technik der Diplomatie, 347.
Wilhelmstrasse: a study of German diplomats under the Nazi regime, P. Seabury, 124.
Will, G. A. , Kleine Beiträge zur der diplomatik und deren Literatur, 763.
Willson, B. , America's ambassadors to England (1785-1929), 581; America's ambassadors to France (1771-1927) 582; Friendly relations, 472; Paris embassy, 473.

Wilson, C. E. , Cold war diplomacy, 681; Diplomatic privileges and immunities, 682.
Wilson, H. R. , Diplomacy as a career, 128; Education of a diplomat, 129.
Winter, H. , Système de la diplomatie, 67.
Without let or hindrance, E. A. Cleugh, 86.
World diplomatic directory and world diplomatic biography, 831; Supplement, 831A.
World peace through diplomacy and law, R. Regala, 229.
World politics, 865.
World understanding, A. H. Flynn, 737.
Wörterbuch der Aussenpolitik, 784.
Wörterbuch des Völkerrechts, K. Strupp, 783.
Wriston, H. M. , Diplomacy in a democracy, 583; Executive agents in American foreign relations, 584.
Wynar, L. R. , Guide to reference materials in political science, 838.

Yearbook, United Nations, 895; United Nations. International Law Commission, 896.
Yearbook of world polity, 897.
Yeh, S. , Privilèges et immunités des agents diplomatiques à l'égard des états tiers, 683.
Young, G. , Diplomacy old and new, 474.
Young, O. R. , Politics of force, 254.
Your career in foreign service, H. E. Neal, 554.
Your future in the Foreign Service, R. F. Delaney, 535.

Zacharias, E. M. , Secret mission, 130.
Zampaglione, G. , Manuale di diritto consolaie, 483.
Zapiski konsula, I. I. Kulyk, 509.
Zawodny, J. K. , Guide to the study of international relations, 839.
Zechlin, W. , Diplomatie und diplomaten, 68; Welt der Diplomatie, 69.
Zimmer, R. , Jurisdiktionsverhältinisse der fremdländischen konsuln in Deutschland, 651.
Zorn, P. K. L. , Deutsches gesandtschafts-und konsularrecht auf der grundlage des allgemeinen völkerrechts, 448.
Zouche, R. , Punishment of ambassaodrs who transgress the laws of countries where they reside, 615.